LAW AND TRUTH IN BIBLICAL
AND RABBINIC LITERATURE

Law and Truth in Biblical and Rabbinic Literature

~

Chaya T. Halberstam

Indiana University Press

Bloomington & Indianapolis

This book is a publication of

Indiana University Press
601 North Morton Street
Bloomington, IN 47404-3797 USA

www.iupress.indiana.edu

Telephone orders   800-842-6796
Fax orders   812-855-7931
Orders by e-mail   iuporder@indiana.edu

⊖The paper used in this publication
meets the minimum requirements of
the American National Standard for Information Sciences—Permanence of
Paper for Printed Library Materials,
ANSI Z39.48-1992.

Manufactured in the United States of
America

**Library of Congress Cataloging-in-
Publication Data**

Halberstam, Chaya T., date
  Law and truth in biblical and rabbinic
literature / Chaya T. Halberstam.
    p. cm.
  Includes bibliographical references
and index.
  ISBN 978-0-253-35411-2 (cloth : alk.
paper)
  1. Jewish law—Interpretation and construction. 2. Truth—Religious aspects—Judaism. 3. Rabbis—Office. 4.
Bible. O.T.—Criticism, interpretation,
etc.
5. Rabbinical literature—History and
criticism. I. Title.
  BM521.H25 2010
  296.1'8—dc22
                        2009025618

1 2 3 4 5   15 14 13 12 11 10

For my parents

CONTENTS

· ACKNOWLEDGMENTS · IX

· Introduction · 1

ONE TRUTH AND HUMAN JURISPRUDENCE

1 Stains of Impurity · 17

2 Signs of Ownership · 42

3 The Impossibility of Judgment · 76

TWO TRUTH AND DIVINE JUSTICE

4 Theologies of Justice · 109

5 Objects of Narrative · 147

· NOTES · 181

· BIBLIOGRAPHY · 205

· INDEX OF SCRIPTURAL VERSES · 213

· INDEX OF SUBJECTS · 217

ACKNOWLEDGMENTS

Steven Fraade and Christine Hayes played a great role in the development of this book. They were both always dedicated and encouraging; as the years have passed, I continue to be inspired by their scholarship and wisdom, and I am extremely grateful for their enduring support. I owe them an immeasurable debt. I also wish to thank Richard Kalmin for his engagement with my work and his ongoing guidance.

I would like to express my gratitude to the Department of Religious Studies at Indiana University for providing a warm, collegial, and intellectually stimulating environment in which I could complete this book. I wish to thank Nancy Levene for helping me frame some of my larger questions, and David Brakke, who, as department chair, always helped me make space for my research. In particular I am grateful to Steven Weitzman, who read drafts of the introduction and served as a true mentor to me even before I arrived at IU. The College Arts and Humanities Institute provided me with research funding for which I am also immensely grateful.

I feel privileged to be publishing my work with Indiana University Press, where the staff has been exceptionally helpful. I would like to thank the anonymous readers for their extremely illuminating and useful comments; Hila Ratzabi for her meticulous copy editing; Michael Lundell, who initially took an interest in this project; and Dee Mortensen, June Silay, and Chandra Mevis who expertly shepherded it through to completion. I would also like to thank Rachel Dadusc for her careful and speedy indexing.

Several portions of this book are revised versions of material that has been published elsewhere; I would like to thank the anonymous readers for *Studies in Law, Politics, and Society; Law Culture, and the Humanities;* and *Prooftexts,* as well as editors Austin Sarat and Matthew Anderson, who have always supported my work and given me invaluable advice. I would also like to thank Elizabeth Shanks Alexander, Jonathan Schofer, and Beth Berkowitz, whose lively conversations with me about the *Sifre* helped shape a portion of chapter 4.

Over the course of this long project, I owe the most to friends and family who have tirelessly supported my seemingly endless work with patience, humor, and love. Ravit Reichman and Lisa Silverman endured countless versions of each of my chapters with unstinting support and infinite generosity; they have each talked me back from the brink more times than I can count, and I am incredibly grateful for their lasting friendship. I would like to thank my aunt, Chani Kleinbart, for always offering help and encouragement, and proofreading much of the introduction. My sister, Batsheva Halberstam, has been there for me from the inception of this project until its end, tirelessly IM'ing, conversing, and trekking out to wherever I happened to be to help me during my life's most trying hours, and for that I owe her undying gratitude. Charles Burnetts appeared in my life midway through this project, but his impact is no less felt. His profound intellect has challenged, sharpened, and improved my work in ways that are incalculable; his love and forbearance seem to know no bounds; I appreciate his presence in my life more than I can ever say. I am also grateful to an adorable and energetic toddler, Aaron William Halberstam Burnetts, who has tried unfailingly to impede my work at every turn, but whose cheeky grin has reminded me over the past two years of life's potential for boundless joy. Finally, I want to thank my parents, Yitzhak and Livia Halberstam, who taught me, by word and example, the value of studying Torah. They have always been eager to discuss my work in progress and read drafts. They have supported me materially and spiritually beyond measure. I could not have reached this point without their constant love and encouragement.

LAW AND TRUTH IN BIBLICAL
AND RABBINIC LITERATURE

INTRODUCTION

> The . . . standard of proof is . . . a concept that incorporates less rigid ideas of justice and reflects the judicial function of resolving disputes in the real world, where values shift and knowledge is uncertain.

It is hard to imagine any leader who would not long for the clarity of divine knowledge. The eschatological vision of the eleventh chapter of Isaiah envisages the ideal leader in these terms: "The spirit of Yhwh shall alight upon him: a spirit of wisdom and insight, a spirit of counsel and valor. . . . He shall sense the truth by his reverence for Yhwh: he shall not judge by what his eyes behold, nor decide by what his ears perceive" (2–3).[1] Looking, listening—these human senses, we are told, often steer decision-makers in the wrong direction. But the spirit of Yhwh imparts the truth, and it is through the truth that the ideal leader "shall judge the poor with justice, and decide with equity for the meek of the earth" (11:4).

Part of the allure of much of the Hebrew Bible is that it offers us a world in which such divine truth is accessible: not only in a moral, pedagogical, or spiritual sense, but also in the sphere of the law. The meaning of each stipulation is clear: "surely, this commandment that I am commanding you today is not too hard for you, nor is it too far away" (Deut. 30:11), Yhwh declares. Not only are God's rules easy to follow, but in the case of a dispute, decision making is aided by divine insight: "If a judicial decision is too difficult for you . . . then you shall immediately go up to the [temple of] Yhwh where you shall consult with the levitical priests and the judge who is in office . . . ; they shall announce to you the decision in the case" (Deut. 17:8–9). Such legal intelligibility and divine aid surely represent myth-making already

1

on the part of the biblical authors; there is much to suggest that jurisprudence among the ancient Israelites was a messy, all-too-human process.[2] The biblical legacy, however, is a rhetorical celebration of the availability of knowledge and truth through "reverence for Yhwh," and of the attainability of true justice through obedience of God's commandments.

The early rabbis, who aspired to Jewish leadership just as the biblical canon was being sealed and its texts venerated as the holy Word, endeavored to shape the divine commandment (as well as centuries of Jewish custom) into a viable sacred legal system. After the destruction of the Temple in 70 CE and the failure of attempts to rebuild it, the rabbis competed with the priests as religious authorities.[3] Whereas priestly authority rested to a large extent upon the notion of immediate divine presence in the temple and the priests as God's earthly representatives, the rabbis submitted that their decision making would not rely on direct access to God—that they, along with the rest of the Jewish community, had to endure what Steven Fraade calls the "*longue durée* between biblical past and eschatological future, . . . the time-between . . . [in which] God is virtually absent as a speaking or acting presence."[4] In other words, they had to act on behalf of God as the priests did, but unlike the priests, they could not rely on the temple service as a means of contacting God and ascertaining God's will.

Even as the rabbis authoritatively offered themselves as the heirs of judicial authority over the divine law, they faced a persistent question: do humans, even the most well-intentioned, competent, and morally righteous among them, ever have the capacity to administer divine commandments? Could they ever discern an unbiased reality and render judicial decisions with the kind of accuracy that would meet a divine standard? And if not— would a solely human administration of the sacred law yield true justice, or its opposite?

A passage in an early rabbinic collection, the *Tosefta* (edited in the third century CE), reflects this rabbinic anxiety:

> Judges should know whom it is they are judging, before whom they are judging, and who judges them, . . . as it is written: "God(s) [*elohim*] stand(s) in the congregation of El [in the midst of gods does he judge]" [Ps 82:1].[5] And thus it is said . . . "He said to the judges, Consider what you do, for you judge not for man, but for Yhwh" [2 Chr 19:6]. And lest the judge should say: Why bother with all this trouble? It is further said:

"He is with you in giving judgment" [ibid.]. You have nothing but what your eyes see. (*t. Sanh.* 1:9)

The opening statement of this intricate midrash alarms the judge with its depiction of divine surveillance, asserting that God closely observes and calls judges to account for any error in judgment. But the rabbis acknowledge that calling judges to contend with this extent of divine stringency when administering God's law may lead them to despair of it entirely.[6] And therefore, in a surprising turn, the midrash mitigates the severe warning cited from 2 Chronicles[7] by re-reading, and in a sense deliberately misreading, the remainder of the verse. Although 2 Chronicles essentially intimidates the judge by stating "He is with you in giving judgment"— watching and recording whether judges take liberties or conform to what is divinely right, the midrash exploits the preposition "with" to unearth a different connotation to the verse. Rather than against you or upon you, God is *with* you, the midrash claims, supporting the kind of limited judgment of which you are capable. The midrash recognizes that a judge cannot aspire to divine discernment, and therefore he must render judgment based only on what his[8] eyes can see. And in this activity of human observing and reasoning, the midrash concludes, God is with him; God sanctions those judgments based upon a fair adjudication of the evidence before the judges' imperfect eyes. In this short midrash, we witness the contradictory impulses of rabbinic jurisprudence: to apprehend and fear one absolute, divine truth to which justice must aspire, and to accept and even sanctify imperfect, human juridical activity. We have come full circle from Isaiah: the leader shall now judge *solely* by what his eyes behold, and the spirit of Yhwh shall shore him up.

In this book, I explore two different modes of juridical rhetoric: the Hebrew Bible, which deploys an authoritative discourse of knowledge, certainty, and divine truth; and tannaitic literature, which assumes a stance of perpetual uncertainty despite the biblical tradition, and demands the authoritative construction of legal truth.[9] I hope to demonstrate how the rabbinic posture of uncertainty in shaping Jewish law promoted energetic legal creativity alongside a residue of anxiety over the consistent possibility of factually wrong and morally wrongful judgment. The chapters that follow trace varying degrees of rabbinic confidence in legal decision making, suggesting that as uncertainty permeates disparate realms of rabbinic law, it fortifies rabbinic legal authority while regularly threatening to topple the very system of law and worldly justice that the rabbis endeavor to establish. I also investigate the theological implications of these legal discourses, demonstrating how the experience of the divine both supplements these earthly concerns and is simultaneously filtered through them.

Until very recently, the study of exegesis, theology, and narrative has largely remained segregated from the study of law and legal reasoning; over the past few decades, a growing number of scholars have sought connections between these two fields. My project owes much to the work of Robert Cover, whose study put language and law on equal footing and suggested that a normative world is built not only through the force of legal decisions, but primarily through the ways in which these decisions are articulated. Cover's work has founded an increasingly fruitful field of study—Law and Humanities—in which literary and legal questions are explored together in order to "illuminat[e] . . . the kinds of cultural work we ask [them] to do."[10] I also draw upon the work of French sociologist Pierre Bourdieu, who reads legal discourse as a process of appropriation and translation, forming a legal universe out of other cultural practices and competing with them for authority and control.[11]

Specifically within the field of rabbinic literature, my work largely follows the model set by Daniel Boyarin in *Carnal Israel*.[12] In bringing together works of various genres and discursive practices throughout rabbinic literature, Boyarin focuses on a set of questions, or a "cultural problematic," rather than a specific text or volume, because "both the halakha and the aggadah represent attempts to work out the same cultural, political, social, ideological, and religious problems."[13] Other scholars of rabbinic literature have begun to integrate law and narrative in their work even more programmatically: Jeffrey Rubenstein has recently examined the structural and thematic connections between narratives and their legal contexts in the Babylonian Talmud,[14] and Steven Fraade has explored issues of community and identity in rabbinic literature and the Dead Sea Scrolls by analyzing both legal and narrative texts.[15]

This book also contributes to a growing number of works on rabbinic authority specifically as it is revealed through discursive analysis of rabbinic literature.[16] Jonathan Schofer in particular lays the groundwork for my emphasis on rabbinic thought in analyzing constructions of rabbinic authority; he maintains that rabbinic literature "represents sophisticated thought about ethics, theology, and other matters that is comparable to the conceptual work done by other intellectual elites. . . . For this reason, I attend . . . to genres, tropes, and concepts."[17]

Because the cultural settings of the tannaitic literature, Talmud Yerushalmi, and Talmud Bavli vary so widely, I have limited my focus primarily to tannaitic texts—though on occasion I do delve into the Talmuds and amoraic Midrashim when they point toward implicit tensions in the Bible or Mishnah, paying careful attention to how they read or misread the texts upon which they comment. I do not limit myself to one topic or tractate *not* because I assume a uniformity of thought among all rabbinic utterances, but rather because I would like to identify a trend in early rabbinic thought and practice that persists despite the *variety* of outlooks and immediate circumstances. It is the continual recurrence of the rabbinic conflict between authority in truth making and encounters with "objective reality" that outlines a pivotal tension within rabbinic culture as a whole.

Shaping the Law

The rabbis, unable to access direct divine communication, turned to the letters of scripture as the source of new divine insight.[18] But rather than offering the simple commandment, the letters and words of scripture yielded a vast and multivocal sea of irreducible utterances, a "synchronic multiplicity of divine voices and their human interpretations."[19] Despite a lack of concern for the "performative applicability"[20] of the proliferating exegeses of scripture for the rabbis, the rabbis conceded that communal practice had to be agreed upon. Not privileging one interpretation over another as closer to some kind of unitary meaning such as the divine authorial intent, truth, or core religious values, the rabbis developed some simple strategies for deciding the right practice[21] and, in doing so, transformed the concept of "divine will" from one unequivocal absolute to a variety of possible truths. Put simply, they believed they could achieve practical, communal uniformity by tallying votes. We might imagine discomfort with the lack of a clear, singular divine intent—an anxiety over whether multiple versions of the divine will amounts to "a sign of deterioration . . . of tradition, which had not been preserved in its purity."[22] But on the whole the rabbis of late antiquity recognized polysemy in the divine word, acknowledging that "this sage forbids, while that sage permits" (*Sifre Deut.* 48),[23] and endorsing their own democratic decision-making process with the confidence of their perceived divine investiture.[24]

If the rabbis, then, rejected a singular, true divine will, seeing each one of their (often conflicting) interpretations of scripture as "divinely authorized"[25] and a way to "enable God to speak to them from between the lines of Scripture,"[26] why then worry about "correct" judgment at all? Why the appeal, in the toseftan passage above, to a singular, absolute, divine standard that a judge's ruling would inexorably be measured against? Why not simply embrace a variety of truths, one of which is expressed in the judge's own application of the law, which would inevitably be "divinely authorized"?

Though the rabbis *did* appeal to this idea of divine authorization of a judge's decision, as we saw above in their interpretation of the passage "He is *with* you in giving judgment," the fact that they seemed to hold fast nonetheless to the notion of one correct decision that could be seen in the light of divine absolutes implies a different hermeneutical stance from the one we saw above. From this position, rabbinic judgment does not affirm polysemy and multivocality but rather the presence of a singular truth which limited human interpreters may approximate but perhaps never fully uncover.[27] In this sense, the rabbis sound less like the poststructuralists to whom they've been compared,[28] and more like Plato, who laments the necessary human administration of the perfect, divine law, writing in *The Laws* that the gods by right ought to rule over the city because "no human nature invested with . . . power is able to order human affairs and not overflow with . . . wrong."[29] So how do we make sense of the rabbinic understanding of truth, in which rabbis could hold different interpretations of the sacred text as divinely true, but could only posit a singular and unknowable truth in the law's implementation?

Two accounts of rabbinic thought, suggested by David Weiss Halivni and Moshe Halbertal, address this question; while they differ, both propose that rabbinic literature can be best understood as having a *dual* understanding of interpretive truth. David Weiss Halivni formulates a rabbinic "double-verity theory," in which the rabbis distinguished between two realms of truth, a heavenly or absolute truth, based upon "logicality" and a practical truth based upon majority rule.[30] Majority opinion may define behavior, thus constituting an alternate, "practical truth," but Halivni himself allows that this position exists rather uneasily alongside the notion of divine truth. As he puts it, "because majority rule is a human verity, a practical verity, *it is an uncertain verity,* subject to limitations."[31] An "uncertain verity," we might conclude, is no verity at all; and indeed, Halivni continues by essentially conceding any "truth" he previously attributed to rabbinic legal decision making, suggesting instead that the rabbis had to accommodate the tension between ideal (objective, absolute, divine truth) and necessity (the practical demands of behavioral conformity). Negotiating this tension ultimately meant that the rabbis maintained that God had given them license to compel and enforce the majority opinion *regardless* of its truth-value on an absolute scale because of the importance of this "practical necessity."[32]

Moshe Halbertal attempts to correct Halivni's overemphasis on the rabbinic adherence to an absolute, divine standard of truth by positing *two different* approaches to authority, interpretation, and truth in rabbinic literature. The majority's opinion is rabbinically authoritative, according to Halbertal, due to two possible lines of reasoning: (1) the "constitutive" approach, which submits that "it is not possible that the court could ever be mistaken, because the court constitutes meanings rather than discovering them"; and (2) the "procedural" approach, in which "it is not possible to question the authority of the court even if it could be mistaken, because of the procedural priority of the institution."[33] Halbertal observes that both the constitutive approach, which *defines* truth via the court (that is, majority) rulings as well as the procedural approach, which affirms an "unalterable reality"[34] yet defers to the majority in practice, are both found in rabbinic literature. The former aligns with midrashic notions of multi-vocal truth, and the latter with the enforcement of majority rule despite the existence of an inaccessible, singular truth. Halbertal gestures toward the notion that these philosophies can coexist without much communal disorder; pragmatically, they both call for adherence to the majority, and the question would simply arise regarding whether one ought to teach and promulgate minority opinions alongside majority practice—or whether these opinions ought to be quashed.[35]

It seems that we might be able to let the question rest here, with these dual (and dueling) conceptions of truth relevant only within the sphere of interpretive theory, and "majority rule" providing an uncontroversial and unswerving guide for rabbinic practice. But regardless of Halivni's or Halbertal's downplaying of the practical import of these differing views, the presence of both in a rabbinic community will inevitably have profoundly real consequences. When does God cease sanctioning a legislative or judicial decision because it is *too much* in error? How closely must legislators and judges align their decisions with socially perceived truths (as opposed to divinely-ordained ones) if they aim to guarantee adherence to their rulings?

Daniel Schwartz and Jeffrey Rubenstein have recently debated this question, examining the extent to which a notion of "unalterable reality" actually influences the formal truth making of law (rather than the other way around). Daniel Schwartz argues that the rabbis "were mainly nominalists,"[36] by which he means that they were essentially formalists, insisting that legal procedures take precedence over other possible truths.[37] As he argues, even if a judicial decision were perceived to conflict with "reality," the formal ("nominal") requirements of law would require that "factual" reality be ignored and the decision be followed—a virtual rephrasing of Halbertal's description of the "procedural approach." As a concrete example of such formalism, Schwartz cites the case of the new moon: if empirical science proves that the 30th of the month is the new moon, but traditional legal procedure of astronomical witnesses testifies that the 29th is the new moon, scientific reality ought to be ignored in favor of "legal reality."[38]

Adding nuance to Schwartz's argument, Jeffrey Rubenstein contends that rabbinic literature "reflect[s a] tension between nominalist and realist tendencies."[39] In other words, Rubenstein rejects the idea that the court authoritatively establishes truth in such a "top-down" way as either the "constitutive" or "procedural" approach describes. Instead, legal authority must to some extent compromise with a-legal truth-claims substantiated by science, common sense, or shifting values. Thus the question of the new moon in rabbinic jurisprudence is more complicated for Rubenstein: there may be some leeway in rabbinic legislation about whether the new moon is proclaimed on the 29th or 30th day of the month but if witnesses declare the 32nd day the new moon, such an "observation" which patently could not be grounded in empirical fact (legal months were known to *always* have either 29 or 30 days) would be rejected. Hence, the rabbis may have exhibited nominalist tendencies by adopting witness testimony over scientific calculation to decide between the 29th and 30th day, but such nominalism was not unbounded.[40]

Rubenstein argues, moreover, that this type of tension between "realism" and "nominalism" is not unique to rabbinic law in late antiquity, but is part and parcel of legal canonization generally, emerging as an integral feature of "just about any society with a living legal system"[41]—hence the tension exhibited in rabbinic texts, and, one might speculate, in rabbinic society as well.

It is precisely this tension that forms the basis of the central question of this volume: what happens when the reality created by divine law conflicts with a person's or society's beliefs about reality? And in which reality ought divine truth to be located? Schwartz and Rubenstein describe one such situation in which human scientific inquiry establishes a perceived "unalterable reality" that clashes with the traditional understanding of the law. In this case, rabbinic legislative activity is pressed either, in a nominal move, to ignore reality, or, in a realist move, to reinterpret biblical law to match prevailing notions of empirical truth. In this sphere, notions of biblical multi-vocality, diffuse ideas of revelation, and Halbteral's "constitutive" theory of authoritative, divine truth may play a role in helping to reshape the divine word into a truth consistent with societal values and scientific inquiry.

Finding Facts

While the scholarship above concerns itself with the rabbinic legislative process, my concern in this book is with the *judicial* process of legal decision making. Here we find a somewhat more commonplace conflict between law and reality that manifests in all "living legal systems." In this instance, it is not the question of how to interpret the law that is tantamount, but rather the dilemma of how to interpret the *evidence* of a case and fairly apply the law so that issues of livelihood, life, and limb are settled in accordance with perceived factuality. In this sphere, open-ended notions of truth and revelation play a much smaller role; as the rabbinic judges are forced to interpret people's private worlds of relationships, bodies, and possessions rather than the intangible Word, the idea of one "objective" reality is much more intuitively felt by rabbis and lay people alike. Only one person can actually have possession of an item; a person either commits murder or does not. The tension between law and reality occurs, then, as law creates and shapes its own, formal reality (damages owed or not owed; guilty or not guilty) while lay individuals make truth claims about their own reality simultaneously.

Legal theorist Hans Kelsen describes this process: "In case a fact is disputed, the judicial decision which determines that the fact has occurred in truth 'creates' legally the fact. . . . In the sphere of law the fact 'exists,' even if in the sphere of nature the fact has not occurred."[42] This "sphere of nature," which is difficult to define precisely, points to other, intuitive understandings of "factual" reality which may pull the definition of truth in other directions. Legal scholar Robert Summers calls this the tension between "formal legal truth" and "substantive truth," and notes that: "In a well-designed system, judicial findings of formal legal truth generally coincide with substantive truth in particular cases, and . . . we can readily see powerful reasons why the two ought to coincide. But formal legal truth may, in a particular case, fail to coincide with substantive truth."[43] This tension is perhaps even more acute in the context of sacred law, because God's law is supposed to engender perfect justice. But as the reassurance of divine intervention is absent for the rabbis in worldly disputes—no lots are cast, no oracles consulted—the divine law compromises with human fact-finding in assigning blame and establishing limited, provisional truth and justice. The rabbis are forced to interpret evidence and compose a body of evidence law, even as the Hebrew Bible offers them little guidance in these matters. At times, I argue, the rabbis are liberated by this turn to evidence, creatively emboldened to pursue legal maneuvering and produce a desired result when access to absolute truth is lacking. At other times, however, the rabbis are distraught at the possibility of wrongful judgment, and question the very foundation of their legal enterprise as the true fulfillment of the divine will.

Part 1 of this book considers instances of evidentiary reasoning in rabbinic literature in three different fields of substantive law.[44] In each case, I examine rabbinic interpretation of evidence as presented, usually obliquely, in various tannaitic texts in order to assess how and to what extent the rabbis establish the "facts" of the case. Because I am interested in the rabbinic understanding of "substantive reality" in contradistinction to legal formalism, I endeavor (when possible) to analyze cases in which the rabbis interpret physical evidence rather than witness testimony because of the inherent textuality of the latter. I then look at the tensions created by the role of rabbinic uncertainty in discerning the "facts" of the case and the unequivocal demands of the divine law. Because the rabbis inevitably invoke the holy writ of scripture not only to ascertain the right law but also to determine the right divinely-authorized hermeneutical strategies they use to interpret the evidence, I also analyze these scriptural sources in order to better understand the conflicting interpretive demands the rabbinic judges face. In general, the muddle of differing truth-claims and uncertainty surrounding the facts and the law in rabbinic texts contrasts with biblical rhetoric, which most often suggests self-assured and certain knowledge of the facts and a clear, divine direction about how to proceed in each case.

The three cases analyzed represent not only three different areas of law but also three distinct approaches to human jurisprudence and uncertainty about the truth. Chapter 1 deals with menstrual impurity law and discusses how perceived reality recedes in favor of rabbinic formal legal maneuvering. It presents a close reading of a decision by R. Aqiba, as described in the Mishnah, to override a woman's claim of observed menstrual blood with a legal presumption of ritual purity. Even as the case is settled, the question of the substantive facts of the case—whether the woman is a menstruant or not—remains open. Nonetheless, this uncertainty does not seem to disturb the edifice of ritual purity law, and the great rabbinic master R. Aqiba quickly dispels the anxiety that the legal pronouncement may in fact be objectively erroneous. Formalism displaces the detection of objective reality, and the law's authority over truth triumphs.

From questions of ritual purity, chapter 2 moves to consider a case of property law in which the rabbis seem far more interested in fact finding; in a departure from biblical law, the Mishnah delineates legal standards of evidence to define ownership through physical "signs" on a found object. In this case, it appears as though the Mishnah is accommodating the law to the demands of the real; but as tangible as they seem, these visible signs upon which the Mishnah relies, in addition to several other demands the rabbis place upon the subject who claims ownership, actually undermine typical notions of "real" ownership. The Mishnah, it seems, attempts to walk a fine line between "real" and legally constructed ownership, and the tension inherent in this approach is best illuminated by the commentaries on the Mishnah in both Talmuds, which I examine to better clarify the issues with which the Mishnah struggles. As both Talmuds strive in very different ways toward more concrete methods of defining ownership we are made more aware of the equivocation in the rules of the Mishnah which never decisively choose formal definitions of ownership over "factual" ones, or vice versa.

Chapter 3 turns to criminal law and investigates the kinds of proof allowed by rabbinic law to assist in establishing guilt at a criminal trial. I focus on the question found in non-mishnaic tannaitic literature of whether or not to admit physical evidence, such as the murder weapon, before the court. Here, the stakes of uncertainty in the interpretation of such evidence are at their highest: because capital punishment is required by scripture, a commitment to human application of the law would literally put bodies on the line. The disputes between various sages on the question of evidence in capital cases reveal differing degrees of commitment to human legal decision making and implementation of this-worldly justice. For some, ultimate uncertainty about the "real" facts is simply part of the system, and infrequent wrongful punishment a necessary evil; for others, this uncertainty is paralyzing, and the divine legal obligation to carry out capital punishment is essentially nullified. In the end we are offered not a univocal rabbinic vision of legal practice but rather a polyvalent portrait of the rabbinic commitment to law, justice, and judicial authority in a highly uncertain world.

In part 2, I turn to the question of how divine truth plays a role in these religious texts which concern themselves not only with human jurisprudence but also with the relationship between human beings and a just God. A common trope of religious thought is to impute to the supreme, divine judge—whether in this world, after death, or in the messianic age—the implementation of a kind of perfect justice of which human judges are incapable. In chapter 4, I turn away from human fact finding and evidence law to explore the possibility of divine justice as a repository for truth in the biblical and rabbinic legal spheres. If God's judgments are unfailingly true, how do the workings of divine retribution intersect with the operation of human justice? Why do ancient Jewish leaders not abdicate responsibility for justice altogether? This chapter explores the limits of divine justice in the Hebrew Bible and tannaitic literature, showing how the unreliability of God's rewards and punishments in both sets of texts requires humans to define and execute justice on their own behalf.

Finally, chapter 5 turns to narrative, another literary genre in which the Hebrew Bible and rabbis confront and explore the dilemmas of establishing truth in the struggle for justice under God's oversight. Biblical narratives offer an interesting counterpoint to the assuredness of biblical law, often indicating that evidence may not generate an accurate apprehension of culpability—it is unreliable and also easily manipulated—while God's truth is unassailable. Rabbinic commentaries on these biblical narratives both heighten these latent ideas in the biblical text and also diverge significantly from them. Rabbinic commentaries underscore the unreliability of interpreting evidence, but they also do something surprising: rather than leaving the characters in states of uncertainty, they uncover distinct moments of divine inspiration which lead biblical characters toward perfect knowledge of guilt and innocence. It is thus through immersion in the sacred biblical past, exploiting the medium of narrative, and adopting the decidedly private perspectives of biblical characters that the rabbis ultimately locate juridical certainty.

PART ONE

Truth and Human Jurisprudence

ONE

Stains of Impurity

Skepticism closes off certain paths to a judicial decision, it is true, but they are snares and delusions. They impart a false confidence; they fog the mind. When they are swept away, the judge is still able to act, but he may reason more clearly and incisively, and perhaps express himself differently.

In the sphere of biblical ritual purity law, we witness a vivid encounter between the realities of human bodies and legal decisions. The physical determination whether or not a person contracts a scale disease or experiences genital flux invokes the legal categories of ritually pure and impure so that a sacred topography is overlaid upon the natural world. As Mary Douglas writes, "the idea of holiness was given an external, physical expression in the wholeness of the body seen as a perfect container."[1] By mandating that a person may approach the Temple only in a state of purity, biblical law requires that physical objects and bodies be objects of constant scrutiny, insisting that one always be cognizant of one's ritual status, responsible for the ritual purity of one's own body. As such, these laws require continual fact finding through the interpretation of physical, bodily evidence in terms of sacred legal categories.

The biblical discussion of genital-flux impurity (Leviticus 15), however, ignores the issue of the interpretive leap required to render physical fact into ritual status. Direct and unequivocal knowledge of one's embodied self, which includes knowing technical details of bodily functions as well as the different ritual meanings they evoke, is assumed by the biblical text. The levitical pericope begins with the clause, literally rendered, "when any man becomes a discharger, he is ritually impure." No biblical stipulations address the method by which one would come to know whether or not one was a "discharger"; the reader is led to assume that the status of "discharger" depends on the seemingly simple observation of the presence of genital flux.

In contrast to these vague biblical rules, the rabbinic delineation of ritual purity laws, which include the laws of menstrual impurity (*niddah*), establishes clear, objective criteria through which one must observe genital flux and then distinguish ritually pure from ritually impure discharge. In so doing, these texts break with biblical precedent, but nonetheless cite Leviticus 15 as the sole source of their authority.

In this chapter, I explore the Hebrew Bible's assumptions about personal, bodily knowledge on the one hand, and the legal creativity of the rabbis on the other as they endeavor to fill the evidentiary gap left by the Hebrew Bible. Two rabbinic innovations come to define the rabbinic standard of proof for menstrual impurity: the requirement of seeing, and the disqualification of the bloodstain as evidence of menstruation. Both innovations suggest the formalist notion that the law can and must determine whether or not a person is a "discharger" despite an individual's private intuitions. The rabbis thus establish legal authority by asserting their own constructions of legal truth over and against a person's intimate knowledge of his or her own body.

Biblical Evidence of Impurity: Negaʿim versus Zabim

Chapters 11–15 of Leviticus constitute a unit on ritual purity. Within this larger priestly composition, the pericope that discusses genital-flux impurity is presented last, immediately following a section on scale-disease impurity. Unlike the dietary laws delineated in chapter eleven, the rules regarding genital-flux impurity have much in common with those for scale disease: a bodily condition must be identified, impurity recognized, a period of time allowed to pass, and a ritual cleansing and sacrifice performed, in order to restore a status of ritual purity.[2] Nonetheless, two entirely different models for identifying and treating these two kinds of bodily impurity are offered. In the case of skin lesions (*negaʿim*), the rules in Leviticus 13–14 prescribe a specific procedure by which an individual is declared impure: he or she must submit him- or herself to inspection by a priest who pronounces his or her ritual status. Because the priest is obligated to distinguish between simple scabs, which are ritually pure, and scale-disease lesions, which are ritually impure, these stipulations delineate precisely how to detect a ritually impure skin lesion by examining its color, shape, and texture. The biblical text specifies:

> The priest shall examine the disease [*nega*ᶜ] on the skin of his body, and if the hair in the diseased area has turned white and the disease appears to be deeper than the skin of his body, it is a leprous disease; after the priest has examined him he shall pronounce him ritually impure. But if the spot is white in the skin of his body, and appears no deeper than the skin, and the hair in it has not turned white, the priest shall confine the diseased person for seven days. (Lev. 13:3–4)

This passage states that the basic criterion for distinguishing between ritual purity and impurity is the appearance of the skin lesion, and this appearance must be inspected and analyzed by a priest.

In genital-flux impurity (*zabim* and *niddah*), however, no inspection procedure is stipulated; the laws in Leviticus 15 require no examination and no priestly pronouncement for determining a person's ritual status. The simple presence of genital blood flow for a woman, and any genital flux for a man, renders an individual ritually impure. God instructs Moses to tell the Israelites:

> Speak to the people of Israel and say to them: When any man has a discharge [*zab*] from his member, his discharge makes him ritually impure. The ritual impurity of his discharge is this: whether his member flows with his discharge, or his member is stopped from discharging, it is ritual impurity for him. (Lev. 15:2–3)

The law for women is similar, though slightly more specific:

> When a woman has a discharge [*zabah*] of blood that is her regular discharge from her body, she shall be in her menstrual impurity [*niddatah*] for seven days. . . . If a woman has a discharge of blood for many days, not at the time of her menstrual impurity, or if she has a discharge beyond the time of her menstrual impurity, all the days of the discharge she shall continue in ritual impurity; as in the days of her menstrual impurity, she shall be ritually impure. (Lev. 15:19, 25)

These laws are uniformly general, especially compared to the stipulations for skin lesions. While the biblical text differentiates between men's and women's genital flux, it nonetheless makes no distinctions among different colors, consistencies, or amounts of discharge.

It is not made clear in the biblical text why the ritual procedure for these two types of impurity differ, as both are contracted bodily and both—at least in the case of some gonorrheal discharges—may be classified as diseases. The language of the text in these three chapters implies single authorship (with some later additions and glosses), and thus the reason behind the divergent practices cannot be attributed to different authorial sources. Jacob Milgrom, in his commentary on Leviticus, notes that because genital-flux impurity is

> a disease of the private parts, only the person can determine if he or she has a flow. Thus, because scale disease is exposed and can be reported by others to the priest, the instruction in 14:1–2 is not addressed to the Israelites; by contrast, the rules of genital discharges must be taught to the Israelites, who are responsible for their own diagnosis; hence these instructions are addressed to them.[3]

The suggestion that the rules for scale-disease impurity are addressed only to the priests because lesions were "exposed" and therefore "reported by others to the priest" does not sufficiently account for the distinction between the role of priestly examination for skin lesions and the lay person's responsibility for determining genital-flux impurity. A skin lesion may often be concealed, but the levitical laws insist instead that it must be brought before the priest. And whereas one could imagine a simple—and modest—procedure of submitting genital discharge for inspection without bodily exposure, such a procedure is not stipulated, but rather, as Milgrom points out, the Israelites themselves are "responsible for their own diagnosis."

Rather than characterizing the distinction between scale-disease impurity and genital-flux impurity as public versus private, one may describe it instead as ambiguous versus straightforward. In other words, the priest is instructed to distinguish a "leprous disease" (or scale disease) from among a wide variety of possibilities; the Israelite, on the other hand, must only recognize, again in Milgrom's words, "*if* he or she has a flow." Most skin lesions are not considered ritually impure; the impure scale disease

is only one of many possible skin abnormalities, and one with which individuals are not generally acquainted—the ancient analogue perhaps of
a malignant skin mole. Such a situation calls for analysis and decision,
and thus an expert, a priest, is called upon. In the model offered for genital-flux impurity, on the other hand, *all* discharge for a man, and all genital blood flow for a woman, would appear to be impure. The simple presence or absence of flux or blood is easily known by any individual, and
thus the Israelites themselves are entrusted with the determination of
genital-flux impurity. Indeed, John Hartley writes that it is, in fact, the
"sparsity of details" that prompts one to deduce that "this information is
formulated for the knowledge of the laity, not the priests."[4] Thus, Israelites
are instructed to *recognize* genital discharge and their own status as ritually impure, while priests are commanded to analyze skin lesions and
decide whether others are ritually impure.

The paranetic rhetoric in Leviticus 15, absent from Leviticus 13–14, underscores the idea that the genital-flux impurity rules are intended to be
carried out by all Israelites, without the involvement of the priests. Leviticus
15 concludes with the admonition, "you shall keep the people of Israel separate from their ritual impurity, so that they do not die in their ritual impurity
by defiling my tabernacle that is in their midst" (Lev. 15:31). Commentators
have suggested that this warning may in fact refer back to all types of impurity
discussed in chapters 11–15,[5] but given the placement of this verse before the
concluding statement for the section on genital-flux impurity ("This is the
ritual for the discharger . . ." [Lev. 15:32]), it seems unlikely that this warning
serves as a general summary. Many scholars do see this verse as a later inser-
tion (possibly H), one which would function as a summation,[6] a bridge to the
next chapter,[7] or a means of situating these laws within the narrative setting
of the wilderness wanderings.[8] Regardless of the intended function of the
placement of this admonition, the biblical text unambiguously entrusts all
Israelites (and not just the priests) with the grave responsibility for a ritual
purity system that is tied to the very foundation of Israel's covenant with
God.[9] This investiture of responsibility to the laity is appended specifically to
the laws of genital-flux impurity, rather than any other, emphasizing again
that unlike scale-disease impurity, *all* of Israel is responsible for recognizing
and keeping the laws of genital-flux impurity. No such warning is found in
the chapters on scale disease, where the onus of determining impurity is
placed upon the priests, who are typically the guardians of temple purity.

Thus, the Bible's rhetoric shifts subtly, though significantly, in Leviticus 15 as it addresses all Israelites rather than just the priestly class. Chapters 13 and 14 instruct the priests in the finer points of examining and recognizing scale-disease lesions, while chapter 15 remains more general and also provides a larger context for observing the ritual impurity laws: maintaining God's presence in the Temple and among the nation of Israel. In this sense, Levitius 15 does not create a hierarchy of authority to enforce genital-flux impurity; it is rather one of the Hebrew Bible's "prototypical compendia of legal and ethical norms"[10] which exhorts all of Israel to act in accordance with the divine will. As such, the pericope assumes that knowledge of genital-flux impurity emerges directly from an individual's close familiarity with his or her own body, and no external, specific criteria for genital-flux impurity need to be demarcated.

Tannaitic Distinctions: Negaʿim and Zabim/Niddah

Tannaitic literature (specifically the *Sifra*, the Mishnah and the Tosefta tractates *Negaʿim, Zavim,* and *Niddah*) thoroughly maintains the distinction between scale-disease and genital-flux impurity laws. They are treated in separate tractates in the Mishnah and Tosefta; Tractate *Negaʿim* continues to invoke the authority of the priest for determining impurity, while Tractates *Niddah* and *Zabim* do not. Nevertheless, the thematic similarity between these two topics and their proximity in the biblical text prompts the rabbinic authors of the Midrash to question whether these two legal subjects may be analogized. A discussion in the *Sifra* maintains that there is a qualitative distinction between *negaʿim* and *zabim,* despite their points of convergence. In this passage, an anonymous rabbi begins the discussion by asking whether ritually impure bodily conditions (scale disease and genital flux) are considered to have imparted impurity even in the pre-Sinaitic era (before the laws of the Torah were commanded):

> A. "When there will be [a discharge]" [Lev. 15:2]: from the pronouncement [of the Torah] and onward.
> B. But is this not logical? [Torah] declared it ritually impure in [the case of] *negaʿim,* and it declared it ritually impure in [the case of] *zabim:* just as [Torah] exempted *negaʿim* before the pronouncement, so [Torah] exempted *zabim* before the pronouncement. [Perhaps there is

also an argument of] *a fortiori:* [In the case of] *nega'im*, in which [the Torah] declared it ritually impure for those under constraint, [the Torah] exempted them before the pronouncement. [*All the more so*, in the case of] *zabim*, in which [the Torah] did not declare it impure for those under constraint, would it not be logical that [the Torah] would exempt them before the pronouncement?

C. No. If you said so in *nega'im*, in which there is no impurity and purity except through a priest, can you say so in *zabim*, in which impurity and purity is through every person? Since impurity and purity is through every person, [the Torah] did not exempt them before the pronouncement! Thus Torah states, "when there will be"—from the pronouncement and onward. (*Sifra Lev., Metsora', Zabim*, 1:2)[11]

In this somewhat opaque *Sifra* passage, the distinction between the cases of *nega'im* and *zabim* is not only maintained, but sharpened. The final formulation of the law under question—that flux before "the pronouncement" was considered pure—creates a correspondence between *nega'im* and *zabim*, but the *Sifra*'s argumentation reveals that it is indeed a correspondence, and not an equivalence. In the first step of the argument, the midrash proposes a provisional hypothesis: the use of the imperfect verb in the biblical phrase with which the laws of *zabim/ nega'im* begin, "when there *will be* a flux" (Lev. 15:2, emphasis added), connotes from the time of the pronouncement and onward—when there *will* be a flux it will render one impure, but when there *used to* be, it had no effect.

But the midrash then objects that a biblical phrase is not needed to impart that particular lesson; rather, it may be a simple, logical inference. First, the midrash suggests that we can assume that the law for *zabim* will be the same as for *nega'im*, and therefore that both began to convey impurity only from the pronouncement of the Torah and onward. This statement by the midrash ("B" above) presumes a simple correlation between these two areas of law—an unsurprising supposition considering the remarkable similarity of these two topics. The midrashic argument continues by showing that in yet another way the teaching that genital-flux impurity is conferred only "from the pronouncement" and onward may be logically deduced, by using an argument *a fortiori:* the law would be the same in the case of *nega'im* not because these two cases are simply analogous, but because scale disease is a more serious subject than genital flux, and therefore its laws are stricter. The midrash offers proof that *nega'im* is treated more strictly than *zabim* by turning to a case in which an individual is "under constraint," i.e., not able to act according to his or her own free will; in such a case, we are taught that *negaʿim* still convey impurity, and genital flux does not. Because our law under question would involve a leniency (exempting the people who lived "before the pronouncement" from genital-flux impurity), one could reasonably conclude that if *negaʿim,* the stricter case, includes an exemption, certainly *zabim,* the more lenient case, would include an exemption as well.

This hypothesis (which is actually refuted in the next line of the midrash) upholds a distinction between scale-disease and genital-flux impurity, even if only a difference of degree: strict versus lenient. The midrash discards this argument, however, in the process trumping this quantitative distinction with a qualitative one. The *Sifra* points out next that in *negaʿim* the very status of pure or impure is achieved only through a priest, whereas in *zabim* any person can determine his or her own ritual status. This observation has the effect of refuting the parallel between *negaʿim* and *zabim* adduced above by pointing out that these areas of impurity law are structured quite differently. *Negaʿim* may be treated more strictly than *zabim,* but that is not the only difference between these two subjects. In fact, those living "before the pronouncement" may be exempted from scale-disease impurity for a very simple reason: this kind of impurity depends upon a priest's pronouncement, and before the Torah was revealed the priesthood had not yet been established. Genital-flux impurity, on the other hand, operates outside of the system of the priesthood, since every individual is responsible to monitor his or her own status of ritual purity. Because the priesthood is unnecessary for ascertaining genital-flux impurity, nothing in the law would have prevented it from being observed "before the pronouncement."

The *Sifra* thus sharpens the distinction between *negaʿim* and *zabim* by demonstrating that the stipulations for determining ritual impurity are different enough that no simple parallel may be drawn between the two subjects. An entirely separate biblical proof (from within Leviticus 15) is thus necessary to show that genital-flux impurity was indeed inoperative "before the pronouncement," and thus the rabbis uphold the initial reading of Leviticus 15:2, "when there *will be* a flux." No parallel between *negaʿim* and *zabim* is inferred, and the legal question of when genital flux impurity took effect is resolved by interpreting biblical texts that pertain exclusively to the subject of *zabim.*

Thus, rabbinic rhetoric distinguishes *zabim* sharply from *negaʿim;* surprisingly, then, the tannaitic rabbis turn around and institute a procedural model for discerning purity from impurity in the case of menstrual impurity (*niddah*) that closely resembles the biblical model for *nega°im*: they posit that some blood is pure while other blood is impure, and one can differentiate between the two by close, physical inspection. While no system of priestly or other authoritative examination is described by the tannaim, by the time the Babylonian Talmud is composed, the rabbis are acting as expert examiners of menstrual blood. Exegetically, then, the rabbis eschew any parallel between *nega°im* and *zabim,* and yet in practice they seem to create a parallel in the appeal to expertise.

I would like to argue that the demands of creating and sustaining a working human legal system out of the raw material of the divine law[12]—with rabbinic authorities at the helm—drove rabbinic exegetes in both of these contradictory directions. On the one hand, the rabbis had to compensate for the fact that these laws are, in the Bible, placed outside of a human legal system, with only the conscience of each individual and God acting as judge and enforcer; if the ancient Israelites failed to carry out these rituals properly, they are vaguely warned that they may "die in their ritual impurity" (Lev. 15:31). But entrusting these crucial matters solely to the laity, using only indefinite threats to ensure their proper fulfillment, would place ritual impurity outside the rabbis' humanly administered sacred legal system, outside any possibility of adjudication. Therefore the rabbis had to create a system for genital flux impurity that resembled the procedure used for *nega°im*—one which was based on clearly delineated rules and easily observable data, but was also complex enough to require expert analysis. The rabbis needed to raise doubt about how to interpret and implement ritual purity laws in order to offer legal solutions to this doubt.

At the same time, having constructed a system resembling the biblical procedure for *nega°im,* the rabbis had to distance their system from *nega°im* because they could not invoke the arbitrary authority conferred upon the priests by divine fiat. Were *zabim* and *nega°im* analogized, the implication would be that only those chosen by God—the descendants of priests—could decide matters of ritual impurity. As the rabbis could not command this divine authority, they would need to persuade their followers that the law of *zabim / niddah* was complex enough to call for expert decision-making, but that it was still not at all tied to the priestly hierarchy.

The rabbis thus make a case for their authority over the divine law precisely by emphasizing the biblical evidentiary silence and perhaps even raising doubt in the very cases that the Bible presents as clear and commonsensical; the rabbis then offer themselves as legal experts who can resolve this uncertainty. By stressing doubt and observable evidence, the rabbis destabilize, and in fact undermine, the rhetoric of simple knowledge in this biblical text which emphasizes the transparency of ritual purity categories—a move which while paving the way for the rabbinic administration of divine law forces the rabbis to construct a different kind of truth from the bodily intuition presumed in the Hebrew Bible.

DETERMINING MENSTRUAL IMPURITY I:
THE APPEARANCE OF BLOOD

Tannaitic rules for determining menstrual impurity are far more specific than biblical ones, and they rely on objective standards of differences in appearance. This divergence between biblical and rabbinic discourses on ritual impurity has been noted, though conclusions as to *why* this is the case differ significantly.

Adrianna Destro argues from an anthropological perspective that the Bible's vague laws about exactly what kind of discharge conveys impurity instilled fear in people, since they were never quite sure whether or not they were ritually impure; the rabbis, realizing that more specific rules would be easier to follow and would offer people more security, defined concrete and objective criteria for determining menstrual impurity. She points out that Leviticus makes impurity "accessible and decipherable exclusively through the idiom of time, and by the mechanism of temporal cycles. . . . [F]or human beings detecting impurity means detecting or structuring times."[13] Impurity is manifest only in time (impure for seven days, wash, wait until sundown, etc.) because "throughout Leviticus impurity appears as something not discernible, elusive and inexorably hidden to everybody, even to the unclean person. Bodily uncleanness is either conceptually and [sic] sociologically vague."[14] Destro argues that the tannaitic rabbis, in Mishnah *Niddah,* elaborate a system of times as well, but add another dimension to the discussion which "concerns the human body." She writes, "In the rabbis' vision, a clear recognition of the necessity of the body and of its material distinctiveness was intended to give practical measures to impurity. Indeed, body condition was linked to time dimension and brought uncleanness under *observation.*"[15] The dimension of "observation" (re'iyah) introduced in the second mishnah of the tractate is foreign to the levitical text, but in tannaitic literature it becomes synonymous with the awareness of impurity.

Moreover, the distinctions drawn by the tannaim between substances which indicate impurity versus those that do not are based entirely on appearance. Again, Destro notes this when she writes that "the tractate of Niddah bases its rules . . . on the external appearance of the contaminating fluids."[16] The way Destro accounts for this shift from the levitical text, however, is not wholly convincing:

> There is no doubt that humans are given a special attention in rabbinic thought. This reflects a need to make impurity more decipherable, and to free people as much as possible from fears and risks. At the very least, it transforms the collective imagination of purity into practical ways to penetrate things that govern usual social life.[17]

The tannaim are certainly attempting to draw clear parameters for the range and reach of menstrual impurity, but while they do succeed in *limiting* the scope of ritually impure blood, they do not necessarily offer easy-to-follow guidelines and hence "freedom from fear." Indeed, there is no evidence in the rabbinic literature on impurity that freedom from fear was any sort of motivating factor. The scriptural verse reads "when a woman has a discharge, her discharge being blood from her body, she shall remain in her menstrual impurity seven days . . ." (Lev. 15:19). The *Sifra* comments:

A. Is it possible that any appearance of flux that flows will be impure?
B. Scripture teaches: "blood."
C. If "blood," I can only deduce that one appearance of blood [is impure]!
D. When [Scripture] says "her bloods" [Lev. 12:17], it teaches that many bloods are impure in her:
E. The red and the black and the shade of the bright-colored saffron, and the color like earthy water, and like wine mingled with water. The House of Shammai says: also like water wherein fenugreek has been steeped, and like the liquid from roasted meat. But the House of Hillel declares these clean. (*Sifra Lev., Metsoraʿ, Zabim*, 4:3)

This midrash severely limits the scope of the biblical passage, only to expand it again by citing another biblical passage. By simply using the word "*dam*" (blood), the biblical text suggests that *all* blood flow is impure, and it does not distinguish between different kinds of blood. The first proposal in the midrash (A and B above) represents a strong, "plain-sense" reading of the biblical text: blood flow is impure, other discharge is not. The midrash then highlights a grammatical detail that may be interpreted to mean that the scriptural verse is restricted rather than extremely broad: because it uses the word "blood" in the singular, it must mean only one appearance (or color) of blood. This is not a necessary reading of the verse, even according to the rules of midrashic hermeneutics, but the rabbis nevertheless choose to limit the scope of the verse, only to expand it again: the word "bloods" appears in the plural (albeit in a different context) and therefore ritual impurity is conveyed in "many" appearances of blood. In other words, ritually impure blood has many different looks, but there are also some kinds of blood which are ritually pure. By naming the colors of ritually impure blood, the midrash limits the possibilities for ritual impurity, but it hardly imparts "practicality" to the act of distinguishing ritual purity from impurity, or even "freedom from fear"; according to the midrash, one need not determine only whether one's discharge is blood, but also whether it is ritually pure blood or one of the many kinds of ritually impure blood.

Thus it follows from these mishnaic laws that interpreting menstrual blood would become an expert science. Charlotte Fonrobert argues that by creating a "taxonomy of blood colors," the Mishnah transforms the determination of menstrual impurity into a specialized skill. She concludes that this shift was not a natural consequence of these laws, but a deliberate rabbinic institution:

> Since with respect to menstrual impurity the Mishnaic ruling [of distinguishing between different colors of blood] does not have a biblical base, it seems that the rabbis looked at Negaᶜim as a model or an analogy. . . . The analogy is a procedural one: just as in the case of skin diseases, which are an integral part of the priestly purity and impurity system in the Bible, the priest is installed as the inspector and, hence, the prime expert, so also they are to be experts in the case of (irregular) genital bleeding of woman. . . . By analogy the successor of the priest, that is, the rabbi, as an expert on the matter of purity and impurity, is installed as the inspector, who like the priest is trained in the differentiation of colors.[18]

Fonrobert's insight that the rabbinic "taxonomy of blood colors" demands expert rabbinic intervention in genital-flux purity matters is undeniable;

however, I suggest that the rabbis did not wholeheartedly create an analogy with *nega'im*. Tannaitic literature ostensibly derives the requirements of determining menstrual impurity not from the priestly inspection of *nega'im*, but instead from close, midrashic readings of levitical texts in which priestly inspection is never mentioned (Leviticus 15, *zabim*, and Leviticus 12, the parturient). Moreover, as we have seen above, the rabbis paint these two subjects as disanalogous precisely on the question of procedure. In discriminating between different types of blood, and choosing appearance as the criterion for discernment, the rabbis may have transferred a concept from the sphere of *nega'im*, or they may have simply chosen the most obvious possibility among several alternatives. Even while the procedure they establish closely resembles the priestly inspection of *nega'im*, however, the tannaim never claim the authority a pseudo-priestly system would demand, in which a certain, divinely-authorized decision is pronounced for each case of impurity. In later centuries, the rabbis do become expert examiners of blood, but that need not have been anticipated by the tannaim. Tannaitic literature (unlike the Talmud) does not impart rules or even stories which depict physical, scientific inspection of menstrual blood.[19] Rabbinic stipulations include a requirement of inspection not by rabbis, but by women themselves.

The Mishnah's detailed rules may not be easily applicable by lay people, but they do replace a subjective standard for determining menstruation with an objective one, insofar as they replace private identifications of "blood" (which may vary) with the decisiveness of an official definition of "blood" (which theoretically remains consistent). One need not posit the rabbinic concern for humanity (Destro) nor the rabbis' direct borrowing from priestly forms of authority (Fonrobert) to explain this exegetical move; the evidence of tannaitic texts supports neither of these claims entirely. On one hand, it seems as though the rabbis are simplifying the biblical text by providing standardized definitions for discernment, giving lay people the tools to take responsibility themselves, and on the other hand it appears that they are hopelessly complicating the biblical rules, with the result that lay people must study in a rabbinic academy before they can recognize impure menstrual blood. These apparently contradictory results may be explained by a broader—and perhaps more obvious—motive: the creation of legally-defined facts that are necessary for the formation and perpetuation of the rule of law. Pierre Bourdieu, the French sociologist, recognizes the centrality of the law's translation of lay issues into specialized discourse while simultaneous presenting this discourse as obvious and natural:

> [T]he juridical field ... completely redefines ordinary experience. ... As is true of any "field," the constitution of the juridical field is a principle of constitution of reality itself. To join the game ... is above all to recognize the specific requirements of the juridical construction of the issue. Since juridical facts are the products of juridical construction, and not vice versa, a complete retranslation of all of the aspects of the controversy is necessary. ...
>
> Juridical language reveals with complete clarity the appropriation effect inscribed in the logic of the juridical field's operations. Such language combines elements taken directly from the common language and elements foreign to its system, but it bears all the marks of a rhetoric of impersonality and neutrality. ... Far from being a simple ideological mask, such a rhetoric of autonomy, neutrality, and universality, which may be the basis of a real autonomy of thought and practice, is the expression of the whole operation of the juridical field and, in particular, of the work of rationalization to which the system of juridical norms is continually subordinated.[20]

In other words, Bourdieu observes that the juridical field operates by constituting its own reality, a reality which must be accepted by the laity who wish to participate in it. While translating experience into "juridical facts," the legal field makes itself seem intuitive by adopting a rhetoric of "universality," which is not a simple "mask" for a particular ideology, such as concern for humanity or male authority, but the very process by which the juridical field sustains itself (and which may embed several ideologies more indirectly). Though Bourdieu bases his reflections on modern practices of French and Anglo-American law, his comments here are easily translatable to the world of tannaitic texts. The mishnah that details the taxonomy of menstrual blood requires no explanation or motivation outside of the acknowledgment that the rabbis attempted to carve out a sphere of human law which need not appeal to outside sources of knowledge or inspiration to render decisions in uncertain situations; as such, the tannaim needed to create the sense that there are objective, observable criteria for deciding one's ritual status, and that only through adherence to these criteria is the "fact" of menstrual impurity established.[21]

What does need to be explained, then, is the discrepancy between the biblical and rabbinic texts. In other words, if the Bible differentiates between public and private law—law that can be enforced by the priests and law that must be monitored only by individuals—why do rabbinic texts blur this distinction? Why are tannaitic rules for impurity uniformly absorbed into a legal field with the rabbis positioned as legal authorities, while the Bible is content to invoke priestly authority for some situations, and yet for others it does not?

The key to the discrepancy between Leviticus 15 and Mishnah *Niddah* 2:6 is the verse quoted above: "you shall keep the people of Israel separate from their impurity, so that they do not die in their impurity by defiling my tabernacle that is in their midst" (Lev. 15:31). Unlike the Mishnah, in which rabbis oversee the law, and unlike Leviticus 13–14 in which priests oversee the law, in Leviticus 15 God himself oversees the law. The consequence of disobeying the laws of menstrual purity in Leviticus 15 is direct and unmediated by human legal authorities: the sinner is punished with death (perhaps as part of a collective judgment on Israel) because of his or her defilement of God's Sanctuary. The biblical text does not require the clear-cut neutrality of legal language nor the reliance upon professionals. Again, Bourdieu remarks: "The [legal] professionals create the need for their own services by redefining problems expressed in ordinary language as legal problems, translating them into the language of the law."[22] The divine strictures here in Leviticus create the opposite effect; the plain language speaks to every individual who is responsible for his or her own ritual purity before God. In the Bible, genital-flux impurity is effectively placed outside of any system of human governance. Indeed, Hartley writes that "[s]ince these matters are very private, there would have been virtually no way to monitor compliance."[23] Though the Bible is concerned with the creation of a human legal system to ensure that the divine laws are kept, ultimately it is God himself who will guarantee and enforce God's own law. Rabbinic literature, however, is oriented toward a human legal system in which the divine is not directly invoked, and thus entire areas of law, such as genital-flux impurity, if left in their biblical form, would be unenforceable and untouched by judicial processes. So the rabbis abandon the biblical imperative that every individual privately determine when they are ritually impure for a system of visible and objective standards—they describe the specific appearance of menstrual blood and insist that it must be *seen* by the woman rather than privately determined. Thus the tannaitic texts depart from the biblical system, insisting that individuals are responsible before *the law*, not God. As divine law is redefined as a human endeavor, all of biblical law must be subsumed under the rabbinic legal field.

DETERMINING MENSTRUAL IMPURITY II: BLOODSTAINS

The rabbinic elucidation of how a woman recognizes the onset of menstrual impurity—actually seeing the impure blood—comprises only the first step in the rabbinic elaboration of biblical law. For just as the tannaim restrict the word "*dam*" to include not all blood, but only certain kinds of blood, they similarly restrict the Bible's perhaps deliberately vague "*ki tiheyeh zabah*" (when she will be a discharger, *lit.*) to refer only to direct knowledge of blood flow (seeing the blood itself) and not to indirect deductions (seeing evidence of blood flow, such as a bloodstain). Again, we see the stark distinction between *nega'im* and *zabim/niddah* in biblical language: in the case of *nega'im,* the status of ritual impurity obtains only through a priest's pronouncement; in *zabim/niddah,* all that is necessary to create the status of impurity is the very existence—"when she *will be*"— of flux. The biblical text's use of this basic "to be" verb emphasizes that the mere *existence* of flux conveys impurity; the way in which one becomes aware of the flux is immaterial within these biblical laws. The biblical stipulation is not concerned with whether one feels a flux internally, sees a stain upon one's bed or clothes, sees the flux directly, or otherwise perceives the existence of flux—all ought to suffice to effect a status of impurity as long as the flux does, in fact, exist. Unquestionably, some methods of ascertaining the presence of blood will produce more uncertainty regarding one's status than directly "seeing the blood" would, but the biblical text does not deal with these questions. Instead, the verse which concludes this section in Leviticus, "you shall keep the people of Israel separate from their impurity . . . ," warns that impurity should be taken extremely seriously, and that a slight doubt as to one's status as ritually impure should not weigh heavily against the enormous consequences of remaining ritually impure: "so that they do not die in their impurity by defiling my tabernacle that is in their midst."

The tannaitic rabbis, as mentioned above, require *seeing* the blood to effect ritual impurity; moreover, they systematize the seeing of blood by instituting a regimen of examinations in which one regularly checks for the presence of blood. As Destro remarks, [the menstruant] is invested with the responsibility of exploring regularly her body, private and secret, in order to find out the onset and the end of the menstrual flow. In rabbinic language, "seeing the blood" therefore has the specific function of determining, *as early as possible,* the exact time at which blood makes the woman defiled and defiling.[24]

In other words, these examinations function as signposts in the Mishnah, allowing the rabbis to carve time up into discrete intervals and thus pinpoint the precise moment of the onset of menstruation, and hence ritual impurity. The "seeing of blood" does not define the onset of impurity; in fact, in several cases developed in the Mishnah, ritual impurity is retroactive to a time before one sees the blood. Nonetheless, this mode of seeing blood directly on a test cloth in the context of an examination does come to define, paradigmatically, the knowledge or awareness of menstruation. Other evidence of menstrual impurity may effect a status of ritual impurity, but these other methods of determining menstruation are ultimately subordinated to the "direct" evidence of blood intentionally collected on a proper test cloth.[25]

The rabbis thus attempt to correlate the onset of impurity with something physically real (the exact moment in which menstruation begins), but they create a legally prescribed procedure to mediate that reality. Outside the arena of examinations and test-cloths, or, as we might say, in an uncontrolled environment, it is more difficult for the law to determine not only the moment of the onset of menstruation, but indeed whether the blood seen is menstrual, that is, ritually impure, blood altogether. Such cases of doubtful impurity may be summed up in the mishnaic case of the *ketem,* or bloodstain.

A bloodstain appearing on a woman's garment or in a woman's immediate environs often conveys ritual impurity, and it may also function as evidence that the woman herself is menstruating and impure. At first, Mishnah *Niddah* appears to set up a standard of "reasonable doubt" to determine the ritual status of the stain and the woman herself. If it is reasonable to assume that the blood came from a source other than menstrual flux, the rabbis permit such an attribution to be made. The mishnah states:

A. She may assign [the cause of the bloodstain] to anything she can possibly assign it to.
B. If she slaughtered a beast, a wild animal, or a bird, if she were engaged with stains, or if she sat beside those engaged with them, if she

killed a louse, she may assign it to [any] one [of these]. . . . And she
may assign it to her son or to her husband.

C. If she had a wound that could open up and let out blood, she may assign it to that. (*m. Nid.* 8:2)[26]

The mishnah's catalogue of possible causes of bloodstains seems lenient, but
not excessively so. Given the biblical admonition to "keep the people of Israel apart" from impurity and the grave consequences that could ensue, one
might assume a more careful approach to doubtful cases of impurity, but
this mishnah's leniency is only intensified in the next mishnah. A story
(*ma'aseh*) is told of a ground-breaking legal decision which defies our expectations of extreme meticulousness in cases of uncertain ritual
impurity:

> It once happened that a certain woman came before R. Aqiba and said to
> him, "I saw a bloodstain." He said to her, "Perhaps you had a wound?" She
> replied, "Yes, but it healed." He said to her, "Perhaps it opened up and let
> out some blood?" She said to him, "Yes." And R. Aqiba pronounced her
> clean. He saw his students staring at one another, and he said to them,
> "Why is this matter difficult in your eyes? For the sages did not say this
> thing to be stringent, but rather to be lenient, as it says, 'When a woman
> has a discharge, her discharge being blood . . .' [Lev. 15:19]—'blood,' not
> 'stain'!" (*m. Nid.* 8:3)[27]

In this mishnah, R. Aqiba's ruling surprises the reader by further extending the leniencies of the previous mishnah. The idea that a bloodstain may
be attributed to a likely, or reasonable, ritually pure source, is surpassed
by R. Aqiba as he privileges a mere possibility (perhaps the wound reopened?) over a known fact (it healed). This rather unlikely possibility that
a healed wound could have reopened suffices for R. Aqiba to declare the
woman ritually pure, a surprising decision considering the high stakes
involved in determining menstrual impurity.[28] The reader's surprise is
mirrored in the students of R. Aqiba, gazing at one another in disbelief;
the audacity of R. Aqiba's verdict is inscribed into the Mishnah itself.[29]

R. Aqiba does not simply push his case beyond the "reasonable doubt"
standard of the Mishnah, however. He effectively neutralizes the force of the
bloodstain as evidence of menstruation by radically separating it from the
blood from which it derives and to which it testifies. He achieves this by
explicating a biblical verse, in which the word "*dam*" (blood) is used. He

claims that because the word "blood" appears in the Bible, one can conclude that only the appearance of blood—and not a dried bloodstain—elicits a status of ritual impurity within biblical law.

This is not to say that a bloodstain had no effect on a person's ritual purity status. The rabbis recognized two different sources of legal authority within rabbinic law: biblical commandments and rabbinic decrees. Of primary legal authority are biblical commandments. Of secondary legal authority are rabbinically authored laws: independent rabbinic decrees and laws derived from scripture through a variety of specified exegetical techniques. The rabbis often would declare something prohibited even while they recognized that biblically it would be permitted. The chief practical difference between these two levels of law relates to deciding matters of an ambiguous case: ambiguous cases of biblical law must be decided strictly, while ambiguous cases of rabbinic law demand leniency. R. Aqiba, in our mishnah above, decides the woman's case leniently because, as he explains, biblical law only confers ritual impurity when "actual" blood is detected, and not when one merely notices a bloodstain. Ritual impurity ensues from the observation of a bloodstain by rabbinic decree only. Therefore, in ambiguous cases involving a bloodstain, one errs on the side of leniency.

Thus R. Aqiba effects a radical separation between blood and bloodstain, defusing the evidentiary force of the bloodstain by declaring it utterly meaningless within biblical law, and viable in rabbinic law only in cases of virtual certainty. As noted above, a simple reading of Leviticus 15 would suggest that ritual impurity is conveyed regardless of how one becomes aware of menstruation; R. Aqiba, however, highlights the question of awareness, teasing out of biblical language the requirement for direct knowledge of menstruation and thereby limiting the possibility of one's becoming ritually impure.

Fonrobert's analysis of the function of the bloodstain in rabbinic impurity law attests to R. Aqiba's ultimate success. She writes:

> Within the larger impurity system of the rabbis the *ketem* is not an unusual phenomenon, since the effort is always made to protect what is in the status of purity and to strengthen the biblical rules by building "protective fences" around them. These principles apply particularly to cases of doubt. . . . Since the bloodstain is recognized as being a rabbinic enactment only, and not derived from biblical legislation (*b. Nid.* 59a), the

halakhic tendency is to be lenient in problems and uncertainties arising from it. *Thus* the mishnah reports the following case: It once happened that a certain woman came before R. Akiva. . . . [30]

R. Aqiba represents himself as rendering a decision in line with a familiar and acceptable principle—that the uncertainty of bloodstains is rabbinic rather than biblical and that doubtful cases must therefore be resolved leniently. But the reaction of the students in the narrative would indicate that this was not in fact a clear and accepted principle, and that R. Aqiba was innovating with his distinction between blood and bloodstain. The story is not proof of the distinction, but rather it is its generating moment. This innovation *subsequently* becomes law (at least according to textual logic, if not historically), and its definitions lay the groundwork for all ensuing rabbinic ritual purity law, enticing us to read the story within the familiar framework which it itself constructed. Because Fonrobert accepts R. Aqiba's claim that the impurity of bloodstains is merely a rabbinic stringency appended to the "core" biblical law, she can state that R. Aqiba's ruling is "not an unusual phenomenon"—which is just the effect R. Aqiba's rhetorical posturing strives to achieve. R. Aqiba's, or the mishnah's, deductive leaps (a stain of blood is not "actual blood") and daring exegetical moves are presented as transparent, objective reasoning. *Basing itself on this mishnah,* the Babylonian Talmud thus states unequivocally that "the impurity of bloodstains is altogether a rabbinical enactment."

The story of R. Aqiba is seen by Fonrobert as reinforcing "the Mishnah's focus on the types of women's genital blood and the bloodstain *as external evidence* of a woman's menstruation,"[31] because he is seen as introducing a further rabbinical enactment for the objective determination of impurity. I would suggest instead that he is *undercutting* the very relationship between external evidence of the bloodstain and a woman's menstruation by declaring that bloodstains may be explained away through the power of an artificial, legal—and indeed linguistic—distinction.

R. Aqiba's legal fiction in our mishnah states that "blood" and "bloodstain" are two discrete entities and concepts. That this marks a significant innovation—and intervention—is indicated by the fact that the word "blood" does not regularly exclude a stain of blood, as demonstrated by the mishnah itself which uses the terms interchangeably. For example, the mishnah states,

A. ... If three women had worn the same garment or had been sitting on a bench, and blood (*dam*) was found on it, all of them are deemed impure.

B. If they had been sitting on a stone bench or on the couch in a bathhouse, R. Nehemiah declares them pure, for R. Nehemiah says: anything that does not accept impurity does not accept bloodstains (*ketamim* [plural of *ketem*]). (*m. Nid.* 9:3)

The "*ketem*" of the last phrase clearly refers back to the "*dam*" of the first sentence, as this "*dam*" in its context must denote a bloodstain: in what other form could blood be found on a garment or on a bench? R. Aqiba's interpretation, in which the word "*dam*" in the Bible excludes the "*ketem*," or the bloodstain, is not a simple definitional observation but a midrash that radically drives a wedge between two nearly synonymous terms: blood and bloodstain.

Conceptually, R. Aqiba's reading of "*dam*" is also counterintuitive. What does it mean to see "actual blood" as opposed to a bloodstain? Even within the rabbinic framework of "seeing the blood" and its system of regular examinations, this conceptual distinction is difficult to grasp. Is blood on a test-cloth—the Mishnah's most esteemed example of "seeing the blood"—not itself a bloodstain? One is compelled to conclude that it is the linguistic, rather than conceptual, dissimilarity between "*dam*" and "*ketem*" that allows R. Aqiba to disassociate these two physical permutations of menstrual blood, creating, in essence, a legal dissimilarity if not a real one. While the bloodstain is, in a real and scientific sense, blood, in a semantic sense it is different from blood in that inherent in the term is an evidentiary nuance: the bloodstain is not blood in that it is the trace or residue of blood, the evidence or sign of blood. It is as if R. Aqiba, in noting that the biblical text writes "*dam*" and not "*ketem*," recognizes that the Bible is indeed unconcerned with evidentiary issues, assuming direct knowledge of the thing itself—the Bible does not discuss the *ketem*, the evidence of blood, but instead *dam*, blood itself. Thus according to R. Aqiba, the biblical law only applies in a case of certain knowledge of menstrual flux—certain knowledge which, for R. Aqiba, is impossible to attain in the legal world, in which physical evidence may always only point toward a particular truth and never offer it directly. The only kind of certainty possible that does not rely upon the interpretation of signs is, for R. Aqiba, legally-constructed fact—which in this case is the arbitrary and artificial procedure of "seeing the blood" by adhering to the rabbinically mandated regular examinations.

In other words, the only difference between "*dam*" and "*ketem*," aside from the linguistic one, is a legal one, one which may be summarized as follows: when *dam* (certain knowledge of menstruation) is present, the biblical criteria for ritual impurity are met, and ambiguous cases must be decided strictly; when a *ketem* (evidence of menstruation) is present, no biblical ritual impurity is possible, and ambiguous cases must be decided leniently.

Interestingly, R. Aqiba's negation of the force of the bloodstain could have been accomplished by a simple explication of the word *zabah,* or "flowing," which occurs in our main biblical text. The term denotes the liquid, flowing form of blood rather than dried blood or a bloodstain. But R. Aqiba does not read the verse this way, perhaps because such a reading would destabilize the rabbis' entire approach to menstrual impurity which isolates *seeing* the blood as definitive rather than experiencing the flow (which would more often be determined by feeling rather than sight).[32] Thus R. Aqiba's focus on the term "*dam*" is in keeping with the rabbinic requirement to keep to a regular schedule of examinations in order to see the blood and determine menstruation—while simultaneously undermining the evidentiary force of the majority of bloodstains discovered outside of this legally-prescribed practice.

The discussion of the bloodstain, centered around this pivotal mishnah, bolsters rabbinic authority, but not in the way in which it is usually understood. Charlotte Fonrobert sees rabbinic patriarchal ideology in the objectification of female menstruation, separating menstrual blood from the woman, and subjecting it to the gaze and authority of the rabbis. She writes, "the story illustrates how the bloodstain becomes the external, visible, and accessible object that is under the jurisdiction of the rabbis. . . . The rabbis . . . are now judges to tell a woman whether she is menstruating . . . or whether she has merely an internal wound."[33] While this mishnah is undeniably steeped in patriarchal attitudes, and it does, in fact, place the rabbi in the position of judge, or arbiter, in this legal question of ritual status (ritually pure or impure), it does so not by making the bloodstain "visible and accessible" but rather by *eradicating* the visibility of the bloodstain—by questioning the very objectivity it is supposed to represent. The woman who comes before R. Aqiba is the one who claims to have seen a bloodstain—*she* brings the objective evidence of menstruation before the rabbinic authority. R. Aqiba does not determine that she has an internal wound; he merely inquires into the possibility, and makes a *legal* decision that she is ritually pure. His invocation of the need for leniency implies that he believes the woman's status as an actual menstruant is *in doubt;* he specifically refuses to decide whether or not the blood she saw was in fact menstrual or the result of an internal wound. He explains that the mere possibility of an open wound triggers the principle of legal leniency for a rabbinic decree. Thus the woman's logical assumption that seeing blood is objective evidence of menstruation is challenged by R. Aqiba's appeal to uncertainty—and he substitutes legal fact for common-sense probability.

This case of doubt is not just acknowledged by R. Aqiba—it is essentially created by him. *He,* rather than the woman, inquires into an alternate possibility for the origin of the bloodstain; she closes off possibilities ("but it healed") and he reopens them ("perhaps it opened up?"). R. Aqiba prevails in this mishnah, seizing control from the woman who approaches him and even the students who, having trained as rabbinic disciples, assume along with the woman that in all probability the stain was menstrual blood, and hence ritually impure. He does so precisely by privileging a slight possibility over any other claims. R. Aqiba dominates not by subordinating personal, subjective sensibility to objective knowledge, but rather by making skepticism the operative principle in rendering his legal decision.

Uncertainty about impurity, which would seem to create fear or helplessness, instead creates a space for rabbinic legal creativity and authority. For if seeing a bloodstain does not necessarily mean that one is ritually impure, simple observations are rejected as a means to ascertaining truth, and legal reasoning is upheld. And thus a legal fiction—that a bloodstain cannot be evidence of menstrual bleeding within biblical law—supercedes the judgment and experience of ordinary people. Bourdieu explains that

> the establishment of properly professional competence, the technical mastery of a sophisticated body of knowledge that often runs contrary to the simple counsels of common sense, entails the disqualification of the non-specialist's . . . naive understanding of the facts, of their "view of the case." The difference between the vulgar vision of the person who is about to come under the jurisdiction of the court, that is to say, the client, and the professional vision of the expert witness, the judge, the lawyer, and

other juridical actors, is far from accidental. Rather, it is essential to a power relation upon which two systems of presuppositions, two systems of expressive intention—two world-views—are grounded.[34]

The biblical law assumes that one can determine menstrual impurity without any recourse to juridical processes; rabbinic law brings these rules "within the juridical order" by emphasizing and indeed exaggerating the depths of uncertainty that attach to any observation of bloodstains and the naiveté of such a "vulgar vision" of ritual impurity. The rabbis thus construct legal truth instead, exemplifying a kind of legal formalism which can serve to establish rabbinic power over the laity.

R. Aqiba's decision is told by way of an *aggadah*, a narrative, rather than simply stated as a legal principle. Through this discursive choice, the mishnah is able to expose the doubt that generates R. Aqiba's legal reasoning and ultimately his decision. In laying bare the process by which R. Aqiba arrives at his ultimate uncertainty, the story invites the reader not only to accept a legal ruling, but to *experience* the frame of mind through which it emerges. The gradual unfolding of this process—witnessed first from the woman's perspective and then in the student's astonishment—reflects the reader's misgivings in order to co-opt them by showing how they are bested by a rabbinic master in a transparent legal process.

In making these legal decisions based on doubt, as R. Aqiba does in the above mishnah, the tannaitic rabbis do not seem concerned that their legal decisions may not correspond to some objectively real state of menstruation or blood flow. Several centuries later, however, as recorded throughout Tractate *Niddah* in the Babylonian Talmud, rabbis act as expert examiners of menstrual blood, and women are expected to consult rabbis so that questionable discharges can be inspected. Here, the rabbis do not make legal decisions as much as scientific ones; they inspect the physical features of the blood to determine its origin, and thereby its ritual status. In the end, then, R. Aqiba's formal legal edifice crumbles—the pressure for the law to adhere to "objective" scientific reality drives the rabbis to begin fitting the law to "substantive" physical reality rather than creating reality through the law. But these later outcomes ought not to influence our understanding of the tannaitic texts which never speak of this kind of "expert science" (even while the detailed laws they delineate augur its development). In the midst of all this concern for taxonomies of blood and procedures for observation, R. Aqiba's story stands as testimony to the centrality of a skeptical attitude about objective reality and of the law's ability to create truth without reservation. In a parallel mode to the enterprise of narrative midrash, the tannaitic rabbis destabilize the notion that there is one true meaning indicated by the physical evidence and invoke divine sanction for the unlikely interpretation offered by the rabbinic sage.

TWO

Signs of Ownership

[O]wnership rights . . . can be made to disappear as if by magic.

In the last chapter, we saw how the rabbinic rules of evidence could intervene in the relationships people have with their bodies, creating skepticism where the Bible defers to intuitive knowledge, and providing legal facts to resolve the resulting cases of doubt. In this chapter, another relationship is examined: the relationships between people and things, given legal significance through the concept of property. Specifically, this chapter will explore the question of whether and under what circumstances lost property must be returned. In this area of law, the rabbis again undermine the force of lay, intuitive knowlede, but unlike in the case of menstrual impurity, clear-cut and divinely sanctioned legal solutions are not provided. As the rabbis experience the counterweight of lived truth against their legal realities, property claims remain in a state of perpetual ambiguity. Even as the Talmuds attempt to refine the Mishnah's vague prescriptions and reach for certainty, the notion of one, true, substantive reality is never dispensed with, and it continues to haunt rabbinic resolves regarding distributive justice.

Lost property provides us with an illuminating case study of the rabbinic approach to property law, because while there are many legal means by which one could come to own an object, the basic reality of possession is undoubtedly the cornerstone of legal ownership.[1] When objects are literally in the possession of owners, the intuitive and legal understandings of property converge. David Hume writes that "the rule favoring possessors has a *natural* prominence"; he continues:

> As property forms a relation betwixt a person and an object, 'tis natural
> to found it on some preceding relation; and as property is nothing but a
> constant possession, secur'd by the laws of society, 'tis natural to add it to
> the present possession, which is a relation that resembles it.[2]

Thus the association of property with possession, in Anglo-American law,
becomes a convention used to resolve conflicts not simply arbitrarily, but by
"exploit[ing] existing associations between claimants and objects. . . . The
maxim that possession is nine points of the law . . . describes a pervasive
tendency in human affairs."[3] Thus, a person who experiences an association
to an object comes to be seen as the owner of that object, and conversely, a
person who feels no relation to an object would likely not claim ownership
of it. In this sense, the felt reality of a subtle, silent relationship between a
person and an object may come to be legally sanctioned.

This chapter examines the biblical and rabbinic understandings of both
the experiences and legalities of ownership, particularly in order to investigate the uncertainties and ambiguities that arise when property becomes
estranged from its owner. In the Hebrew Bible, ownership never dissolves
even when it has been disturbed by loss; a lost object is seen merely as a case
of possession gone awry, a setback which must be rectified. Biblical lost
property law thus assumes a stable relationship between an original owner
and his or her property in the absence of any documentation or other evidence—affirming and relying upon people's lived realities of the relationships between themselves and their possessions. In the case of lost property,
biblical law does not equivocate about its status as the property of the original, or "real," owner; the biblical rules require that a passerby even take
temporary possession of a lost object in order to return it to its rightful
owner.

The tannaitic discussions of lost property, however, represent a significant shift in the concept of ownership from this biblical perspective,
and seem to correspond much more closely with a modern understanding
of property. The main preoccupation in these laws is the problem of the
unobserved and unspoken relationship between the original owner and
the lost object—again, the question of *how* one can come to know the facts
that the biblical text takes for granted is what is foregrounded by the rabbinic texts. As a rule, the Mishnah requires clear evidence of ownership:
simanim (signs upon the object) and *shinuy* (something unusual about the

object). These markings upon the object testify—in the absence of witnesses—to care that has been taken with the object and to its status as property. Without these markings, the object presents itself merely as an enigma; the Mishnah wonders how anyone would know whether the item was lost or discarded, or who the owner might be. Thus the objects are presumed ownerless—a category which is never invoked by the biblical texts and so can only be informed by reconceiving biblical concepts.

The ambiguous case of the "unmarked" object would seem to provide precisely the kind of factual vacuum that may enable the rabbis to allow legal definitions to create reality, akin to R. Aqiba's assertion of the legal fact of ritual purity in the face of doubt, as discussed in the last chapter. And indeed it is here that the rabbis break most notably from biblical precedent, creating the legal category of ownerlessness, and allowing a finder to acquire the object rather than requiring him or her to return it.

But the story of lost property does not end here, with two easily distinguished categories of ownership, owned and ownerless; instead, the tannaitic rabbis focus on marked objects, objects that bear "signs" of ownership, and destabilize the relationship between these items and their purported owners by directly challenging common experiences of the relationship between owner and object. Again, rabbinic legal maneuvering intervenes where common sense might easily be serviceable, demanding that a seemingly simple deduction of ownership be approached with great skepticism. Just as in the case of ritual impurity, the intricate machinations of rabbinic law are positioned at the *center* of the requirement to return lost property by using a two-tiered approach: (1) formulating laws that help adjudicate in cases of doubt and (2) insisting that in almost any case that arises, the apparent truth must be doubted.

In this chapter, I first examine the biblical commandments to return lost property, again uncovering the presumptions of knowledge in the biblical text. I then turn to the tannaitic texts—both the Mishnah and the Midrash—to analyze how they expose and disrupt this certain knowledge and complicate ownership relationships such that the basic biblical imperatives of returning lost items can no longer be easily carried out by a typical finder. Because the tannaitic texts leave the question of returning these lost items with "signs" of ownership unresolved, I look to the Talmuds' understandings of the Mishnah's rulings. Both Talmuds exceed the

Mishnah in attempting to further guide the finder's actions toward fulfillment the biblical lost property law. The Talmuds help illuminate the struggle of the tannaitic texts by making explicit what is implied in the Mishnah and Midrashim: that the tension between an observable and legally definable mode of ownership and lay, intuitive senses of property relationships felt by "real" owners permit the rabbis neither to construct their own legal truth with abandon nor to legally sanction personal knowledge of ownership for which no observable evidence can be produced.

Certain Ownership in the Hebrew Bible

While various property laws are scattered throughout the Pentateuch, many of them are found in the Book of the Covenant in Exodus 20–23, including the law that stipulates the return of lost property. Many of these laws are restated and expanded in Deuteronomy in a somewhat "miscellaneous" collections of rules. In fact, the lost property law seems out of place both in Exodus and Deuteronomy. What little organization is apparent seems interrupted by the lost property law (as well as the rule requiring a person to help a beast with its burden):

> You shall not spread a false report. You shall not join hands with the wicked to act as a malicious witness. You shall not follow a majority in wrongdoing; when you bear witness in a lawsuit, you shall not side with the majority so as to pervert justice; nor shall you be partial to the poor in a lawsuit. When you come upon your enemy's ox or ass going astray, you shall bring it back. When you see the ass of one who hates you lying under its burden and you would hold back from setting it free, you must help to set it free. You shall not pervert the justice due to your poor in their lawsuits. Keep far from a false charge, and do not kill the innocent and those in the right, for I will not acquit the guilty. You shall take no bribe, for a bribe blinds the officials, and subverts the cause of those who are in the right. You shall not oppress a resident alien; you know the heart of an alien, for you were aliens in the land of Egypt. (Ex. 23:1–9)

Brevard Childs, in his commentary on Exodus, points out the odd location of the laws contained in verses 4 and 5, noting that they "interrupt a series of laws . . . which prohibit various abuses connected with the court."[4] Unlike the verses on judicial ethics, these laws lie outside of the court and . . . [are] chiefly under the control of the conscience. The shift from the prohibitive style into a positive formulation points to the paranetic style of the homily.[5]

Martin Noth expounds this idea in even starker terms: "the regulations of vv. 4 [and 5] . . . deal not with conduct in the legal assembly but with *extra-legal conduct* towards an 'enemy' or 'one who hates you.'"[6] Because the demand to help one's enemy is one among a list of divine imperatives, it seems rather arbitrary to differentiate between the categories of "legal" and "extra-legal"; nonetheless, the stipulation is indeed addressed not to the judiciary but to the individual member of God's covenant—expressed, indeed, as a matter of "conscience."

The laws of lost property receive a somewhat fuller treatment in Deuteronomy, and it is this pericope which animates the rabbinic laws of lost property. This deuteronomic version of the lost-property law is also placed among a series of seemingly unconnected rules. Unlike the Exodus version, the law in Deuteronomy does not specify "your enemy's" object; in the words of Gerhard Von Rad, "this ordinance has been reduced to the most general terms. It applies to every fellow-countryman."[7] Thus we read:

> You shall not watch your neighbor's ox or sheep straying away and ignore them; you shall take them back to their owner. If the owner does not reside near you or you do not know who the owner is, you shall bring it to your own house, and it shall remain with you until the owner claims it; then you shall return it. You shall do the same with a neighbor's ass; you shall do the same with a neighbor's garment; and you shall do the same with anything else that your neighbor loses and you find. You may not hide yourself. (Deut. 22:1–3)

The laws in Deuteronomy not only generalize "your enemy" to "your brother,"[8] but they also provide for a situation in which one is not acquainted with the person who has lost the object, a scenario which is not envisioned in Exodus. In such a case, one must safeguard the object until someone claims it. In other words, even when the object is not recognized as a particular person's property, it must be held for the owner rather than acquired by the finder.

The biblical imperative to actively restore lost property requires individuals never to leave a stray object where it is found: if the owner is not known, the finder must take the object with him and safeguard it until the owner claims it. While the finder is safeguarding this object, it is still not considered his property even though it is in his possession. This unwavering presumption is demonstrated in the Deuteronomist's choice of language—the biblical text consistently refers to the lost object in the possessive, i.e., the stray animal "of your brother" or "of your enemy"; the object may be lost or stray, but it is nonetheless still owned by the one who lost it. Thus the distinction between "safeguarding" and acquiring an object is essentially one of intention rather than deed: in either case, the finder takes the object and brings it to his home. The observance of this law, then, hinges on a moment of interiority, of conscience—something which cannot be observed or known by any human judge. Just as the finder's intention to simply safeguard the object is definitive in the Hebrew Bible for property law, so the unspoken intention of the original possessor—without any clear communication—allows him or her to remain the object's owner *ad infinitum*.

The wording of the biblical text implies an awareness that lost property law hinges on several moments that cannot be observed or witnessed, with silent, interior property relationships occurring between people and objects. The text is not bothered by this difficulty for enforcement, and no provisions are included which would lay the groundwork for judgments to be made by others.[9] Instead, the hortatory verses appeal to the conscience of the individual: "You may not hide yourself."

That these laws are interspersed among different rules from various spheres of law merely underscores the Bible's lack of regard for distinguishing enforceable law from moral imperatives: one is accountable before God equally for all infractions. As Moshe Greenberg writes, "[t]he entire normative realm, whether in law or morality, pertains to God alone."[10] As such, the command to return lost property, though found among legal and procedural material, may nonetheless be understood as a "moral" law incumbent on the individual conscience alone, unable to be placed before a judiciary for human interpretation. And thus there is no effort made to define property in terms of the observable, or to legislate a procedure for lost property that would require evidentiary standards.

Thus the simple imperative in Exodus to return a lost object to its owner is complicated in Deuteronomy not by enforcement or evidentiary concerns, but rather by the acknowledgement that a person may not always know whose lost object he has found; according to the passage, the finder is still required to search his or her conscience and return it anyway.

As the text asserts that the finder may "not know" the owner of the object (*lo yeda'atiw*), it highlights all the other facets of property ownership which are understood to be *known*: we know that the object, though lost, is not abandoned but owned; we know that the person who lost the object is its rightful owner; we know that the finder may not acquire the object, no matter how long he keeps it in his possession. In fact, the finder of the lost object is permitted to do only one thing—to *return* (*hashib*): this verb is used consistently throughout the pericope, and it is the same verb used in Exodus as well. Thus in the Hebrew Bible, the notion of property always connotes a relational status—an object belongs *to* someone—and the absence of an identifiable owner does not disturb the relationship of ownership: the object is still considered possessed, even if its *owner* is lost. Lack of knowledge about the owner's identity does nothing to mitigate the unremitting imperative to restore the lost property to him.

Biblical law, then, does not require the reality of possession or any kind of deed of ownership, nor does it necessitate observable traces—evidence—of ownership to keep the property relationship intact. The fact of ownership never has to be made clear; it is, rather, unfailingly presumed. These legal relationships that cannot be fully articulated are left to the realm of the conscience, to be intuitively known rather than demonstrated.

Communicating Ownership in Rabbinic Law

Biblical discourse suggests a stable and indissoluble bond between owner and object, a stance which implies two crucial certainties: first, that every piece of property has an owner, even if that owner cannot be found, and second, that this ownership status is not altered even when the property is lost. The Mishnah challenges both of these convictions, and requires that these property relationships be interpreted and established rather than assumed.[11] The turn toward evidence—evidence of both the very fact of ownership as well as the identity of the owner—represents a significant divergence from biblical lost property law, and a parallel to contemporary legal practice. Today, the law generally requires a "clear act" to define one's first claim of ownership and furthermore, it demands subsequently that "the acquiring party ... *keep on speaking,* lest he lose his title...."[12] In other words, what may be necessary for *legal* ownership, instead of an unspoken, sustained proximity between person and object, is some visible, verbal, or tangible attestation of the existence of a property relationship. This externally perceivable evidence is required not only at the initial moment of acquisition but also throughout the term of ownership; it is this evidence which prevents possession relationships between other people and the same object from being legally recognized, from another person legally gaining ownership by "adverse possession" (one may think of borrowers or squatters). In other words, without a continued, documented connection between owner and object, the owner's hold on the object begins to disappear.

Thus as biblical law speaks of knowing and returning, mishnaic law insists on observing and discerning. But while the rules of evidence are prominent in the tannaitic texts on lost property, they are not overly standardized. Though one could easily imagine a highly legalistic practice for establishing ownership when one's property is lost, including the bringing of witnesses or signing of documents, no such procedures are stipulated in the Mishnah. One need not even imagine such procedures; Mishnah *Baba Metsiʿa* describes such legal procedures for settling other types of property disputes:

> If one person says, "The whole is mine" and the other says, "The whole is mine," one shall swear that not less than one half of it belongs to him, and the other shall swear that not less than one half of it belongs to him, and they shall divide it. . . . Whenever they make an admission, or if they have witnesses, they shall divide it without taking an oath. (*m. B. Metsiʿa* 1:2)

In a case in which there is a conflict regarding the ownership of property, the tannaitic rabbis provide a legally prescribed compromise rather than allowing the parties to work out the dispute to their own satisfaction. This compromise is facilitated by the personal testimonies of the disputants accompanied by oaths—legal methods for proceeding in the face of uncertain facts. Two other alternatives for demonstrating ownership are offered: an admission of one of the parties and the testimony of outside witnesses. In the case of lost property, however, none of these evidentiary procedures are stipulated and no compromises are offered.

Instead, the Mishnah requires a different kind of proof; namely, character evidence and physical evidence. The Mishnah simply states:

> If [the claimant] stated the object lost but did not describe its signs, [the finder] may not give it to him; and if the [claimant] is a deceiver, then even

though he described its signs, [the finder] may not give it to him. (*m. B. Metsi'a* 2:7)

According to the mishnah, a claimant must describe the object's "signs" (*simanim*) in order to reclaim possession of the lost object, but how specific this description must be remains undefined. While rabbinic rules of lost property remain somewhat imprecise, they nonetheless introduce an aspect of visibility that was absent in biblical law: the object must have identifiable signs, and a claimant must indicate his familiarity with the lost object through the medium of these visible signs. Moreover, the mishnah adds the possibility of the "deceiver"—a person who may manipulate the uncertainty of the situation for his own benefit. The simple relationship between owner and object is thus challenged by the Mishnah, and must be reestablished by recourse to the visible. Yet the turn to these "signs" is something of a double-edged sword: because physical signs on the object, as opposed to a real history of past experience, now establish ownership, they can be manipulated to benefit a deceiver.

These elements for proving ownership of lost property are elaborated and emphasized in the various tannaitic interpretations of Deuteronomy 22:1–3. In the *Mekilta,* three explanations are offered for the words "until your brother's inquiry." Within the context of the biblical verse, this phrase stipulates that one must safeguard the lost object until one's brother seeks it. The *Mekilta* presents three alternative readings:

> *Until your brother's inquiry.* Until you inquire after your brother. Another explanation: *Until your brother's inquiry.* You must find out whether your brother is a deceiver or not. Another explanation: *Until your brother's inquiry.* Until a public announcement has been made about it. (*Mek. Mishpatim, Kaspa,* 2)[13]

If the biblical law requires activity rather than passivity on the part of the finder ("You may not hide yourself"), it nonetheless allows the finder to passively await the arrival of the owner to claim his property. The *Mekilta,* conversely, demands that the finder actively seek out the original owner. The midrash's surprising reading highlights a grammatical ambiguity inherent in the grammatical form of *semikhut*—a genitive construct in this case. Much like in English, the phrase "your brother's inquiry" may denote two distinct ideas: either the brother is the subject inquiring into something, or he may himself be the object of inquiry (a less intuitive reading). The phrase, as it appears in its biblical context, is clarified by the addition of a masculine singular direct object, the word ʾoto ("it"): not "until your brother's inquiry," but "until your brother's inquiry [into] it." But the midrash characteristically atomizes the text, and thus derives an unusual—but nonetheless grammatically plausible—reading of the biblical phrase "until your brother's inquiry": rather than waiting until your brother searches for the object, you must inquire after your brother.

The midrash's second reading bases itself not only on the grammatical ambiguity of semikhut, but an alternative meaning of the root DRSh. While this Hebrew root can simply denote "to seek out," it often has a more intensive meaning of "to investigate" or "to examine." This interpretation imparts an even more active role to the finder, requiring him not only to seek the owner, but to examine him, and to find out whether he is trustworthy. Finally, the Mekilta's third interpretation offers a more specific understanding of how one would "inquire after" one's brother: the finder must make a public announcement regarding the object.

The investigation or interrogation presented in the second interpretation recalls the formal procedure of bediqat ʿedim (the examination of witnesses) in criminal cases. The root DRSh is not regularly used for this procedure, but rather a synonymous root: BDQ. Nonetheless, the Mekilta here draws a clear parallel to this formal procedure by glossing the term employed in the biblical verse (DRSh) with the term "libdoq" (BDQ). The Mekilta does not explicitly mention a formal legal inquiry in the case of lost property, but it does evoke it by using the same terminology: the claimant is being cast by the Mekilta as a witness submitting testimony, and much like a witness in formal court proceedings, he is subject to tests of credibility.

In extending the biblical injunction by placing a burden of rigorous discernment of the facts of ownership on the finder, it may seem as though rabbinic law insists even more vigorously on the need to restore the lost object to its proper owner. In fact, a closer look at the rhetoric of these midrashim suggests the opposite. In the biblical text, no activity is required on the part of the finder to seek out the owner because it literally is not needed—the owner is presumed to inevitably seek out those objects which unambiguously remain his property. In the rabbinic texts, on the other hand, the owner has virtually no agency; the finder, instead, becomes the dominant figure in the narrative of lost property. The owner, much like in the deuteronomic scenario, is "unknown"; but unlike the biblical case, the owner is also entirely absent and inactive, a near non-entity, and possibly a corrupt "deceiver." If the biblical text has offered an example of uncertainty, the rabbinic text has maximized that uncertainty. In the second comment in the *Mekilta,* the owner is present, but objectified—both grammatically and pragmatically. The owner is himself inquired into, challenged, and made uncertain. The *Mekilta,* implicitly, infuses serious doubt into the Bible's version of events: do we really know that the "brother" who seeks the found object is the owner? By virtually erasing the owner from the narrative of lost property, the *Mekilta* discursively severs the bond of ownership so clearly presented in the biblical text, and threatens the foundation of the strong biblical position that every object is property that must be restored.[14]

The *Mekilta* chiefly upsets the biblical concept of ownership by invoking an established evidentiary procedure: the examination of witnesses. By insisting that what is unsaid must be spoken and what is unseen must be made manifest, the rabbis invoke the cornerstones of legal evidentiary discourse not, ironically, to dispel doubt, but precisely in order to inscribe it into the concept of property. Comprehensive property laws, just like ritual purity regulations, are here made necessary because intuited relationships of ownership are eclipsed by uncertainty.

The *Sifre* furthers the position of the *Mekilta* in a subtle but striking way. Not content to allow the rabbinic concern with outward, legally authenticated communication of ownership to appear as a rabbinic innovation, the *Sifre*'s commentary elucidates the nature of the evidence required of the claimant, and further disrupts a simple reading of the biblical text. It reads:

> *And it shall be with you until your brother's inquiry.* Would you possibly think that you are to surrender it to him without his describing its signs? [Of course not!] Why then is it said, *until your brother's inquiry*? Until you find out whether your brother is a deceiver or not. (*Sifre Deut., Ki Tetse, Piska* 223)

The *Sifre,* like the *Mekilta* above, reads the phrase "your brother's inquiry" as requiring an examination of the claimant. Here, this understanding is implicit; this midrash endeavors to ascertain the nature of this inquiry. The most obvious method for verifying ownership of an object would be to ask a claimant to describe its contours, shape, size—its "signs." But for the midrash this procedure is, in fact, too obvious; invoking the midrashic principle of verbal economy, the midrash asserts that the Bible would not need to teach us explicitly that which we would infer from common sense. Thus the midrash asks: to what does the phrase "your brother's inquiry" really refer? The midrash's answer parallels the second interpretation of "your brother's inquiry" in the *Mekilta*: scripture requires further inquiry, beyond what common sense would demand: not merely the claimant's description of the object's distinguishing features, but also the examination of the credibility of the claimant.

This midrash's conclusion is no different from the *Mekilta*'s, but a rejected hypothesis is dangled intriguingly before the reader: "Would you possibly think that you are to surrender it to him without his describing its signs?" That the claimant must describe the signs on a lost object cannot be the teaching conveyed by the biblical verse because, according to the midrash, it is such a self-evident step in the recovery of lost property it would never need to be overtly stated—it is surely *presumed* by the biblical laws. The overall sense of the biblical pericope is thus subtly—but significantly— transformed by this midrash. Deuteronomy ignores any discussion of describing signs or proving ownership perhaps in an attempt to appeal to conscience and to the trust one must have in one's brother—it attempts to cast the requirement of returning lost property more as a moral demand, regardless of verifiability or legalities. The midrash, however, understands the absence of evidentiary concerns in these laws as suggesting not their insignificance but their blatant obviousness: scripture naturally ignores these issues, the mishnah argues, because who could possibly imagine any other alternative? Following this midrash, the biblical laws must be read not as blanket statements of trust and fraternal obligation (you must return lost objects) but as statements entirely *contingent* upon the presence of "signs" in an object, and upon the claimant's ability to authenticate his position as owner through an appeal to these visible markings. This midrash not only adds a new dimension to the biblical pericope; it insists that one read the passage in no other way but through the rabbinic interpretation by ridiculing any other reading: "Would you possibly think that you are to surrender it to him without his describing its signs?"

For the rabbis, then, true ownership cannot be assumed but must be proven or shown; the finder cannot be passive, but must act like (or consult!) a lawyer (examining claimants, issuing public statements, verifying signs).

The mishnah therefore attempts to systematize the divine law of lost property, as interpreted by the rabbis. It even begins by veering sharply from scripture, simply listing those objects that are subject to the rules of returning lost property and those that may be kept by the finder or left alone. While the biblical text always uses the possessive to describe the lost property ("*his* ox," "*his* sheep"), the mishnaic text begins with, simply, "*ʾeleh metsiʾot . . .*"— "these *finds*." The "find" is divorced from any possessor, betraying the mishnah's sense that ownership has been disrupted. As possessed objects are now just "finds," some may be considered still owned, while others may be acquired by the finder. The mishnah derives the guidelines by which to differentiate between owned and stray objects from the Bible itself, appealing to Deuteronomy 22:3: "You shall do the same with a neighbor's ass; you shall do the same with a neighbor's garment; and you shall do the same with anything else that your neighbor loses and you find. You may not hide yourself." Deuteronomy here expansively defines what may be deemed a lost object; even though the passage began by referring to "your brother's ox or sheep," this verse states that the rule is not limited to these animals—rather, it applies to "*every lost thing* of your brother."[15] By repetitively listing objects—ox, sheep (22:1), ass, garment (22:3)—the biblical text emphasizes the wide application of this law: any object whatsoever that a person finds must be returned.

The mishnah, however, perceives a wholly different significance in this verse.

> A garment was also included among all these; why was it mentioned separately? To compare it [to other lost objects] to tell you that just as a garment is distinguished in that it bears signs and has claimants, so also anything that bears signs and has claimants [and even anything that has claimants][16] must be proclaimed [when found]. (*m. B. Metsiʿa* 2:5; see also *Sifre Deut.,* §224)

Employing the principle of verbal economy, the mishnah wonders: if the verse states explicitly "every lost thing," why must it also enumerate specific lost things, such as a garment, a sheep, or an ass, since this list is simply redundant? The midrash focuses on the most suggestive item, the garment, deducing that it holds a special significance, and thus highlights it as the key to understanding the parameters of lost property. This midrash reasons that a garment characteristically has both identifiable signs and claimants, and extends these criteria to all forms of lost property. In short, lost property, like the garment, is both identifiable and significant enough for a person to want it back. The Bible's admonition not to "hide yourself," to act morally in a situation in which it may be easy to rationalize inaction, is not replicated in the Mishnah. The tannaitic rabbis instead devise criteria which would allow for ownership to be established, and thus ultimately for lost property to be integrated into an enforceable system of law.

While the presence of identifying signs becomes a rabbinic method of distinguishing lost property and connecting it with its owner, it is not the only condition that must be met for the purported owner to reclaim his lost property. As stated in the *Mekilta* and *Sifre,* the claimant must also meet a certain standard of credibility—he must not be a person of disreputable character. The mishnah relies upon the biblical exegesis seen above ("until your brother's inquiry" signifies "until you have inquired into your brother") in order to make sure the property is returned to the correct person, the actual owner of the object and not a defrauder. The mishnah adds one clause not mentioned in the midrashim: that a deceiver should not be given the object *"even though he described [the object's] signs"* (*m. B. Metsi'a* 2:7). In other words, the mishnah warns that even though the identification of signs may be seen as a test of the claimant's credibility, in fact it is not—the recognition of signs is independent of any process used to determine whether or not the claimant is a deceiver. The function of the identification of signs is thus clearly articulated by the mishnah: it is simply the primary method of demonstrating ownership. If an object bears signs it may be considered property; if a claimant identifies these signs he may be considered an owner.

The Mishnah thus puts a visible face on the rather invisible and imagined relationship of ownership. Ideally, one would envisage a consistent clear line of ownership through, for example, the proximity of possession, or the renewal of deeds. But when this chain of ownership is broken, the Mishnah insists that there be *signs* of this relationship: it does not presume that such a tie exists as the Bible does, and it does not trust the personal testimony of the claimant. The language of the Mishnah reflects this perspective. Rather than *returning* the object to its owner, one *gives* it to him—the verb here is not *hashib* as it is in the Bible, but *yiten* (see *B. Metsi'a* 2:7). There is thus no presumption of ownership: the Mishnah essentially avoids the entire matter of prior possession by framing the exchange as a form of gift-giving. A fundamental change has occurred between the Bible and the Mishnah in conceiving of ownership: Deuteronomy appears to rely upon personal knowledge and intuitive experience for claims of ownership while the Mishnah turns external signs into basic requirements for ownership.

But though the Mishnah requires evidence of ownership in defining property rights, it nonetheless uses the vague concept of "signs" in different—though compatible—ways, compromising between the formal and the real. On one hand, the presence or absence of signs defines whether an object is considered owned or simply stray—signs point toward an intention on the part of the owner to keep or abandon his property.[17] In this case "signs" function in a binary way: they are present or absent, they indicate ownership or abandonment, and they require the finder to return the object or allow him to keep it. Such signs of ownership need not be overwhelming; any sign that may distinguish owned property from a mere stray object may suffice. Signs may be as inconsequential as the arrangement of items, as in the mishnah's example which distinguishes between "scattered money" (*m. B. Metsiʿa* 2:1) and "three coins on top of each other, heaps of money" (*m. B. Metsiʿa* 2:2). The arrangement of the latter testifies to the existence of an arranger; the disorder of the former cannot. Such detection of ownership relies essentially on legal distinctions; absent the "real" owner, the finder relies on the oftentimes arbitrary boundaries created by law to categorize lost objects as "owned" or "unowned."

On the other hand, the Mishnah looks not only for the presence or absence of signs to legally classify objects, but looks at the signs themselves to function qualitatively as evidence of a particular person's prior relationship with the object. Signs no longer simply establish one side of a legal binary (owned or unowned); they now function as the only means by which a claimant can establish his ownership. As such, signs cease to function in a legally formal way, and instead serve as conduits to the real, visible manifestations of an owner's experience of possession and loss.

By employing the category of "signs" in both of these ways, the Mishnah does not simply construct formal, impermeable legal boundaries of ownership (as we saw regarding menstrual impurity), but instead calls for a compromise between legal truth and lived experience. It offers the multifaceted category of "signs" to govern ownership in both general and particular terms, allowing the concept of property to be understood on a case-by-case basis. How does a claimant describe the object's signs? Does the claimant appear trustworthy? The Mishnah asks the finder to make these determinations in every instance, allowing the relationship of ownership to be repeatedly interpreted and assessed rather than mechanistically applied.

The tannaitic texts on lost property, in the end, are caught between the urge to interpret ownership along clearly defined, legal lines and the need to respond to real claimants who feel a personal connection to their property even when there is no incontrovertible proof to establish their ownership. Much as in the case of ritual impurity discussed above, experienced reality is challenged by the introduction of persistent suspicion and doubt, and the insistence upon a more concrete legal hermeneutic of physical signs and witness credibility. At the same time, however, unlike the case of ritual impurity, felt realities are not swept away by legal pronouncements. Ownership is never conclusively proven or constructed; instead, the Mishnah equivocates: one must interpret signs and motives and act according to one's inferences, but one must follow legal guidelines in order to do so rather than naively trusting one's intuition.

Talmudic Directions

As the Mishnah attempts to mediate between the unspoken lived reality of property relationships and the need for observable guidelines for human decision making, its refusal to offer unchanging rules of behavior, that is, its insistence upon leaving the final decisions of ownership in the hands of lay finders, impel both Talmuds to further concretize the Mishnah's rulings. In failing to firmly define ownership in lost property cases, the tannaitic texts compromise both the firm moral stance of Deuteronomy (in which *every found object* must be returned) and the comfort of unyielding legal categories that allow a society to judge with certainty in property disputes. The Talmuds, commenting on these mishnahs, seek ways out of the Mishnah's perpetual uncertainty, attempting to set normative courses of action for lost property and to define ownership more clearly. I now turn to both Talmuds in order to illuminate more fully the two poles that the Mishnah seeks to avoid, and the anxiety that may result from insisting upon moral or legal certainty in an imperfect world.

Both the Babylonian and Palestinian Talmuds begin to refine the vague mishnaic concepts of ownership by describing the relationship between owner and object as a psychological or intentional bond, an owner's expectation either of recovery or permanent loss.[18] They then turn to the obligation of the finder in interpreting signs and restoring the lost object, and, like the Mishnah, understand the function of these signs in two different ways: first, signs function as evidence of the owner having not despaired of recovering the object; second, signs function as evidence to establish the identity of the owner. Common to both Talmuds is an appeal to a source of knowledge or decision making beyond the interpretive discretion of each individual finder. The Yerushalmi (Palestinian Talmud) contains a series of *aggadot* (narratives) that appeal to individual conscience and private knowledge beyond the possibility of verification; the Bavli (Babylonian Talmud) contains a *sugya* (pericope) which attempts to clarify how one may render legally binding decisions based on signs.[19] The Talmuds' attempts to lay the groundwork for generalized decision making in the face of uncertainty in cases of lost property are dramatically different, but both reveal the problems inherent in acting decisively in the midst of uncertainty about substantive reality. The remainder of this chapter is devoted to these divergent visions of lost and found objects in order to examine how these visions of justice present a world as fraught and anxious about responsibility to the divine commandment as it is steeped in desire to obey it.

NARRATIVE CLARITY IN THE PALESTINIAN TALMUD

The Yerushalmi does not extend the laws of the evidence of signs far beyond the tannaitic texts. The commentary in the Yerushalmi on the mishnah which discusses signs ("just as a garment is distinguished in that it bears signs and has claimants, so also anything that bears signs and has claimants must be proclaimed [when found]" [*m. B. Metsiʿa* 2:5]) consists of a series of *aggadot,* or stories, about returning lost property—not stories which exemplify carrying out one's legal duties, but rather stories that depict sages going *beyond* the letter of the law and returning lost objects even when it is not required of them. While the Yerushalmi acknowledges that the law allows for the finder to keep an object in certain situations, it stresses the idea of returning the object nonetheless, thereby glorifying

God's name. The Yerushalmi's narratives echo the simple biblical imperative to return property to a previous owner, even when ownership cannot
be legally proved.

The first *aggadah* describes an incident in which Simeon b. Shetaḥ, a
sage of the Second Temple era, defies his students' expectations by restoring property that need not have been returned according to the law:

> Simeon b. Shetaḥ was employed in flax. His disciples said to him, "Rabbi,
> remove [this work] from yourself, and we shall buy for you an ass, and you
> will not have to work so much." They went and bought him an ass from a
> Saracen. Hanging on it was a pearl. They came to him and told him, "From
> now on you do not have to work anymore." He said to them, "Why?" They
> told him, "We bought you an ass from a Saracen, and hanging on it was a
> pearl!" He said to them, "Did its master know about it?" They said to him,
> "No." He said to them, "Go and return it." Did not R. Huna Bibi bar Goslon
> in the name of Rab state: They replied before Rabbi, "Even in accord with
> the one who has said, 'Stealing from an idolater is prohibited,' all parties
> concur that it is permitted to retain what he has lost"? Now, do you think
> that Simeon b. Shetaḥ was a barbarian? Simeon b. Shetaḥ preferred to hear
> 'Blessed be the God of the Jews' over all the money in the world. (*y. B.
> Metsi'a* 9a)[20]

In this story, Simeon b. Shetaḥ, depicted as working laboriously, is confronted with the possibility of instant riches: a precious pearl is attached to
an animal he has purchased. When he discovers, however, that the previous
owner of the animal was not aware of the pearl's presence, he considers the
item lost property and insists on returning it. The circumstances related in
this half of the story exemplify the Bible's concern that one not "hide yourself"; as the owner did not even know about the pearl, Simeon b. Shetaḥ
could easily have "hidden himself" and kept the object, releasing himself
from strenuous work. Instead, he follows the biblical prescription and re-
turns the item.

The second half of this narrative, though, introduces a new perspective,
supplied by R. Huna Bibi bar Goslon, on Simeon b. Shetaḥ's act. The students
are said to cite a rabbinic law: all agree that one is permitted to keep a found
object belonging to a non-Jew, even those who do not exclude non-Jews from
the scope of the laws of theft. (As the ass was from a Saracen, one could
reasonably assume that the owner of the pearl was not Jewish.) Though
emphasis is placed upon this law of the non-Jew, one of the Mishnah's main
requirements for ownership of lost objects would be missing as well—the

object would have no claimants, as the ass's owner did not even know about the pearl. Thus, Simeon b. Shetaḥ, in returning the pearl, is portrayed not as following the law's demands but as exceeding them—in essence, responding to the broad biblical imperative rather than the rabbinic legalities of ownership. This story, then, could easily have been about the greatness of Simeon b. Shetaḥ and his unsurpassed code of personal ethics, which exceed both the requirements of rabbinic law and the instincts of the ordinary person. Instead, the story concludes on a different note. The rhetorical question posed in the narrative—"Do you think that Simeon b. Shetaḥ was a Barbarian?"—implies that Simeon b. Shetaḥ's actions were not exemplary but common to all who are not "barbarians." In other words, to go beyond the letter of the law in such a case is in fact normative[21]—it is not the exceptional act of a well-known sage.

The narrative then explains why one would naturally go beyond the dictates of the law in such a case: the reward for acting ethically is to glorify "the God of the Jews" among the gentiles. Along with broader connotations about general Jewish / non-Jewish relations, the story suggests that only a barbarian would prefer money—however much—to this lofty goal. Much like the biblical text, then, this narrative in the Yerushalmi appeals to the conscience of the individual to return lost property even when it would be easy not to do so. It makes the reader keenly aware of the great benefits of returning lost property not just for one's own reputation but for God and the Jewish people; it also implies that one who chooses not to act in such a manner is no better than a barbarian.

This second story offered in the Yerushalmi describes in more detail how God may be glorified specifically through the return of lost property even when one is not required to do so legally. Abba Oshaiah, a poor worker, finds jewels belonging to a wealthy woman. He attempts to return them to her, and she refuses them, telling Abba Oshaiah, "What are these worth to me? I have many which are even better than these." The story continues: "He said to her, 'The Torah has decreed that we should return [what we find].'" She said, "Blessed be the God of the Jews" (y. B. Metsiʿa 9a).[22] Abba Oshaiah, a humble worker, refuses to accept the legal ruling that if a person renounces ownership of an object—through despair of recovery or otherwise—the finder may keep the now ownerless item. When Abba Oshaiah attempts to return the jewels, the woman essentially bequeaths the jewels to him—she says, "They are yours." The objects are worthless to her, and the mishnah makes it clear that a lost object must have claimants—a requirement this time *explicitly* not met in this case. Thus even though Abba Oshaiah would presumably benefit greatly from keeping the jewels, and even though legally he could be viewed as actually owning them, he insists on returning them to the woman. Lest his act be construed by the woman as testifying to the exceptional nature of his character, Abba Oshaiah clearly states his reason for surrendering these riches: the Torah requirement to return lost objects. Even though according to the rabbinic interpretation Torah law does *not* require the return of property under these particular circumstances, in this story "Torah law" is invoked as the very reason behind Abba Oshaiah's moral act. This narrative, through the character of Abba Oshaiah, who is not a prominent sage but a common man, understands the Torah law of lost property in a much broader sense than tannaitic texts do: the narrative draws upon the paranetic style of the biblical commandment, exhorting the reader not to act according to rabbinic law and keep what he or she has found. Instead, the text implores the reader *never* to "hide oneself"—to act upon personal knowledge and conviction (rather than legally established rights) and thereby glorify God. Proper conduct is not cast as doubtful or ambiguous; it is presented as a simple choice, so much so that even a mere laundryman can quickly ascertain the proper course of action.

The narrative that follows that of Abba Oshaiah again involves a queen's loss of her jewels, but in this story she is concerned to retrieve them. The sage who has found the jewels does not return them immediately, however, realizing that he may glorify God's name by defying the queen's wishes:

> R. Samuel bar Suseretai went to Rome. The queen had lost her jewelry. He found it. A proclamation went forth through the city: "Whoever returns her jewelry in thirty days will receive thus and so. If after thirty days, his head will be cut off." He did not return the jewelry within thirty days. After thirty days, he returned it to her. She said to him, "Were you not in town?" He said to her, "Yes." She said to him, "And didn't you hear the proclamation?" He said to her, "Yes." She said to him, "And what did it say?" He said to her, "It said, 'Whoever returns her jewelry in thirty days will receive thus and so. If after thirty days, his head will be cut off.'" She said to him, "And why did you not return it within thirty days?" "So that people should not say, 'It was because I was afraid of you that I did so.' But it was because I fear the All-Merciful." She said to him, "Blessed be the God of the Jews." (*y. B. Metsiʿa* 9a)

In a near repetition of Abba Oshaiah's story, we find here another individual, this time a sage, returning lost property for the sake of God's glory. In this story, however, more than property is at stake: R. Samuel bar Suseretai risks his life in order to elicit praise of God from a non-Jewish queen. While the message of this story may not just be limited to the subject of returning lost objects, as it addresses the value of performing all commandments for the sake of God rather than out of fear of earthly retribution,[23] its focus on the return of lost objects is telling: the lost property law may be uniquely positioned to glorify God among the gentiles, since it legislates a kind of universal ethic that all people would value. Again, the man at the center of the story, R. Samuel bar Suseretai, is not satisfied to adhere to the letter of the law. There is clearly no requirement to glorify God through the return of lost property—both biblical and rabbinic texts seem concerned merely that an owner retrieve his rightful possessions. R. Samuel bar Suseretai may in fact be bending the law by not returning the item when the owner made a claim on it, and instead holding on to it for thirty days.

Yet while in the other narratives the characters seem to want to fulfill the Torah's lost property law as fully as possible by returning possessions despite overwhelming incentives to the contrary, R. Samuel bar Suseretai's story carries a somewhat different message. For he desires not only to fulfill the law, but to proclaim his reason for doing so: not for material gain or fear for his life, but because God has commanded it. It is only by doing so that he gains the significant reward of the queen praising "the God of the Jews." R. Samuel bar Suseretai needs to take these further steps—holding on to the objects for thirty days, risking his life—to glorify God because in his case, returning the lost jewels is in no way an extraordinary act; in fact, considering the authority of the owner and the threat of punishment, the return of the objects would be nothing if not expected. The story suggests that the Torah command to return lost property is not about money, distributive justice, or the fear of being discovered and punished. It is, rather, an ethical demand, a moral imperative that has everything to do with one's relationship to God and less so with enjoying one's own material goods.

A final story furthers this idea that enjoying material items is not, in fact, the value that drives the sacred property laws. It depicts a conflict over lost property in the context of a visit by Alexander (of Macedon) to a non-

Greek (and non-Jewish) court. The different approaches to property disputes reveal many of the tensions inherent in rabbinic thinking about lost property:

> Alexander of Macedon went to the king of Qasya. He [the king] showed him that he had a great deal of gold and silver. [Alexander] said to him, "I don't need your gold and your silver. I came only to see your customs, how you distribute [alms], and how you judge." While he was speaking with him, someone came with a case against his fellow. He had bought a piece of a field with its garbage dump, and he had found a trove of money in it. The one who had bought the property said, "I bought a junk pile; a trove I did not buy." The one who had sold the property said, "A junk pile and everything in it is what I sold you." While they were arguing with one another, the king said to one of them, "Do you have a male child?" He said to him, "Yes." He said to his fellow, "Do you have a female child?" He said to him, "Yes." He said to them, "Let this one marry that one, and let the treasure-trove belong to the two of them." [Alexander] began to laugh. He said to him, "Now why are you laughing? Didn't I judge the case properly?" He [the king] said to him, "If such a case came before you, how would you have judged it?" He [Alexander] said to him, "We should have killed both this one and that one, and kept the treasure for the king." He said to him, "Do you people love gold all that much?" (*y. B. Metsi'a* 9a)

The narrative clearly represents a parodic rabbinic critique of Hellenistic materialism by depicting Alexander as "loving gold" and executing judgments in accordance with this lust for money. Through the vehicle of a generic non-Jewish kingdom this narrative depicts a proper approach to material wealth, one which places other values above monetary gain, such as compromise and community. At the center of this story is a case of "lost" property: a treasure-trove that was transferred, along with a field, unbeknownst to its owner. Here the disputants argue about what may be considered lost property that must be returned, much as the Mishnah does. Whereas the other stories suggest a kind of certainty about the rightful owner of the lost object, this narrative finally acknowledges a case of doubt— it is made perfectly *un*clear to whom this treasure-trove belongs. The ownership of this item must therefore be legally decided, but in this highly improbable story, each disputant interprets the law in a way that would maximize the *other* party's material gain. They seem to do this for no other reason than their belief that it is the correct and ethical understanding of the law, and the idea, similar to that in the previous story, that the lost property rule has more to do with celebrating a special relationship to the divine than with material objects.

Unlike the previous three stories, in which the actions of exemplary individuals are portrayed as remarkable, this story extends its vision to an entire community. In a decidedly utopian turn, this community is comprised of individuals who are all too happy to relinquish objects in their possession—a community in which judgment is suspended and replaced by a wedding. The situation is so remote from any real-world analogy that it is difficult to determine precisely how it could be understood as normative. And perhaps this is precisely what the story is getting at: not the determination of what one should do, but the feeling—the conviction—with which one should do it.

In narrating these convictions, the redactors of the Yerushalmi, who chose these narratives to follow the mishnah which states the requirement of signs to determine the owner of lost property, subtly undermine the Mishnah's legal distinctions. They instead underscore the idea, much like the biblical text does, that while legal parameters may be drawn and the boundaries of property defined on the basis of observable evidence, a decent and honest person, a true servant of God, will set aside the desire for material gain and will not be concerned with these legal details. These narratives substitute personal conviction for visible evidence, and moral sensibility for legal definitions—and as such, they replace the focus on property relationships with an emphasis on the godliness of morality.

These narratives, much like the biblical texts, define ownership in the broadest, most unwavering terms: even if a person gives up his or her property (as the woman does in the second story), even if one does not know of the loss (like the owner of the pearl in the first story), a natural bond still persists, and the return of the item becomes an ethical—if not legal—imperative. But these narratives, and especially the final one, uphold the stability of ownership not to strengthen the bonds between people and their things, but to deny the importance of these very ties. The only people in the Yerushalmi's stories that request their property back, unlike in the biblical text, are non-Jews; the Yerushalmi suggests that the Torah of the Jews, and in particular the lost property law, discourages an attachment to material wealth. And therefore even when a case of uncertain ownership arises, such as in the last narrative, property considerations become secondary to that which is certain: the moral certitude that one must place God's name and other people's happiness above any material considerations. Thus the mish-nah's case-by-case interpretive process is replaced by the unyielding demand to give up one's property rights in service of a higher calling.

But as the Yerushalmi's series of narratives makes the case for clear-cut moral behavior, the connection to real situations—and indeed even to prop-erty law—becomes ever more tenuous. In demanding extra-legal conduct, the Yerushalmi resorts to idealized characters and improbable situations. By the time one reaches the final narrative, with its absurdly generous liti-gants and matchmaker judge, one realizes that the Yerushalmi's attempt to define a divine standard of behavior can be nothing but utopian. In adhering to presumed and unseen property relationships and jettisoning the observ-able and legal, these narratives, in the end, serve only to underscore the gap between abstract, biblical, divine imperatives and real humans with their attachment to the material world. When one comprehends how unrealistic the Yerushalmi's stories are, one recognizes all the more the need for rules to pragmatically manage the doubt that accompanies real cases of lost prop-erty. The (moral) certainty of the Yerushalmi inheres in the ideal rather than the real.

LEGAL CLARITY IN THE BABYLONIAN TALMUD

If the Yerushalmi's narratives downplay or altogether ignore the Mish-nah's legal maneuvers which limit the Bible's moral imperative to return lost property, the Bavli takes the opposite approach, honing the Mishnah's legal categories and developing them further. As we have seen, the Mish-nah (*B. Metsiʿa* 2:5) understands signs on a lost object as indicating or pointing toward ownership; the Amoraic sages, however, understand signs along much less oblique lines: they do not merely *suggest* ownership; they offer legal proof of it—and they establish legal facts. As noted above, signs provide evidence designed to resolve two different types of uncer-tainty: whether an item must still be considered owned even though it is lost, and whether an object can be shown to belong to particular indi-vidual who attempts to claim it. The Bavli takes up each of these issues, and through the challenges and debates on its pages, the difficulties inher-ent in seeking legal solutions to uncertainty are exposed.

The topic of *yeʾush*, despair or mental abandonment of property, is noted by the Yerushalmi, but it is further developed in the Bavli. While the mishnah that distinguishes between owned and unowned lost objects may be read to imply that an owner despairingly renounces his ties to his property, both Talmuds explicitly rationalize lost property rules of ownership according to this concept of *ye'ush*. It would seem that the Talmuds understand the owner's relationship with the object as definitive, even when clear communication is lost: if the owner maintains his felt relationship to the object by imagining that he may recover his item, the lost object is considered owned; if the owner despairs of any hope of recovery, severing his relationship to the object, the object is considered abandoned. Deuteronomy 22:3 ("so shall you do with any lost thing of your brother's, which he loses and you find . . .") is interpreted in the Yerushalmi as alluding to the owner's state of mind:

> Whence do we know the law of the owner's despair (*ye'ush*) from the Torah? . . . That which is lost by him and found by you are you liable to proclaim, and that which is not [perceived as] lost by him and found by you, you are not liable to proclaim. This [verse] then excludes that for which the owner has despaired, which is lost to him and to everyone. (*y. B. Metsi'a* 2:1)

The idea of an object that is "lost to him and to everyone" is the case in which *ye'ush* obtains according to this *beraita* in the Yerushalmi, referring to an item lost at sea or washed up on a riverbank, which would be understood to be officially "lost" rather than just mislaid. True despair of recovery on the part of the owner may occur in such cases in which recovery is nearly impossible—this text describes an extreme case of *ye'ush* which would not seem to apply in most instances. At the same time, it seems to indicate that *ye'ush* is a real state of mind experienced by the owner who knows that his item has truly vanished.

The Bavli, however, has a more expansive application of *ye'ush*. The Bavli *sugya* comes soon after the quotation of the mishnah describing the various kinds of "finds," and whether they can be kept by the finder:

> These goods belong to the finder: if a man found scattered fruit, scattered money, small sheaves in the public domains, cakes of figs, bakers' loaves, strings of fish, pieces of flesh, wool-shearings [in the condition in which they have been] brought from their country [of origin], stalks of flax, and strips of purple wool; these belong to the finder. So R. Meir. R. Judah says: Whatsoever has in it anything unusual must be proclaimed: thus if he found a fig-cake with a posherd in it or a loaf with coins in it [he must proclaim it].

R. Simeon b. Eleazar says: [New] merchandise need not be proclaimed.
(*m. B. Metsiʿa* 2:1)

Even if this mishnah is explained through the concept of *yeʾush*, it is still the appearance of the object itself which allows one to deduce whether an owner would have despaired of recovery or not. Items which are "scattered about" indicate a lack of identifiability—there is nothing to distinguish the object allowing it to be returned. Therefore, the Talmud suggests, one can reasonably assume that the original owner has despaired of ever recovering the object. This presumption of the attitude of the owner toward his property—whether he perceives his item as lost but recoverable or whether he gives up the prospect of finding it altogether—determines whether the owner has a legal claim on the item. One wonders, then, whether *yeʾush* is tied to the *actual* state of mind of the owner, or whether the legal distinctions between the appearances of items, derived from the idea of *yeʾush*, become legal categories that diverge from and even overrule the owner's real state of mind.

As the *sugya* develops, the notion of *yeʾush* as a formal, legal construction which can be determined on the basis of observable evidence is drawn out to its radical extreme; ultimately, the idea of "despair" becomes divorced entirely from its reality as a state of mind and becomes instead a legal fact based entirely upon the physical features of the object. The topic of an extended *sugya* in Bavli *B. Metsiʿa* (21a–22b) is *yeʾush sheloʾ midaʿat*, "despair that is unconscious." As Louis Jacobs points out, "translated thus baldly into English the term makes no sense. How can abandonment of property be otherwise than conscious?"[24] The point, however, is that "despair" need not actually take place in the mind of the owner but instead be a general legal concept: a case in which in general, "if a person had been aware of his loss he would certainly have abandoned all hope of recovery."[25] Because "despair" is thus divorced from any internal, psychological state, the property status of an object would depend entirely on its physical features: where it was found, how it was arranged, its signs. Raba argues at length for this definition of *yeʾush*, though his position is ultimately refuted. But even Abbaye, who requires "conscious despair," generalizes from the physical state of the object and what a typical person would experience; he does not require, in the end, that the owner *actually* despair of recovering his property.[26] For example, lost "cakes of figs and baker's loaves" (mentioned in the Mishnah) are heavy, and thus an average owner of these items would quickly realize that his load has been lightened, know that he has lost the objects, and despair of recovering them (*b. B. Metsiʿa* 21a). The evidence of signs in determining whether an object is owned or unowned, then, may be derived from the assumed intent of a typical owner, but it is that general, legal assumption, rather than the case-by-case reality, which is ultimately definitive.

After discussing signs as a means of determining whether an object is owned or abandoned, the Bavli takes up the other function of signs—to serve as a means of identifying a particular individual as the true owner of the object. One question governs a long *sugya* in Bavli *Baba Metsiʿa* (27b–28a), which navigates through various subjects from distributive justice to divorce law to the identification of bodies:[27] do signs have the force of biblical or rabbinic law? This very question presupposes that signs do, in fact, have the force of law—that the identification of these signs amounts to a kind of legal proof, an establishment of fact. Indeed, Louis Jacobs writes,

> In the whole of the second chapter of *Bava Metziʿa* . . . it is accepted as the rule that a lost article must be returned . . . if the [claimant] substantiates his claim either by producing two witnesses . . . or by declaring the distinguishing marks of the article. . . . *Simanin* [signs] are thus treated as a reliable means of identification. But it is not clear whether reliance on *simanin* has Biblical warrant . . . or whether such reliance is by Rabbinic enactment only.[28]

Whether biblical or rabbinic, signs are considered legal proof and enable the return of an object to a claimant. Thus, what difference does it make to know the source of the authority of the rule of signs—biblical or rabbinic? The anonymous redactor (*stam*) of the *sugya* answers this question by reminding us that a rabbinic enactment cannot override a biblical prohibition. The Talmud can envisage situations in which the return of a lost object might lead to the violation of a biblical prohibition; for example:

> [In the case of] returning a woman's divorce decree on the basis of signs: if you say they [signs] are biblically valid, one returns it. If you say they are rabbinically valid, the rabbis enacted this for monetary matters, but for ritual prohibitions they did not enact it.[29] (*b. B. Metsiʿa* 27b)

The case imagined here is one in which a husband lost a divorce decree (*get*). He may have changed his mind about delivering the *get*, or simply had one prepared with no intention to deliver it immediately. Were such a *get* to be found and returned to the woman whose name appears on the document (following the lead of the signs on the object), she might believe herself to be divorced. But in fact, she would still be married: rabbinic divorce law requires intent on the part of the husband to divorce his wife. She might then remarry, and so violate the serious biblical prohibition against adultery. How, then, should one proceed if one finds a *get*? Should one give it, on the basis of its signs, to the woman and risk the scenario described above in order to fulfill the lost property law? Or, should one refrain from returning it? If the basis of signs is rabbinic, then rabbinic enactments do not outweigh biblical strictures—one does not risk returning it. If, however, the basis of signs is biblical, the conflict, and the question, remain.

Another mishnah concerning signs (quoted in this *sugya*) does imply that when the stakes involve a biblical prohibition, signs are not a sufficiently reliable form of evidence: "[Witnesses] do not testify [regarding the identity of a body] except on the basis of the whole face with the nose, even if there are signs on his body or on his clothes" (*m. Yebam.* 16:3). Here, in order to establish a person's death and, within the context of *Yebamot*, permit his wife to remarry, signs are not considered adequate proof. This mishnah is consistent with other tannaitic material, in which signs are not presented as legally binding but rather as mere indications of particular facts. But for the Bavli, which takes signs as legal proof, this mishnah may indicate that signs are not a biblically sanctioned mode of evidence, but rather a rabbinic enactment.

In contending with the apparent conflict between this mishnah in *Yebamot* and our mishnah, *Baba Metsiʿa* 2:7, which implies the reliability of signs, the Talmud begins to explore the nature of these signs, assessing what kinds of signs would constitute valid evidence. After quoting the mishnah in *Yebamot* and deducing that signs must not have the force of biblical law, the Talmud raises an objection:

A. Come and hear: Testimony may be given only on proof of the face with the nose, even if the body and the garment bear signs. This proves that signs are not biblically valid.

B. Let us say: in respect of the body, [the signs were]: it was short or long, while [the signs] of the garments [are rejected] because we suspect they might be borrowed. (*b. B. Metsiʿa* 27b)

Perhaps signs are in fact biblically sanctioned, the Talmud argues, but in this mishnah, the signs referred to were "his body is long or short," and as for recognizing his clothes, "we suspect [they might be] borrowed." In positing these alternatives to *valid* signs, the Talmud describes those signs which one would never accept as sufficient: general descriptions such as "long" or "short," and signs not on the item itself but on an auxiliary object which may have been transferred or borrowed. By specifying these kinds of signs as patently invalid, the Talmud achieves a degree of specificity lacking in Mishnah *B. Metsi'a* which seems to leave the acceptance and interpretation of signs in the hands of the finder. Moreover, the Talmud here neutralizes the force of this mishnah in *Yebamot,* which implies that mere signs should not be relied upon as evidence in matters of crucial importance, by limiting "mere signs" essentially to general descriptions.

The Talmud then quotes a *baraita* which contains a dispute about the legal viability of a specific sign: "One may not testify on the basis of a mole. Eleazar b. Mahabai said: one may testify on the basis of a mole" (*b. B. Metsi'a* 27b). Since the *baraita* questions whether a body be identified on the basis of a mole, the talmudic commentary seeks to resolve whether its overarching question—are signs biblical or rabbinic?—is represented here. If so, the question would have no definitive answer, as even the earliest rabbinic texts were conflicted over the issue. In the process, the Talmud further refines the character and definition of signs:

> Are they not arguing about this [whether signs are biblical or rabbinic]? The first tanna holds that signs are rabbinically valid and Eleazar b. Mahabai holds that signs are biblically valid? . . . Perhaps all agree that signs are rabbinically valid, and [they differ] here as to whether a mole is a distinctive sign: one holds that a mole is a distinctive sign, and one holds that a mole is not a distinctive sign. (*b. B. Metsi'a* 27b)

The idea that a mole may or may not be a "distinctive sign" is provided by the anonymous *stam* of the Talmud, and it is only one of the many alternatives offered to contest the idea that this tannaitic text concerns the question of the biblical or rabbinic force of signs. Nonetheless, the possibility of the "distinctive sign" reveals a further clarification of the category of signs: it excludes not only those signs which are too general as to be meaningful, but also those signs which are so specific ("distinctive") that the truth is self-evident.[30]

While the talmudic *sugya* further defines the parameters of the evidence of signs, the amoraic statements (attributed mostly to Raba) grapple with the interpretation of the biblical text, investigating whether the evidence of signs has biblical force because the principle is derived from a biblical verse. First, the anonymous *stam* quotes *m. B. Metsi'a* 2:6 in which signs are derived from the inclusion of "a garment" among objects which are lost, and offers an alternate interpretation:

> "Just as a garment is distinguished in that it bears signs and has claimants, so also anything that bears signs and has claimants must be proclaimed." [No.] The tanna needed [this verse to teach the principle of] claimants; signs are incidental. (*b. B. Metsi'a* 27b)

This biblical verse, according to the stam, is not rendered redundant if one considers signs rabbinic, rather than biblically derived, because it teaches that claimants are required for an object to be considered lost property; the rule of signs may have simply been mentioned along with the need for claimants, even if it was not derived directly from the biblical verse. While this reading seems rather forced, Raba provides an alternate way to contend with the issue of the place of signs in lost property law; his logical argument regarding the status of signs seems reasonable, though it is rebutted:

> Raba said: if you should say that signs are not biblically valid, how do you return lost [property] based on signs? Because one who finds a lost object benefits if it should be returned on the basis of signs, since if he loses something himself, it will be returned to him on the basis of signs. R. Safra said to Raba: can one confer benefit upon himself with money that is not his? (*b. B. Metsi'a* 27b)[31]

Raba attempts to argue that the acknowledged use of signs as a basis for returning lost property implies that it is biblically valid (a rather circular argument!). But he then surmises that perhaps the rabbis would have decreed the use of signs for the return of lost property, even if it was not biblically sanctioned, because it works toward the well being of society. Through the use of signs, more people would recover lost property and, though it appears that the finder would lose out in the immediate situation, he benefits in the long run from a society in which people know that they may recover their lost goods. R. Safra's rebuttal of this argument, however, is noteworthy; he asserts that no matter how important or beneficial the value is, the rabbis ought not allow for the redistribution of items because, quite simply, it is inappropriate for a person to benefit from someone else's property. R. Safra suggests that the reality of the property relationship is so essential that it cannot be disturbed through rabbinic legalities, even if such law would benefit the whole of society.

But R. Safra's observation is not dwelt on by the Talmud. Raba continues to conclude that signs are indeed biblically valid after citing a midrash similar to the one found in the *Sifre* and appending a different conclusion:

> Signs are biblically valid because it is written "'And it shall be with you until your brother's inquiry into it.' Would it enter your mind to give it to him before he sought after it? Rather, inquire into him, whether he is a deceiver or not." Would that [inquiry] not be through signs? Conclude. (*b. B. Metsi'a* 28a)

In this midrash, the "inquiry into" the claimant regarding his credibility is not an additional requirement aside from the identification of signs, but rather alludes to that very procedure. How would one know whether one's brother is a deceiver? Ask him to identify the signs on the object. Thus Raba concludes that the seemingly needless phrase "until your brother's inquiry" is required to teach one thing: that the evidentiary procedure of identifying signs on an object is a *biblically valid* mode of proof, and action could be taken, no matter how dire the consequences, on the basis of such evidence.

Raba goes on to specify precisely how the evidence of signs may be weighed against other forms of biblically sanctioned evidence, such as witnesses, and how different forms of signs (e.g., length versus width) may be measured against each other, providing the kind of unambiguous guide to behavior that the Mishnah omits:

> A. Raba said: Should you resolve that identification marks are biblically valid . . .
> B. ("Should you resolve"? But he has proved that they are biblically valid! That is because it can be explained as it was above.)
> C. If two sets of signs [are offered by disputing claimants], [the lost object] must be left [in custody]. If [one claimant] states signs and one [produces] witnesses, it must be surrendered to him who has witnesses. If [one claimant] states signs and another also states signs and [produces] one witness, one witness is as though non-existent, so it must be left [in custody]. [If one claimant produces] witnesses of weaving, and another witnesses of losing, it must be given to the latter, because we argue: [the first] may have sold it, and another lost it. If [one claimant] states length, and another its breadth, it must be given

to [him who states its] length, because it is possible to conjecture the breadth when its owner is standing and wearing it, whereas the length cannot be well conjectured. [If one claimant] states its length and breadth, and another its square area, it must be surrendered to the former. If the length, breadth, and weight [are stated by different claimants], it must be given to [him who states] its weight.
(b. B. Metsi‛a 28b)

In each case listed by Raba, a legal rule is generated and the freedom of personal judgment is limited; in other words, private uncertainty is replaced with legal certainty. But this legal certainty (of ownership, or identity) adduced by Raba and given the full authority of biblical, and hence divine, sanction, is simultaneously undone by the anonymous *stam* in both his additions to and arrangement of this *sugya*. The redactor introduces the *sugya* with a series of tannaitic texts that imply the validity of signs and proceeds to offer alternative readings of each. One of these texts is the very midrash Raba uses to conclude that signs are biblically valid: "'inquire into him, whether he is a deceiver or not.' Would that [inquiry] not be through signs? Conclude." In the *stam*'s version, the conclusion reads differently. The rhetorical question is actually answered, in a surprising manner. "Would [that inquiry] not be through signs? No—through witnesses!"[32]

This text is referenced again at the very end of the *sugya*, negating the decisiveness of Raba's conclusion. Raba's final remark in the *sugya*, after deducing that signs are in fact biblically valid, begins "if you should say that signs are biblically valid . . ." (b. B. Metsi‛a 28a). This statement of Raba, which continues by delineating the weight different forms of evidence are to be given, may have been imported from another text,[33] or it may be presented out of order, or the preface "if you should say" may simply be a way of introducing the idea that signs may indeed be biblically valid, but are still subordinated to the testimony of witnesses. In any case, the *stam* interrupts immediately after the introductory phrase and asks why it is phrased this way: "'If you should say'! But he has proved that they are biblically valid! It can still be explained as it was explained above" (b. B. Metsi‛a 28a). The *stam* reminds us, at the very conclusion of the *sugya*, that there is a different way to explain Raba's centerpiece text, and that the biblical validity of signs is in fact still open to question.[34]

Raba hopes that the legal facts that result from the evidentiary transactions facilitated by signs will impart a sense of certainty in one's fulfillment of the divine law (much as R. Aqiba's legal decision of ritual purity did in the last chapter). But though R. Aqiba's students' unspoken challenge of the woman's "real" ritual status is swiftly quelled, here R. Safra's question remains unanswered, haunting the seemingly decisive conclusion of the *sugya:* ought one benefit from money that is not *really* his? No matter who authorizes the legal correctness of the transfer of money or property—even if it is the divine law—and no matter what positive outcome may result, one cannot escape the lingering doubt that perhaps, in the end, the money was not rightly his—that the truth of property ownership, known personally and intuitively, can intrude on the demonstrable legal decision of ownership.[35] In refining and specifying the unequivocal legal standards of evidence by which money and property can and must be transferred, the talmudic *sugya* is simultaneously undermined by the notion of the real—a relationship of ownership which can never be perceived by outside observers with certainty, but which nonetheless may represent substantive truth. The ambiguity created by the *stam* allows for the certitude of the legal sanction of signs to be second-guessed. The commitment to rabbinic property law as a definitive fulfilment of the divine will is shaken.

While the Mishnah creates space for different understandings of property and ownership, the series of narratives in the Yerushalmi and the legal *sugya* in the Bavli each strive toward differing approximations of certainty. The narratives in the Yerushalmi endeavor to create a sense of the certainty of ethical obligation, but it is undermined by the idealistic nature of the narratives, and their lack of applicability to real situations. A general moral may be derived from these incredible stories of men returning lost property at all costs, but they are hardly a helpful guide in cases of actual property disputes and real-world fulfillment of the divine law. The legal argument in the Bavli emphasizes that ownership may be defined by its observable traces, striving for legal certainty in ambiguous situations; indeed, legal rules are elaborated for making firm decisions in a variety of discordant circumstances. But the redactor of the Talmud refuses to make this biblically-sanctioned certainty the final word: he arranges the text to underscore that these decisions may still be challenged. In sum, the *sugya* in the Yerushalmi attempts to ignore the real need for legal guidelines in property disputes, and Raba in the Bavli attempts to ignore the possibility of an experienced reality that would undermine legal verdicts. Each talmudic text, then, can be seen to supply what the other is lacking, as each chooses between observable signs and felt truth, legal facts and moral imperatives, human decisions and divine sanction. And each text gestures toward the other perspective, revealing the inaccessibility of substantive truth and the problem of the human application of the divine commandment.

THREE

The Impossibility of Judgment

The undecidable remains caught, lodged, at least as a ghost—but
an essential ghost—in every decision, in every event of decision.

The rabbinic texts that we have seen so far question, undermine, or overrule
lived experience, offering legal solutions while maintaining a stance of
doubt. While ambiguity about substantive reality may be tolerated in regard
to ritual law and even to some extent in property law, as we saw in the Mishnah, criminal law would seem to demand more precision, especially with
the divinely mandated punishment of death for various offenses. Rabbinic
law is well known for its enactment of multiple legal safeguards to ensure
that there be no false convictions, but the specter of wrongful judgment—in
an absolute sense—nonetheless remains ever present. For if sages like R.
Safra voice misgivings about the possibility of a clash between legal and
substantive truth with regard to the transfer of property, this anxiety becomes even more consuming in matters of life and death. I therefore turn in
this chapter to biblical and rabbinic discussions of truth seeking in capital
cases to examine how the rabbis harmonize their commitment to fulfilling
the divine law on the one hand with their doubts about the human ability to
discern certain truth on the other.

Biblical law, once again, offers little guidance to later rabbinic jurists.
In the biblical texts that discuss criminal procedure, witnesses are represented as rather straightforwardly establishing the facts of a crime in all
but the most difficult cases; these rare cases that completely stymie the
courts are resolved by appealing to agents of the divine cult, the priests in
the Temple. Rabbinic sources, however, fundamentally complicate this

biblical picture; the "normal processes of lawyerly handling of the laws," according to Michael Fishbane, include "a concern with scrutinizing the content of laws for real or anticipated deficiencies."[1] The most apparent "deficiency" in biblical criminal procedure is the possibility of mistaken judgments, whether through deliberate falsification by witnesses or an innocent error, neither of which is taken into account in biblical law.[2] Thus the rabbis develop an extensive criminal procedure, I maintain, not necessarily out of some philosophical or theological aversion to the death penalty,[3] but due to the need to incorporate criminal law and construct legal truth within the uncertain discourse of a human, living legal system. Uncertainty and a formal notion of truth in capital cases, however, can hardly be tolerated. To admit the presence of doubt in a death penalty case is to acknowledge the possibility of authorized murder.[4] Establishing the facts—indeed, the truth—in capital cases, therefore, has tremendous implications for fashioning a juridical world in the face of uncertainty—for authorizing human juridical action in the absence of certain, divine knowledge. In shaping this legal sphere, the rabbis' dangerous judicial authority—and weighty responsibility—disturb the careful balance between the commitment to justice in fulfillment of the divine will and the recognition of continuing doubt as to an unalterable and ultimate truth. As such, the sphere of capital, criminal law challenges the rabbinic faith in the viability of the human administration of divine law in an uncertain world.

Biblical Criminal Law: A Life for a Life

The rabbinic encounter with capital punishment stems from the unequivocal biblical sanction of, and indeed demand for, capital punishment for several grave crimes. As Elie Spitz asserts, "the death penalty is commanded in the Bible with no moral qualms. It is presented as a just penalty which facilitates a realignment of God with creation, provides retributive justice, and serves as a deterrent."[5] This basic requirement of retributive justice is found in the biblical law of *talion,* in which a just world order must be restored after injury or murder by subjecting the criminal to the very injury he inflicted upon the victim. This talionic rule for murder is stated explicitly in all five books of the Pentateuch.

The biblical principle of "a life for a life" is clearly stated in Exodus and Leviticus:

> Where injury ensues, you are to give life for life, eye for eye, tooth for tooth, hand for hand, foot for foot, burn for burn, bruise for bruise, wound for wound. (Ex. 21:23–24)

> If one person strikes another and kills him, he must be put to death. (Lev. 24:17)

These texts simply lay out the talionic principle, ignoring the question of how one establishes that the crime has been committed by a particular individual before punishment is administered. The levitical text alludes to the need for evidence—specifically, the requirement of witnesses—in a short "case study" about a blasphemer which precedes the talionic pronouncement:

> When the Lord spoke to Moses he said: The man who blasphemed is to be taken outside the camp, and let *everyone who heard him* lay a hand on his head, and let the whole community stone him to death. (Lev. 24:13–14, emphasis added)

Though this text does not explicitly discuss calling witnesses, or in this case "hearers," as part of a court procedure to prove a case, it makes clear that there are indeed those that have heard the blasphemer and that these individuals have a special role to play in punishing the sinner.

Other biblical texts, however, inscribe the precondition of witness testimony within the law of the injurer. The chapter in Numbers which treats in depth the crimes of intentional (and unintentional) murder outlines the basic elements of criminal law: what kind of act constitutes murder, who executes punishment, what modes of punishment are sanctioned, and finally why punishment is necessary altogether. The text elaborates:

> A. But anyone who strikes another with an iron object, and death ensues, is a murderer; the murderer shall be put to death. Or anyone who strikes another with a stone in hand that could cause death, and death ensues, is a murderer; the murderer shall be put to death. Or anyone who strikes another with a weapon of wood in hand that could cause death, and death ensues, is a murderer; the murderer shall be put to death. The avenger of blood is the one who shall put the murderer to death; when they meet, the avenger of blood shall execute the sentence. Likewise, if someone pushes another out of ha-

tred, or hurls something at another, lying in wait, and death ensues, or in enmity strikes another with the hand, and death ensues, then the one who struck the blow shall be put to death; that person is a murderer; the avenger of blood shall put the murderer to death, when they meet. . . .

B. These things shall be a statute and ordinance for you throughout your generations wherever you live. If anyone kills another, the murderer shall be put to death on the evidence of witnesses; but no one shall be put to death on the testimony of a single witness. Moreover you shall accept no ransom for the life of a murderer who is subject to the death penalty; a murderer must be put to death. Nor shall you accept ransom for one who has fled to a city of refuge, enabling the fugitive to return to live in the land before the death of the high priest. You shall not pollute the land in which you live; for blood pollutes the land, and no expiation can be made for the land, for the blood that is shed in it, except by the blood of the one who shed it. You shall not defile the land in which you live, in which I also dwell; for I Yhwh dwell among the Israelites. (Num. 16–21, 29–34)

Many biblical scholars view the last section of this pericope (B), which consists of the requirement of witnesses and the rationale behind capital punishment, as "appended, or possibly adapted from another source."[6] Still, by attaching it at the end of the law of the murderer, "the priestly author brings basic deuteronomic principles about witnesses into direct association with the law of blood vengeance and asylum."[7] The pericope then ends with an admonition that is characteristic of priestly concerns; according to Jacob Milgrom, "it is a basic [priestly] theological postulate that the divine Presence cannot abide in a land polluted by murder; the offense leads to the pollution of the earth and the abandonment by God of His sanctuary and people."[8] As a corollary, the death of the murderer atones for the shedding of innocent blood and allows the divine presence to abide in Israel. Humans are "charged with the primary responsibility of punishing the murderer . . . [and] God is the final guarantor that homicide is ultimately punished."[9]

This passage in Numbers offers a comprehensive treatment of the law of the murderer; unlike the succinct pronouncements of Exodus and Leviticus, the lengthy and detailed pericope rhetorically persuades the reader that treatment of a criminal can be fair and decisive, and that after a serious crime order can be restored and justice dispensed. However, Levine notes, what is missing from Numbers 35 is any provision for the total exoneration of the one accused of murder, for a determination that the wrong person had been accused. It is assumed that the one accused is the true perpetrator, the actual homicide. It remained to determine the status of his crime under the law.[10]

"The evidence of witnesses" suffices in Numbers, then, for an accused to be put to death; one must turn to Deuteronomy for a consideration of—and provision for—doubt about the veracity of testimony, for the total exoneration of the accused:

> But if someone at enmity with another lies in wait and attacks and takes the life of that person, and flees into one of these cities [of refuge], then the elders of the killer's city shall send to have the culprit taken from there and handed over to the avenger of blood to be put to death. Show no pity; you shall purge the guilt of innocent blood from Israel, so that it may go well with you.... A single witness shall not suffice to convict a person of any crime or wrongdoing in connection with any offense that may be committed. Only on the evidence of two or three witnesses shall a charge be sustained. If a malicious witness comes forward to accuse someone of wrongdoing, then both parties to the dispute shall appear before Yhwh, before the priests and the judges who are in office in those days, and the judges shall make a thorough inquiry. If the witness is a false witness, having testified falsely against another, then you shall do to the false witness just as the false witness had meant to do to the other. So you shall purge the evil from your midst. The rest shall hear and be afraid, and a crime such as this shall never again be committed among you. Show no pity: life for life, eye for eye, tooth for tooth, hand for hand, foot for foot. (Deut. 19:11–21)

This passage in Deuteronomy echoes the one in Numbers, but it has a significantly different approach to two elements of the law of the murderer. First, the question of evidence is highlighted, nuanced, and more fully explored. A similar two-witness rule is stipulated, but Deuteronomy entertains the possibility of false ("malicious") witnesses and legislates and prescribes severe punishment for perjurers. According to these laws in Deuteronomy, then, it is not simply the testimony of two witnesses that "establishes the matter" and calls for punishment, but the testimony of two *true* witnesses. Deuteronomy allows for the possibility that was ignored in Numbers: that the accused is wholly innocent.

Deuteronomy thus postulates a judicial procedure that can distinguish between true and false evidence; specifically, it requires that judges make "a thorough inquiry"[11] (19:18). Evidentiary procedures are foregrounded here in a way that they are not in the other biblical passages that legislate on murder. Bernard Levinson notes that Deuteronomy emphasizes evidentiary procedures not only in regard to murder but to most other capital crimes as well—it becomes a characteristic motif of deuteronomic criminal law. He writes:

> Strikingly, the requirement of a minimum of two witnesses becomes a precondition to conviction even in the case of the most heinous offense imaginable, apostasy as the breach of the first commandment of the Decalogue. Even in such a case, normative witness law must be scrupulously implemented.... That capital offenses, even in the gravest of cases ... are subordinated to a general law of evidence clearly gives a powerful theme-setting demonstration of the injunction with which the unit as a whole opens:... "they shall judge the people with righteous justice." (Deut. 16:18)[12]

In other words, Deuteronomy is concerned not only with the task of punishing the criminal and purging the land of evil, but also with the process of "judging righteously," which means insisting that legal judgment correspond to *substantive reality* and not be applied readily when apparent legal criteria are met. Though the procedures by which judges could distinguish true from false evidence are left entirely vague by the biblical text, some kind of divine arbitration—either oracle, divination, or priests acting as agents of the deity—may be implied; the inquiry takes place "before Yhwh, before the priests and judges" (19:17). Thus, the sanctuary serves as a locus of judicial authority for the verification of evidence; furthermore, it functions as a final recourse when evidence is scarce or ambiguous. As we have seen, Deuteronomy legislates as follows:

> If a judicial decision is too difficult for you to make between one kind of bloodshed and another, one kind of legal right and another, or one kind of assault and another—any such matters of dispute in your towns—then you shall immediately go up to the place that Yhwh your God will choose, where you shall consult with the levitical priests and the judge who is in office in those days; they shall announce to you the decision in the case. Carry out exactly the decision that they announce to you from the place that Yhwh will choose, diligently observing everything they instruct you. You must carry out fully the law that they interpret for you or the ruling that they announce to you; do not turn aside from the decision that they announce to you, either to the right or to the left. (Deut. 17:8–11)

Here, the biblical text explicitly acknowledges the uncertainty that may arise in adjudication, and provides a solution: consultation with agents of the divine cult.

Aside from the emphasis on the verification of evidence, the deuteronomic text differs strikingly from the one in Numbers in the reasons given for capital punishment. While Numbers specifies that the blood of a murderer would cleanse the land of the defilement of innocent blood that had been shed, Deuteronomy offers several subtly different justifications for the execution of a criminal. Most frequently, Deuteronomy explains capital punishment with the phrase "and you shall purge the evil from among you" (cf. 13:6; 17:7, 12; 19:19; 21:21; 22:21, 22, 24; 24:7). In the case of murder, a similar statement appears, but "[guilt for] innocent blood" is substituted for "evil"— the execution of the murderer "purge[s] the [guilt for] innocent blood" from the community (19:13, 21:9). Moreover, a classic deterrence argument appears in several passages: "Then all Israel shall hear and be afraid, and never again do any such wickedness" (13:11; see also 19:20, 21:21). The purging of evil and the guilt for innocent blood may be harmonized with the deterrence argument—and simultaneously differentiated from the priestly idea of cleansing the defilement of spilled blood—through the larger rubric of the solidarity and health of the community of Israel. Indeed, the purging of the guilt for innocent blood called for in 19:13 is justified by the result of this act: "it may go well with you."

Even the ancient law of *talion* ("a life for a life") is transformed in Deuteronomy—the classic formulation of exact and equal retribution is applied to the law of false witnesses, extending its application from an injury inflicted to one intended but never carried out (because, presumably, the false witnesses are identified before the accused is executed).[13] This deviates from a true talionic understanding of punishment which is precisely equal and exact retribution; here, one is commanded to punish *as though* an act was realized, when it in fact was not. What Deuteronomy demands is an imaginative leap: it insists that intending to cause harm is equivalent to causing it. This equation is made even more strongly by a rhetorical sleight of hand as the familiar formulation of the talionic law concludes this section on false witnesses, suggesting that the mandate to execute a false witness is not an innovation but merely the application of precedent. Deuteronomy does not justify its stipulations but merely states: "then you shall do to the false witness just as the false witness had meant to do to the other. So you shall purge the evil from your midst. . . . life for life, eye for eye, tooth for tooth, hand for hand, foot for foot" (19:19, 21). Though the act of attempted murder does not correspond to the act of murder, what remains the same whether a victim is killed or not is the malignant intent of one member of the community to harm another. The deterrence argument, appended here alongside the law of *talion*, rationalizes the death penalty yet again in a different way: "The rest shall hear and be afraid, and a crime such as this shall never again be committed among you" (Deut. 19:20)—the community will thus be cured of its malignancy.

It is likely no coincidence that where room is made for the possibility of wrongful accusation, the rationale for capital punishment relies less on a literal equality between deed and retribution and more on values that seek to protect the community as a whole.[14] The passage in Numbers presumes certainty about the guilt of the accused, and the shed blood of the criminal is considered the only means for expiation. Deuteronomy, however, entertains the possibility of false evidence, the consequence of which is the possibility of a wrongful execution. According to the text's reasons for capital punishment—deterring crime and ridding the community of those who intend it harm—such "collateral damage" does not threaten the efficacy of the entire penal system.

The logical extension of Deuteronomy's case of false witnesses is indeed the unstated case in this biblical pericope, a case in which false witnesses are successful in putting an innocent person to death through the instrument of the court. The biblical text's emphasis on the witnesses' intention, rather than deed, conveys the sense that the deed has not occurred, that no wrongful death has taken place. Deuteronomy's rhetoric demonstrates a confidence in the ability of courts to ascertain the truth in criminal cases and identify the guilty party. Another instance of this confidence occurs in reference to the sin of idol worship, and incitement to idol worship; the text reads, "and if it is reported to you or you hear of it, and you make a thorough inquiry, and the charge is established as true [*emet nakon*] [that] such an abhorrent thing was done in Israel, then you shall bring out to your gates that man or that woman who has committed this crime and you shall stone the man or woman to death. . . ." (Deut. 17:4–5; see also Deut. 13:11, 15). Deuteronomy does not provide a legal standard of evidence, such as "beyond a reasonable doubt." Instead, one must investigate until the *truth* is uncovered. The text emphasizes this point three times in the Hebrew: "*emet*" (truth) "*nakon*" (it is established) "*ne'estah ha-to'ebah*" (the abhorrent thing was done). Such turns of phrase leave little room for continuing uncertainty. Strikingly similar language is used in conjunction with the laws of murder and false witnesses: "you shall diligently inquire," "the matter is established." The deuteronomic stipulations for capital crimes thus require nothing less than absolute certainty regarding the guilt of the accused.

Indeed, certainty is virtually guaranteed by the provision in Deuteronomy that we saw above to repair to the Temple should a court lack the necessary discernment for a decision to be rendered. Besides providing an avenue through which a clear decision may be reached, this stipulation also reinforces the idea that most matters are not too difficult to judge, that the truth may be known and understood in most cases. Only in specific, and one would assume rare, instances will the truth not become apparent. And in such cases, certitude is nonetheless provided by the agents of the divine cult.

The biblical sources, as a whole, consist of criminal law codes in which evidentiary rules are not heavily emphasized. When they are invoked, the testimonies of more than one witness are deemed sufficient for conviction provided that the witnesses are not "malicious." In fact, what is stressed in the biblical sources more than concrete modes of evidence is the requirement incumbent on the court or the community to reach certainty on the matter; the means through which one might reach a decision are left unstated. When uncertainty lingers, a verdict may be "handed down" to the court by priests acting as God's mediators.

None of the biblical law codes we have examined envisage judicial error. While Deuteronomy does admit the possibility of falsified evidence by lying witnesses, it does not consider the prospect of a wrongful conviction on the basis of this evidence. In the law of the false witnesses, the witnesses are exposed and punished *before* their testimony perverts justice; no provision is made for dealing with witnesses whose falsified evidence has actually resulted in a wrongful conviction and execution. The Bible's legal texts[15] refrain from imagining the successful manipulation of the judicial system by malicious witnesses who falsify evidence; moreover, they do not even consider cases of erroneous evidence provided by well-intentioned witnesses, an extremely common occurrence in contemporary jurisprudence. Biblical rhetoric advances the sense not merely of the court's authority but also of its near-divine omniscience: according to these biblical passages, *all* can ultimately be known. Because certainty is portrayed as the end result of due diligence, disputes may be resolved conclusively and justice done without exception.

Burdens of Proof: Rabbinic Criminal Procedure

The mishnaic legal material on capital cases is primarily collected in Tractate *Sanhedrin*. The rabbinic discussion dwells in the interstices of the biblical sources, expanding and lending concrete meaning to the Bible's sparse and vague evidentiary rules, demanding that prescribed procedures be followed prior to judgments being rendered. The Mishnah establishes that, in accordance with the biblical stipulation, at least two witnesses are necessary for a conviction. Beyond the biblical prescription, these witnesses must also meet certain requirements for their testimony to be admissible: they must be of upstanding character, they must be men, and they must not be related to the accused (*m. Sanh.* 3:3). Examination of the witnesses, implied in the biblical directive to "diligently inquire," is given specific contours: the witnesses must be separated, interviewed individually (3:6), and even intimidated (4:5) according to the procedures delineated by the Mishnah. It divides the questioning into two categories: *ḥaqirah*, investigation, and *bediqah*, examination. The investigations establish basic facts of the case, and the examinations inquire into details of the event. The testimony is entirely nullified if one witness cannot answer even one of the investigations, or if a contradiction arises between the witnesses during the examinations (5:1–2). The Mishnah emphasizes that these interrogations are not intended to be a formality but rather a thorough inquiry; the Mishnah states that "whoever increases examinations is worthy of praise" (5:2).

Unambiguously placing the burden of proof on the prosecution, the Mishnah thoroughly delineates the rules of evidence, extending them beyond the particulars of witness testimony. Proof and arguments for the defense are always submitted first (4:1), and a judge who has argued for acquittal cannot reverse his argument to one for conviction even before the verdict has been rendered (5:5). An accused can be acquitted—but never convicted—by a majority of one (5:5).

Mishnah *Sanhedrin* fills out biblical criminal law with specific procedural rules, and in doing so, it concomitantly deserts the Bible's rhetoric of certainty and guarantee of justice. But is that all there is to it? Many scholars and commentators have discerned a programmatic energy on the part of the tannaim to deliberately eliminate the death penalty from the Jewish legal tradition by imposing strict procedural rules that could never lead to a conviction, thus creating a *de facto* moratorium. Gerald Blidstein famously argues that "Jewish law abolished capital punishment in fact not by denying its conceptual moral validity but rather by allowing it *only* this conceptual validity."[16] This division between theory and practice, also maintained by David De Sola Pool in his well-known essay on Jewish capital punishment,[17] is complicated by others such as Richard Block, who rightfully points out that "inasmuch as Jewish courts were deprived of their authority to impose capital punishment . . . the talmudic restrictions on capital punishment must be regarded as theoretical rather than practical."[18] Block then observes a conflict in rabbinic thinking about capital punishment:

> The tradition is at war with itself. It embodies the tension between two compelling theoretical positions and two competing sets of values. There are, tradition tells us, crimes heinous enough to warrant death as the just and appropriate punishment. Society needs and deserves the full protection of criminal sanctions, including capital punishment. Yes, tradition answers itself, but, every person bears the divine image, and society cannot be too careful when it seeks to take a life. In the final analysis, these two antithetical bodies of talmudic material reflect the classic tension between *midat hadin* and *midat harachamim,* the attributes of justice and mercy.

Block sees both sides of the death-penalty debate reflected in the rabbinic upholding of capital punishment, on the one hand, and erecting almost insurmountable procedural hurdles to attaining a death-penalty sentence, on the other. But for Block both sides of the argument, in the end, support an abolitionist perspective, since the rabbis'

> primary concern was [not] practical Halacha. . . . Their primary concern was to penetrate and replicate God's mind through the study and exposition of "Torah," in its most comprehensive sense. Ultimately, the talmudic discussions of capital punishment are part of the messianic enterprise.[19]

In other words, whichever theoretical position the rabbis' were to take on capital punishment, the idea of actually putting it into practice and executing criminals was anathema.

But can we really read these rabbinic *legal* texts as an abstract, idealistic debate? Aaron Kirschenbaum writes that such an

> explanation . . . ignores the great piety of the Rabbis and their extreme conservatism when it came to preserving traditional teachings. It also ignores the feverish activity with which R. Akiva sought to achieve the restoration of Jewish independence. . . .[20]

The rabbis were not willing, according to Kirschenbaum, to relegate their legal traditions to theoretical positions about values, but rather wanted them to be a serviceable part of the Jewish religion. His central question, then, speaks to the issue of rabbinic practice: "How did the Rabbis understand their legal system which, on the one hand, makes the punishment of criminals well-nigh impossible and, on the other, contains so many capital crimes?"[21] Kirschenbaum turns to pedagogy, again, for the answer. He contends that the rabbis understood the biblical requirement of capital punishment, along with the tradition of evidentiary restrictions and the difficulties for conviction, as educative and thus a deterrent: "Punishment was . . . rarely meted out, but the serious nature of the infraction was duly impressed upon the people."[22]

One might ask, then, how this pedagogical aim is not merely theoretical—in what sense "education, refinement, and spiritual elevation"[23] as the end results of the criminal code could be reconciled with the rabbinic efforts to restore Jewish independence and enact Jewish law. Kirschenbaum himself raises this question: "what of the maintenance of law and order? What of men of violence and murderers?"[24] To settle this dilemma of the impending failure of the rabbinic justice system, Kirschenbaum reaches for the same answer as the authors of Deuteronomy: "a third arm of the judiciary function[s] concurrently with [human jurisprudence]: the Heavenly Court presided over by the Lord of Justice Himself. This Tribunal was invoked (especially, but not only) when the other two institutions were unable or unwilling to cope with crime."[25] In the end, then, Kirschenbaum must concede that capital punishment was intended to be nothing more than theoretical, as criminal law had to be delegated to God himself.[26]

What all of these scholars take for granted is the complete unfeasibility of the Mishnah's rules of criminal procedure, and as such they each look beyond the sphere of human jurisprudence to understand it. The

Mishnah itself, though, never indicates that its model for a criminal trial is unworkable or too lenient. In fact, as we shall see, the Mishnah assumes that its procedures may even lead to the wrongful convictions of innocents. Nevertheless, it never invokes God, the messianic age, or theoretical concepts such as the attribute of mercy to complement or complete the legal practice it outlines—rabbinic criminal procedure may be presumed to be self-sufficient. But for many scholars, Mishnah *Sanhedrin* is not read on its own terms but instead through the lens of a famous mishnah which seems to reflect rabbinic opposition to the death penalty, particularly when certain statements are emphasized over others:

> A Sanhedrin [high court] that executes one person in seven years is considered destructive. R. Eleazar b. Azariah says: one in seventy years. R. Tarfon and R. Aqiba say: had we been in the Sanhedrin, no one would ever have been executed. R. Simeon b. Gamaliel adds: they multiply murderers in Israel. (*m. Mak.* 1:10, emphasis mine)

As many scholars either ignore entirely or give less weight to the final statement in this mishnah, they deduce a general rabbinic opposition to the death penalty.[27] Beth Berkowitz, however, in her recent book, suggests that we must avoid readings of Mishnah *Sanhedrin* that assert "comprehensive explanations that predicate the rabbinic death penalty on a particular idea"[28]—such as a philosophical discomfort with capital punishment. Instead, she argues that "even though rabbinic criminal law may exist as 'theory' rather than 'practice,' that is, as a law on the books rather than law applied and enforced, it may still in some sense be understood as practice."[29] By this she means that rather than posit an intellectualized "attitude" toward capital punishment on the part of the early rabbis, one must "[suppose] the rabbinic laws to be overdetermined and contradictory rather than unitary and coherent, asking about their construction of authority. . . ."[30] One of the main questions she asks is "What work does the ritual of execution do?"[31]

It is precisely this question of what work rabbinic criminal laws do that I would like to take up, and I would extend Berkowitz's analysis beyond the execution of punishment to the performative framework of the trial process itself—a topic she does not dwell on because it has been so overemphasized by previous scholarship on the rabbinic death penalty.[32] I would like to examine the discursive practice of the Mishnah in constructing authoritative, legal truth when the facts are uncertain. Though one may perceive in the Mishnah an attempt to align legal verdicts with the real or substantive facts of the crime, the law nonetheless inevitably establishes its own unequivocal decision of guilt or innocence, its own determination of the "facts" which are supposed to ultimately prevail. In this sense, Mishnah *Sanhedrin* does not differ from other spheres of mishnaic law. But as a law code which is "overdetermined and contradictory," particularly because there is so much at stake in capital punishment, the triumph of legal truth is consistently and subtly challenged if not undermined, undone by the persistent awareness of the fault line between the legal construction of guilt and the inaccessible reality of the past.

In highlighting the discursive work of rabbinic criminal law, however, I would not like to neglect the rabbinic "attitude" to the death penalty. Mishnah *Makkot* 1:10 offers us a rare glimpse of the rabbis' view of and commitment to their own legal system. The painful awareness that "the truth of the matter" is deeply buried if not entirely unreachable creates a juridical crisis when it comes to capital punishment, and Mishnah *Makkot* 1:10 may be read as the reflection of the crumbling edifice of rabbinic law when faced with the dreadful power it may wield.

LEGAL TRUTH AND WRONGFUL JUDGMENT

Alongside the careful elaboration of criminal procedure, rabbinic legal discourse in Mishnah *Sanhedrin* implicitly acknowledges the difference between meeting a legal standard for conviction and uncovering the truth about the facts of the case and the guilt of the accused. Indeed, the Mishnah from the outset deals only with *legal* possibilities. Tractate *Sanhedrin* never insists that judges unearth the "truth" or "establish the matter," even though the biblical texts from which these laws derive speak exclusively in these terms. Instead, testimony stands (*qayemet*) or is nullified (*betelah*). If the testimony is found legally viable, each individual judge either acquits (*mezakeh*) or convicts (*mehayeb*), pronouncing legal verdicts which do not claim to be statements of fact, but which stand, instead, as legal constructions.[33]

The Mishnah then openly admits that an innocent could be wrongfully convicted. It raises the issue not to warn judges about avoiding such a scenario at all costs, or as an example of a corrupt court, but rather as a matter of fact to be considered when a convict is urged to confess his or her crime as part of the "last rites" before execution. The judges are told to prompt the convict to utter the following words: "may my death be an atonement for all my sins." The mishnah then continues, "*If he knew that he was falsely accused,* he says, 'may my death be an atonement for all of my sins, aside from this one'" (6:2). This certainty ("he *knew*") casually asserted in this mishnah, is set apart from the legal proceedings, having no bearing on the progress of the execution. It disrupts neither the continuing force of the conviction nor the impassive language of the Mishnah, which continues with yet another practical concern: perhaps the convict should not be urged to say these words, lest "all confess thus, in order to clear themselves" (6:2). While the sages appear to accept unanimously the possibility of an innocent convict, they disagree over whether such innocence should be proclaimed in public. There is no disagreement, again, on whether the punishment should be carried out regardless of this certainty which, simply put, renders meaningless the entire framework of this mishnah—the confession, the atonement, the punishment. All may be canceled out by the specter of the convict's knowledge and thus, the rabbis imply, this certainty ought not affect the legal establishment of criminal guilt.

The closest the Mishnah comes to the notion of objective truth, the use of the word ʾ*emet,* is in stipulating the reaction of the convict's family after the execution. The relatives are required to ask after the welfare of the judges and the witnesses, "as if to say that we have nothing against you in our hearts, that you have judged a *true judgment*" (6:6). The word "truth" is never applied by the rabbinic authors of the mishnah to describe the legal decision, but such a validation of the work of the court is placed in the mouths of the convict's family, thus requiring not that the judgment *be* true but that it be *said* to be so—the authority of the court must be accepted as "true" (i.e., in good faith and according to procedure) even when its judgments do not cohere with others' knowledge (i.e., of substantive truth). In this mishnah, the rabbinic authorities seem to want unchecked authority to render and enforce their verdicts and to simultaneously absolve themselves of responsibility for wrongful convictions—but these two postures may be more mutually exclusive than the Mishnah would care to admit. If authority is absolute, then the court must be held absolutely responsible for its errors in judgment; if it admits these errors, then its claim to authority can only be undermined. The Mishnah's attempt to acknowledge the messy world of uncertain reality and simultaneously tame it through language and law, illustrated in its effort to control not only the confessing convict's words but his or her family's as well, betrays perhaps the innate and profound contradiction between these two positions, and the inevitable failure of the rabbinic endeavor to have it both ways.

PHYSICAL EVIDENCE AND JUDICIAL RESPONSIBILITY

The trial procedure outlined in the Mishnah implies a kind of comprehensiveness, a thorough investigation into the crime such that no detail is left out. But there is a whole sphere of evidence that the Mishnah strangely ignores. The obvious and basic idea that the murder weapon and the body ought to be present before the court—a requirement which would effectively mean acquittal for every case in which these objects were missing—is never even entertained. The Mishnah's exclusive reliance on eyewitness testimony as evidence in criminal law may be presented in unremarkable rhetorical fashion, but it stands, in the end, as a legal choice that is never explained.[34]

The explicit rejection of physical evidence from criminal trials by R. Aqiba is recorded in Tosefta *Sanhedrin*. Simeon the Temanite suggests that the judge should immediately acquit, despite the presence of valid witnesses, in cases in which the murder weapon cannot be found and submitted to the court. He states:

> Just as a fist is known to the assembly of the judges and the witnesses, so also a stone should be known to the assembly of the judges and the witnesses, which excludes the case where the stone was lost. R. Aqiba said to him: This would only apply to a case in which the stone was lost. From where would one derive that [the judgment] would depend on a stick [were it used as a weapon] being in the courtroom? And would the judges know whether he hit [the victim] upon his thigh or upon the tip of the heart? And if he threw him from the top of a building and he died, should we say bring the building to the courtroom? And if you say the court can go and see the building—if it collapsed, should we say that the owners would have to rebuild it? Rather, just as witnesses are believed in these matters, so in criminal judgments, all depends upon witnesses. (*t. Sanh.* 12:3)

Simeon the Temanite interprets, quite simply, the verse in Exodus which opens "When individuals quarrel and one strikes the other with a stone or fist..." (Ex. 21:18).[35] He argues that just as a person's fist would be seen by the court and the witnesses when the accused is brought before the assembly, so also, if he used a murder weapon such as a stone, it ought to be seen by the assembly and witnesses. He then proceeds to explain the legal consequence of this observation: when the murder weapon is lost, the accused must automatically be acquitted. It is unclear from this short statement whether Simeon the Temanite calls for the actual inspection of the murder weapon by the judges for further evidence that could illuminate the case. We might understand his statement as drawing upon Numbers 35:23 which specifically legislates that for an assault to be considered murder, the attacker must have "a stone in his hand capable of causing death," implying that a small pebble might suggest an intent to injure, but not to kill. This biblical stipulation strongly indicates the need for a judgment about the murder weapon itself, which could most easily be accomplished through the inspection of the murder weapon by the court.

However, Simeon the Temanite's words do not overtly call for such examination of or decision about the murder weapon; rather, his brief pronouncement succinctly conveys the requirement that the murder weapon be "known"—*yaduʿa*—to the witnesses and the assembly. This word is ambiguous: does it mean merely that the murder weapon be seen by the court, entered into evidence, or does it mean that it must be known, i.e., examined by judges and determined to be capable of causing death? A parallel passage in the early midrashic compilation on Exodus, the *Mekilta* of Rabbi Ishmael, may help explain Simeon the Temanite's cryptic statement. The *Mekilta* comments on the biblical phrase "when a man hits another with a stone or with his fist" (Ex. 21:18):

> R. Nathan says: This is to declare that a stone must be like the fist, and the fist must be like a stone. Just as the stone is something that can produce death, so also the fist must be such as to be capable of producing death. And just as the fist is something that can be identified, so also the stone must be such as can be identified. Thus, if the stone with which he struck him became mixed with other stones, the assailant is free. (*Mek. Neziqin* 6)

There are two elements in R. Nathan's comment, both of which endeavor to explain why the biblical verse specifies "stone or fist" as possible murder weapons and not anything else. R. Nathan provides two reasons: (1) Numbers 35:23 specifies that a person is considered a murderer only if he "has thrown a stone *capable of causing death*," which excludes a case of a small or light stone which may have caused death in an unusual manner; "stone" is connected to "fist" in this verse to require the same standard of "capable of causing death" for the fist as well. (2) Just as a fist is "known," so a stone must be "known." This sounds much like the reasoning of Simeon the Temanite, but fortunately another clause helps explain what is meant by "known": because a fist is attached to a person, one knows which fist caused the death—one can determine the identity of the murder weapon. A stone, however, may be mixed up with many other stones; unless the identity of the actual murder weapon is known, a conviction cannot be procured.

Simeon the Temanite's statement in the Tosefta—that the murder weapon must be "known"—thus has a more extensive parallel in the *Mekilta*. But the Tosefta version includes one detail the *Mekilta* omits: that the murder weapon must be submitted to and identified by *the court and the witnesses*. And it is precisely this issue of *who* must inspect the murder weapon which fuels the argument between Simeon the Temanite and R. Aqiba.

A brief form of this disagreement—which appears to have been expanded in our Toseftan text—is found in the *Mekilta* of Rabbi Simeon b. Yoḥai. Here, R. Aqiba's rebuttal consists of only one point:

> R. Aqiba said to him: if a man was pushed from the top of a building, and he fell and died, should we say that we must bring the building to the court? Rather, everything depends on witnesses, and criminal judgments depend on witnesses. (*Mek. of R. Simeon, Exod* 21:18)

R. Aqiba's position is essentially one of jurisprudential equity—if the instrument of death cannot be brought into the courtroom in every case, it cannot be a mandated part of trial procedure. R. Aqiba's argument is more rhetorical than logical, however. While buildings cannot be moved to the courtroom, the court, or an agent of the court, could be required to view the scene of the crime and ascertain whether the roof was high enough for the building to be deemed "capable of causing death."

In fact, the expanded version of R. Aqiba's argument, found in the Tosefta, entertains this very idea, and dismisses it. This longer version mounts a substantial case against Simeon the Temanite's opinion by raising several arguments against the inspection of the murder weapon. The first is exegetical: R. Aqiba points out that the verse only mentions fists and stones—how could one ascertain that the same requirement would apply to sticks as well? Second, he argues, examination of the weapon could not substitute for witness testimony, since the judges would still need witness information to ascertain how the weapon was used—whether on a vital organ, or merely on the thigh. Third is the question found in the *Mekilta* of what one must do if the murder weapon were a building, which clearly cannot be brought into the courtroom. Fourth, and finally, the idea that the judges could visit the building is dismissed by R. Aqiba because buildings fall down, and in such a case one clearly cannot expect that the building be rebuilt for the sake of the trial.

That Simeon the Temanite's three-phrase exegesis is followed by a paragraph-long rebuttal by R. Aqiba highlights the fact that R. Aqiba's argument holds little more than rhetorical power. Each of R. Aqiba's arguments is easily rebutted by anyone familiar with rabbinic midrash or evidence law; even the overarching point of equality before the law—that the weapon would not be able to be inspected in the case of the building, or the building's having collapsed—is little reason to exclude important evidence in a case when it is available. Indeed, rabbinic criminal trial procedure allows for vast inequity: the absolute requirement for conviction of two witnesses who are not relatives of the accused, not minors, women, or gamblers would allow the man who killed someone in front of twenty women to be acquitted, while the one who killed someone in front of two strange men to be convicted. Is it any more unjust to acquit someone who, as luck would have it, pushed his victim off the roof of a building which had subsequently collapsed and to convict someone else because his building remained intact? The mounting of *reductio ad absurdum* arguments against Simeon the Temanite's opinion lends rhetorical weight to R. Aqiba's own opinion, but does not present a good legal case for it. But after so many arguments against Simeon the Temanite, R. Aqiba's conclusion appears logical and necessary: that in cases of criminal law no evidence outside of eyewitness testimony ought to be considered: "all depends on witnesses."

R. Aqiba's opinion is, in the end, supported by little more than rhetorical posturing. In contemporary legal systems, for example, the inspection of the murder weapon by the court and the reconstruction of the scene of the crime are fundamental steps for securing a conviction in murder cases. Nonetheless, R. Aqiba's position that "all depends on witnesses" is the dominant voice in rabbinic criminal law. As I mentioned earlier, Mishnah *Sanhedrin* outlines the details of criminal trial procedure: while specific requirements for trying blasphemy and idolatry are mentioned, no special stipulation for murder is included—there is no mention of the examination of the murder weapon by the court. The Mishnah, and the Talmuds based on the Mishnah, which provide the grounding for all of subsequent Jewish law, consider nothing for the conviction of murder aside from the testimony of eyewitnesses. In fact, Simeon the Temanite's opinion is taken up only once in "mainstream" rabbinic literature and used as the basis for subsequent Jewish law; it is cited in the Babylonian Talmud as a tangential point in a different context, and R. Aqiba's opinion is given ultimate authority.

What is most intriguing about the absence of Simeon the Temanite's opinion from the Mishnah and Talmuds is that the Mishnah's exclusion of this leniency flies in the face of the once-prevailing scholarly opinion that a motivating impulse behind the rabbinic law for criminal proceedings was to virtually guarantee acquittal, to eliminate capital punishment in practice if not in theory. Simeon the Temanite's argument that without the murder weapon an accused could not be convicted certainly provides more opportunity for acquittal—if the weapon could not be produced, an acquittal would be automatic. Moreover, it introduces the possibility of finding evidence outside of witness testimony that could corroborate or dispel the witnesses' claims, imparting more authority to rabbinic judges in rendering verdicts. Would this increased judicial latitude not provide even further opportunity to acquit, and thus do away with capital punishment in practice?

This unexpected failure to exploit an opportunity for leniency may be explained not by a rabbinic faith in eyewitness testimony (the many discussions dedicated to false witnesses and wrongful conviction belie that notion), but rather by the lack of faith the Aqiban sages had in *any* kind of evidence for assessing "the truth of the matter."[36] If evidence is understood as a means of ascertaining legal facts rather than objective reality, the type of evidence admitted is irrelevant; what matters is that there are clear legal procedures which allow judges to distinguish between innocence and guilt, and that the vast majority of cases will not lead to wrongful conviction—a position which echoes and parallels what we have seen in R. Aqiba's approach to ritual purity law. While R. Aqiba's arguments against Simeon the Temanite do not really stand up to scrutiny, they have one theme in common: there is much that one does not, or cannot, know about the circumstances of a crime when one examines the evidence. Stones can be used to hit a person in numerous ways; buildings fall down and cannot be reconstructed. In fact, another tannaitic text attributed to R. Aqiba—a *baraita*—conveys the same skepticism for examining physical evidence, here regarding a post-mortem examination for signs of puberty.

> It once happened at Bene-Beraq that a person sold his father's estate, and died. The members of the family, thereupon, protested [that] he was a minor at the time of [his] death. They came [to] R. Aqiba and asked whether the body might be examined. He replied to them: You are not permitted to dishonor him; and, furthermore, [the] signs [of maturity] usually undergo a change after death. (*b. B. Bat.* 154a)

R. Aqiba determines that a post-mortem examination should not be done because it would dishonor the dead, but also because one cannot trust the physical evidence present on the body, since physical signs, according to R. Aqiba, change after death. Once again, then, according to the Talmud, the only type of admissible evidence is witness testimony (oral or written).

I would like to argue that the skepticism[37] displayed here regarding physical evidence, the staunch upholding of significant doubt which underlies its rejection from rabbinic criminal law, provided the rabbis with an opportunity to begin settling their chief anxiety about the commitment to human lawmaking and judging in the face of uncertainty. If one despairs of being able to ascertain the truth through the examination of evidence—of any kind—one may as well abdicate the responsibility for the facts to human, rational agents who claim to have seen the truth first hand. Witness testimony has the advantage of being explicitly biblically mandated (as opposed to the inspection of physical evidence, which is alluded to in several biblical texts but never directly stipulated as part of criminal procedure).[38] Moreover, the turn to witnesses has another advantage: in the absence of all other evidence, witnesses alone may bear responsibility for the outcome of the case. The reliance exclusively on witnesses effectively ties the hands of the judges in independently corroborating or disproving their testimonies, making the witnesses the primary shapers of the case's outcome.

WRONGFUL DEATH AND WITNESS ACCOUNTABILITY

The rabbinic redactors of the Mishnah limit, rather than expand, judicial latitude in ascertaining the facts of a crime. Far from accepting the dangerous and overwhelming power inherent in adjudicating capital crimes, the rabbinic authorities, especially as presented in the figure of R. Aqiba, seek to reduce their own responsibility when it comes to prosecuting and convicting criminals, sharing with, if not altogether transferring responsibility to, the witnesses. Beth Berkowitz argues that "the Rabbis strategically represent an ambivalence towards power. The closer they get to representing themselves in the role of executioner, the more they appear to back away from it."³⁹ Her argument focuses on the methods of execution and the rabbinic obscuring of the identity of the executioner in the "ritual" of execution as part of the rabbinic "negotiation for authority."⁴⁰ She writes,

> On one hand, the Rabbis assert control over the executioner, defining who he is and what he must do. On the other hand, the Rabbis sometimes withdraw, leaving the executioner anonymous, obscuring the agent of execution. . . . In defining the executioner—but also refusing to—rabbinic authority confronts its own limits, the outer boundaries of its claims to exercise force.⁴¹

Berkowitz thus shows how the rabbis' legal control over executions confronts the realities of deadly power, from which they wish to withdraw. I suggest that this argument equally applies to the criminal trial itself. It is through the recruitment of other responsible individuals not only to perform the execution but to serve as the sole conduits between the judges and the facts of the case that the rabbis maintain their exclusive control over verdicts without being exclusively responsible for erroneous decisions that lead to death.

The responsibility the witnesses bear for the outcome of the case is made explicit in several tannaitic texts. Mishnah *Sanhedrin* prepares potential witnesses for their testimony not by stressing the importance of telling the truth or the penalties for perjury, but rather by conveying that by testifying they are making themselves accountable for the outcome of the verdict, which may be death. An oft-quoted midrash on Genesis 4:10 is offered as a grim warning:

> In civil suits, a person can make monetary restitution and thereby effect his atonement; but in capital cases he is held responsible for his blood and the blood of his [potential] descendants until the end of time, for thus we find in the case of Cain, who killed his brother, that it is written: "the bloods of your brother cry unto me": not the blood of your brother, but the bloods of your brother, is said—his blood and the blood of his [potential] descendants. . . . For this reason was man created alone, to teach you

that whoever destroys a single soul, scripture imputes [guilt] to him as though he had destroyed a complete world. (*m. Sanh.* 4:5)

This passage may well apply to the alleged crime of the accused, if he is on trial for murder, but it is addressed to the witness as part of a technique for intimidating him, suggesting that if his words lead to an execution, he will be responsible for the destruction of "an entire world." This passage ought not be read as a simple opposition to the death penalty, equating it with murder, because the mishnah ends with the opposite sentiment:

> Should you say: why should we incur this anxiety? [know then:] is it not already written, "and he being a witness, whether he has seen or known, if he does not utter it [he shall bear his punishment]" [Lev. 5:1] and should you say: "why should we bear liability for the blood of this [man]?"—surely, however, it is said, "when the wicked perish, there is joy." [Prov. 11:10] (*m. Sanh.* 4:5)

This mishnah relates witness testimony directly to the outcome of the case—the death of the accused. The first half of the mishnah emphasizes the overwhelming power of the judicial process, suggesting that it may take not only one life but the lives of "an entire world"; the second half of the mishnah expresses both the anxiety that accompanies this power and the need to overcome that anxiety for the well being of the community. The mishnah quotes an excerpt from a verse in Proverbs which describes the prerequisites for the well being of the city: "When it goes well with the righteous, the city rejoices; and *when the wicked perish, there is jubilation.* By the blessing of the upright a city is exalted, but it is overthrown by the mouth of the wicked" (Prov. 11:10–11).[42]

The double-exhortation in this mishnah progressively aggrandizes not only the reason for testifying but the role of the witness in the judicial process. First, the mishnah imagines that the witness feels anxiety because he is called to testify; to that, the mishnah responds that he should testify anyway because of a biblical commandment to do so. But while Leviticus 5:1 establishes the basic biblical requirement to testify it simultaneously provides a motive to do so: if a witness does not come forward, he shall "bear his punishment." The mishnah then echoes this language in its next phrase, which literally reads "and perhaps you will say: what [is it] to us *to [become] liable for the blood* of this one?" (emphasis added). In this rhetorical question placed in the mouths of the witnesses, the mishnah both intensifies Leviticus' language and appends it to a different circumstance: the witnesses who *do* testify. Leviticus indicates that only witnesses who refrain from coming forward will bear punishable sin, and that those who testify are exempt from guilt. But the mishnah places the witnesses in an insoluble dilemma, as those who do not testify will bear sin and those who do testify face the even worse prospect of blood-guilt.[43] And thus the mishnah can offer no personal motivation for the witness to testify and resorts, instead, to the value of civic duty.

I would like to suggest that this mishnah's deliberations on why a witness should or should not come forward are a displacement, that the rabbinic anxiety about judging capital cases is here played out on the canvas of the reluctant witness. Indeed, the Tosefta offers a slightly different version of this passage:

> The judges should know whom they judge and before whom they judge and who it is who judges with them. And the witnesses should know about whom they give testimony and before whom they give testimony and with whom they give testimony and who it is who is a witness with them, as it is said, "both the men between whom the controversy is shall stand before the Lord" [Deut. 19:17] and it is said "God stands in the congregation of the Lord and in the midst of gods he judges" [Ps. 82:1]. . . . Now perhaps a *judge* might say, for what do I need this anxiety? But has it not been said, "He is with you in the matter of judgment" [2 Chron. 19:6]. (*t. Sanh.* 1:9, emphasis mine)

The beginning of this passage places the witnesses and judges on equal standing—both judge and witness play an important role in an arena in which the stakes are at their highest. But unlike the mishnah examined above, in this toseftan passage the ultimate anxiety of judgment resides with the judges, rather than the witnesses. A further significant difference is the manner in which the anxiety is relieved. While the mishnah exhorts witnesses to bear great risk because of the value of civic duty, the tosefta assures judges that there is, in fact, no risk at all. For when the judge, rather than the witness, asks "for what do I need this anxiety?" he is assured that his decision is seconded by the divine presence.[44] While the tosefta appeals to divine guidance in the juridical process to alleviate the judges' anxiety regarding wrongful conviction, the mishnah inserts a conflict between bearing punishment and risking blood-guilt. At the same time, it removes the judges from the equation, shifting the tension—and responsibility—to the witnesses.

If the above mishnah subtly shifts accountability for verdicts from judges to witnesses, a narrative in the Tosefta raises the stakes of this shift in a profoundly emotional way. In this text, the rabbis directly blame the witnesses for a convict's being led to his wrongful execution.

> It once happened that there was a person who was led out to be stoned. They said to him, "Confess." He said, "Let my death be an atonement for all my sins, but if I did this thing, let God not forgive me, and let the Israelite court be innocent." Now when this report came to the sages, their eyes flowed with tears. They said, "To reverse this is impossible, for there will be no end to the matter. But lo, his blood is on the hands of his witnesses." (t. Sanh. 9:5)

This brief narrative dramatizes the rabbis' uneasiness, even their torment, with the implementation of law, to which they adhere in spite of possible error in judgment. Their commitment is challenged by the possibility of innocence: by sensibility rather than legal logic, and ultimately by the presence of the divine. We may begin to explore the contours of this anxiety by noting what the rabbinic sages actually say: that they want to reverse the ruling but are constrained, and that in any case the witnesses are liable for the death of the convicted man. The sages—the judges—shift responsibility for the wrongful death twice over. In the first statement they blame the dictates of the law, the need to preserve a system in which absolute action is possible even without absolute knowledge. As Berkowitz writes, "The Sages . . . have created a legal Frankenstein, a monster of laws over which they are no longer master. It is this Frankenstein, not his creator, who has the power of execution."[45] They realize, in other words, that when one begins to second-guess the court's decisions "there is no end to the matter"—every ruling may be reversed. But rather than simply leaving it at that, at the acknowledgment that any legal system requires certain sacrifices, the rabbis lay blame for the wrongful judgment. For the rabbis, the blood-guilt incurred by wrongful death is not be explained away or shrugged off as a kind of "collateral damage"—it ought to be acknowledged, assigned, and eventually expiated. To accept such culpability upon themselves would place rabbinic judges in an untenable position, in that it would force them to admit the failure of their legal enterprise, which, because of their inability to access the real truth of transgression and righteousness, turns rabbinic authorities into murderers themselves as they try to rid the community of evil. And therefore the witnesses, who are privileged with *private* knowledge, are made accountable.

But why, we might ask, do the sages admit this anxiety in the first place? What prompts them to speak within this toseftan narrative; what drives the composition of this narrative as a whole? In answering these questions, it is crucial to note that this rabbinic shifting of blame is preceded by a non-verbal response: "their eyes flowed with tears." This sensibility, this grief, is not a resigned sadness but a deep distress,[46] which provokes not a detached acceptance or righteous anger but rather an ethical, normative response.[47] The first word the rabbis utter is "*lehaḥaziro* (to reverse it)"—the feeling they experience urges them, first and foremost, to act, to repair the injustice. Their sense of injustice is also a feeling of responsibility—a moment in which they glimpse, however briefly, the possibility of a different decision, a different course of action. Even as they immediately withdraw this alternative—"to reverse this *is impossible*"— the mere fact of its recognition already broadens the legal imagination, compelling a vision of a world in which clemency for this man is possible, a world in which things might have been otherwise, the lost world of divine presence and the assurance of unimpeachable justice.

This feeling of responsibility for wrongful death is prompted not only by the overarching injustice of the circumstance but by the convict's words—specifically, his confession before the divine. His short prayer is more convoluted than the mishnaically prescribed confession for the innocent man, "let my death be an atonement for all my sins aside from this one." The Mishnah imagines the innocent man directing himself exclusively to God in the last moments before his execution, but the tosefta triangulates this final moment of truth, as it were. For the innocent convict's confession—his confrontation with the divine—necessarily involves and implicates those responsible for the injustice of his death. In this tosefta the convict ignores the witnesses entirely, and he accuses "the court of Israel": "if I did this . . . let the court of Israel be innocent." His words imply, of course, that since I did not do this, the court of Israel is guilty. It is significant that unlike the rest of the rabbinic judicial proceeding, this final confession directly invokes the presence of God, for it is only in this context that the court of Israel, the rabbis as judges, can be said to be guilty. They are not assumed to have violated the law or corrupted God's Torah; within the sphere of human justice that the rabbis have constructed, they are presumed above reproach. But before God, in the face of the absolute arbiter of guilt and innocence, the process of adhering to imperfect human justice is found wanting. Before God, according to this tosefta, judges who meticulously follow the rule of law still inexorably incur guilt. In this context, before the presence of the divine, the strident and jarring rabbinic deflection of guilt onto the witnesses hardly masks the rabbis' fear of the very power they seek to wield.

Uncertainty, Responsibility, and Commitment

Thus far, I have outlined an innate conflict in the normative world of the rabbis between a commitment to doing justice and an ultimate uncertainty about the world around them. I have argued further that this insoluble tension was not always easily tolerated or even articulated by the early rabbinic sages because it cut to the heart of the rabbinic project—it threatened both the viability of a human legal system devoid of divine arbitration, and the possibility of justifying human action before God. I now turn to one well-known mishnah which reveals differing rabbinic responses to this central anxiety. Not surprisingly, the point of tension in this mishnah is the question of capital punishment—an issue that provokes an intense, varied, and impassioned array of voices. I quote it again in full:

> A Sanhedrin [high court] that executes one person in seven years is considered destructive. R. Eleazar b. Azariah says: one in seventy years. R. Tarfon and R. Aqiba say: had we been in the Sanhedrin, no one would ever have been executed. R. Simeon b. Gamaliel adds: they multiply murderers in Israel. (*m. Mak.* 1:10)

As I mentioned above, this text has most often been used to support the notion that the rabbis were opposed to capital punishment, or to show the conflict of rabbinic voices on the issue of the death penalty. I would like to view this mishnah, however, especially its latter half, as an illustration of the struggle over the rabbinic commitment to the divine law in general. The first two opinions speak of the court personified, noting that though capital punishment is infrequent, "the court" does, periodically, find a person guilty of a capital crime and sentences him to death. Both the anonymous opinion and R. Eleazar b. Azariah note the infrequency of such rulings, demonstrating that, in general, "the court" does not put people to death, wrongfully or not. R. Aqiba and R. Tarfon, however, do not speak of "the court" in the abstract but take responsibility themselves, considering themselves the agents behind the execution of the criminal: "had *we* been in the Sanhedrin," they say. Perhaps because they recognize themselves as personally responsible for the taking of life through the instrument of the court, they say they would never issue a guilty verdict. It is no accident that this stance is attributed to the very same R. Aqiba who argued vehemently that physical evidence be kept out of the courtroom—that objective reality, truth, could never be the end results of legal inquiry. It is perfectly consistent that R. Aqiba, who espouses a radical skepticism regarding certainty within the law, would also find paths to acquittal for all who were tried for capital crimes in his court. Indeed, the amoraic comment on this statement of R. Aqiba and R. Tarfon in the Babylonian Talmud says that it is precisely epistemological uncertainty underlying this stance, rather than any particular view of capital punishment. It reads:

> R. Tarfon and R. Aqiba say: had we been in the Sanhedrin, etc. How would they do this? Both R. Johanan and R. Eleazar say: "Did you see whether an injured person or a healthy person was killed?" R. Ashi said: And if you should say, "he was healthy," perhaps in the place of the sword was an internal lesion? (*b. Mak.*7a)

R. Johanan and R. Eleazar wonder whether the witnesses could ever know that the murderer really killed the person—perhaps he died of failing health? But even if the victim appeared "perfectly healthy," R. Ashi adds a question that can never be answered with absolute certainty—perhaps the exact place where the sword hit already contained a fatal injury? Seeing one man fell another with a sword still does not decisively mean that that man has murdered the other—absolute certainty is only possible through divine omniscience.

R. Johanan and R. Eleazar illustrate how a judge could nullify any testimony through legal maneuvering; they need simply stymie the witnesses with questions that they would not be able to answer, creating doubt at every turn. When the standard of proof is set so high as to essentially require certainty, then any doubt, no matter how remote, will prevent a conviction. Interestingly, R. Johanan and R. Eleazar do not use the example found in the mishnah in which a judge, ben Zakkai, presses a witness about the leaves of a fig tree (*m. Sanh.* 5:2). In this instance, ben Zakkai is praised for his acumen in seeking the most minute details of a crime. This remarkable attention to detail attempts to vet the witnesses by looking for gaps in their memory, but R. Johanan, R. Eleazar, and R. Ashi in the text just cited seem, instead, to actually manufacture doubt. R. Ashi's question, as opposed to ben Zakkai's, highlights the inherent doubt in *every* case, no matter how cut and dried it appears.

According to the amoraic commentators, then, the failure of R. Aqiba and R. Tarfon, in *m. Mak.* 1:10, to convict anyone was due to their tendency to point out the ultimate uncertainty that accompanies any witnessed event. Given this uncertainty, we are left with formal, legal constructions of truth, which R. Aqiba and R. Tarfon here reject. As judges, they see themselves, rather than witnesses or the abstract "court," as risking blood-guilt for capital punishment; hence, they refuse to administer death sentences, acquitting instead, and remaining innocent before perfect divine judicial standards. Nonetheless, by committing to inaction in the face of anything less than certainty, R. Aqiba and R. Tarfon choose to resolve only one side of the tension between admitting to perpetual uncertainty and acting decisively—a tension we have uncovered in two other spheres of law as well. In this case, however, this tension amounts to a choice between allowing the proliferation of bloodshed and incurring personal blood-guilt. And at this moment, when law is tested in the most extreme circumstances, R. Aqiba's and R. Tarfon's commitment to human jurisprudence falters. The truth that the law constructs is revealed to be no truth at all.

R. Simeon b. Gamaliel's reply, however, represents the pull of the other side of this basic conflict between commitment to the truth of the legal system and risking the possibility of having innocent blood on one's hands. He accuses R. Aqiba and R. Tarfon of "multiplying murderers in Israel"—by refusing to risk incurring guilt themselves, they allow evil to flourish in the community, and in fact indirectly cause the very wrong they wish to avoid. The undecidability of guilt is thus echoed in the undecidability of the appropriate normative response; obliged to act justly, the rabbis, responsible before God, are faced with the "experience of the impossible"[48]—whichever path they choose, their human limitations lead them to perpetrate injustice.

As the rabbis recognized that human adjudication would inevitably result in wrongful decisions and injustices, they struggled with the implications of such an application of the divine *Torah,* as these tannaitic texts attest. But as these texts invoke the truth of a divine presence that cannot be known or accessed, they gesture toward something beyond the realm of human jurisprudence that, while segregated from rabbinic law, was integral to rabbinic Judaism. Perhaps God could put right what humans inevitably get wrong.

PART TWO

Truth and Divine Justice

FOUR

Theologies of Justice

Do you think that he has emerged vindicated from My
Court as he has emerged vindicated from yours?

(*MEK. KASPA* 3)

In the last three chapters, we saw that the Hebrew Bible maintains a rhetoric of certainty regarding the enactment of the divine law because it can rely upon divine omniscience as an aid in the pursuit of worldly justice. Conversely, the early rabbis develop a stance of uncertainty when it comes to implementation of the divine law, insisting that divine knowledge is largely inaccessible and therefore irrelevant to jurisprudence. The rabbis develop evidence law as a strategy for constructing legal truth, and thus pursue a kind of provisional justice. At the same time, they gesture toward a higher, more certain truth that cannot be accessed through legal maneuvering but that must, nonetheless, be acknowledged.

Yhwh is known as the God of justice in both the Hebrew Bible and rabbinic literature. So far, I have only hinted at God's role in the jurisprudence of the Bible and the rabbis, suggesting vaguely that Yhwh himself enforces covenantal law according to the Hebrew Bible, and that God is significant in rabbinic jurisprudence only to the extent that his absence symbolizes a lost, absolute truth. In this chapter I would like to look at this subject in greater detail and explore the jurisprudence of the heavens. Alongside the human justice systems we have so far investigated, both biblical and rabbinic authors imagine the God of Justice implementing his own rewards and punishments, vindicating his own knowledge of human behavior, and intervening in human history in a purposeful way. Though much has been written about the subject of divine justice, I would like to focus on one specific question: how does God's role as an executor of justice interact (or interfere) with the comprehensive human religious legal systems of the Bible and the rabbis? If the Hebrew Bible envisages an active divine role for God in his supervision of the covenant, is this supervision always executed in line with human notions of appropriate justice? If the rabbis are forced to implement an incomplete, provisional human jurisprudence owing to the limits of their knowledge, how did they imagine God's role in meting out justice given his omniscience and alignment with ultimate truth?

Bernard Jackson's article "Religious Law in Judaism"[1] provides a schema for the roles of the divine and human in jurisprudence in both the Hebrew Bible and rabbinic literature. I accept his general assertions about the allocation of roles and responsibilities within these religious legal systems, but Jackson's ambitious goal to elucidate these intertwined and overlapping spheres of justice sometimes drives him to overstate their seamless cooperation. I begin each of my discussions of biblical and rabbinic notions of divine justice with Jackson's astute observations and proceed to illuminate some of the disjunctions and incongruities that Jackson does not fully develop. I argue that it is precisely those moments which disrupt the vision of perfect harmony between divine and human justice that allow human jurisprudence to flourish despite the vision of a more capable, omniscient deity presiding in the heavens.

God and Justice in the Hebrew Bible

Jackson begins his discussion of religious law in the Hebrew Bible by noting the intersections between its human and divine elements:

> In Biblical literature the legal roles of man and God have much in common. God is depicted as judge, and the forms of divine law and judgment, whether mediated through Mosaic revelation or prophetic inspiration, owe much to human models. Moreover, the planes of human and divine legal activity interconnect: Abraham acts as advocate in the divine adjudication of Sodom and Gomorrah (Genesis 18), and man, not God, is assigned the role of judge as regards much of the divine law. Moreover,

divine legal activity is . . . brought to bear only where there is a special need, arising from the limits of human capacity.[2]

According to Jackson, then, the Hebrew Bible offers us a multifaceted relationship between the human and divine in jurisprudence. First, we encounter a relationship of similarity: the depiction of God borrows from human juridical activity, imagining God as a supreme legislator and judge—human in kind, but greater than human in scale. Second, we witness an interdependence of humans and God in jurisprudence: God may require human advocates to shape his own judgments; he in fact delegates many of these judgments to humans; he acts on his own initiative when humans are hampered by their own limitations.

In essence, the Hebrew Bible presents an idea of the achievability of worldly justice because of this divine–human partnership in legislation, judgment, and enforcement. The book of Deuteronomy stresses the importance of human institutions of justice, linking it to earthly reward:

> You shall appoint judges and officials throughout your tribes, in all your towns that Yhwh your God is giving you, and they shall render just decisions for the people. . . . Justice and only justice, you shall pursue, so that you may live and occupy the land that Yhwh your God is giving you. (Deut. 16:17, 19)

Concomitantly, it emphasizes Yhwh's role in guaranteeing that just deserts (whether reward or punishment) are issued whether humans enforce the law or do not, by tying juridical processes to the vicissitudes of nature and history:

> If you will only obey Yhwh your God, by diligently observing all his commandments that I am commanding you today . . . blessed shall be the fruit of your womb, the fruit of your ground, and the fruit of your livestock, both the increase of your cattle and the issue of your flock. . . . Yhwh will cause your enemies who rise against you to be defeated before you. . . . But if you will not obey Yhwh your God by diligently observing all his commandments and decrees . . . Yhwh will make the pestilence cling to you until it has consumed you off the land that you are entering to possess. Yhwh will afflict you with consumption, fever, inflammation, with fiery heat and drought, and with blight and mildew; they shall pursue you until you perish. . . . Yhwh will cause you to be defeated before your enemies; you shall go out against them one way and flee before them seven ways. (Deut. 28:1, 4, 7, 15, 21–22, 25)

As J. G. Griffiths succinctly summarizes, "virtuous obedience to God results in security and prosperity, while sinful disobedience produces failure
and suffering: this is the view of history put forward in Deuteronomy and
it is equally present in the books from Joshua to the Second Book of Kings,
books thus properly called the 'Deuteronomic History.'"[3]

The idea that Yhwh acts in the world in order to balance the scales of
justice when humans have not is prevalent not only in these works, but in the
prophetic works as well. It hardly bears mentioning that Israelite prophets
(especially before the destruction and exile of Israel and Judah) were preoc-
cupied with humans' failure to enact justice, and consequently with the in-
exorableness of divine justice. Griffiths begins his discussion of divine judgment with a discussion of Amos, because "his book is replete with judgments
that are imminent."[4] Indeed, while the entirety of the Hebrew Bible cannot
be said to uphold the centrality of divine justice (the books of Job and Ecclesiastes being the most notable exceptions), Griffiths nonetheless concludes:

> If we attempt a broader (and inevitably sketchier) view of Old Testament
> literature in search of this theme, we find that it occupies a *dominating
> place* throughout. That God controls history with a moral motive is im-
> plied from the very beginning in the interpretation of the creation stories
> and their sequel; in particular he is said to exact penalties firmly and
> consistently for sins committed.[5]

That Yhwh's retributive justice in particular is "firm and consistent" corresponds to Jackson's notion of a divine "supreme court" which acts when
the capacities of the lower courts are reached. When, exactly, we must ask,
is divine justice activated? Jackson provides several examples of divine
capacity to judge and reward or punish beyond the limits of human jurisdiction. First, as god of "all the earth," Yhwh judges and exacts retribution
on an international scale.[6] Second, Yhwh, as the judge of the covenant to
which he is a party, demonstrates a divine "capacity beyond human
reach—the ability to judge fairly in his own case."[7] Third, only Yhwh, according to Jackson, can rise above the "arbitrariness and injustice" of
implementing the law of *talion* for injuries, applying it with "perfect justice"[8] (Jackson claims it was rarely used in human courts in ancient Israel).
Fourth, Jackson maintains that in cases of "evidentiary difficulty . . . divine justice is appropriate because the situation demands divine omniscience; human knowledge will not suffice."[9]

Given the "dominating place" of divine judgment in the Hebrew Bible, and the intensity and thoroughness with which Yhwh is shown to react to human disobedience, one has to wonder whether divine justice can possibly be viewed merely as a helpful complement to human jurisprudence, as Jackson would have it. I would like to examine two of Jackson's examples more closely: Yhwh's purported unique abilities to "judge fairly" on his own behalf and to implement *talion* perfectly, because if we look beyond what the Hebrew Bible confidently asserts to the divine retribution it actually describes, such biblical claims of perfect divine justice begin to look like empty rhetoric. As James Crenshaw writes, "the problem with this type of [theology] is the way it ignores facts."[10]

DIVINE VICTIMHOOD: YHWH JUDGES HIMSELF—FAVORABLY

Scholars have long noted Yhwh's awkward role as both a party to the covenant and its guarantor, casting Yhwh as both plaintiff and judge in the case of any Israelite transgression.[11] Some, such as Jackson, prefer a charitable reading, seeing Yhwh as always acting in accordance with truth, because he is not susceptible to human bias. Thus even though God is acting on his own behalf, his often violent punishments of the Israelites may be seen as just: "however harsh the penalties [Yhwh metes out]," writes Alan Bernstein, "they are due for breach of contract."[12] Andrew Davies observes, however, that at least in the book of Isaiah, this "blurring of the borders between . . . various functions, particularly those of judge and prosecutor, . . . always seems to work in [Yhwh's] favor."[13] He comments that while many scholars excuse Yhwh's dual role as inescapable, he himself finds it "troubling."[14] "It is difficult to see why Yahweh can permit himself to act injudiciously for his own sake while refusing that privilege to the leaders of Israel,"[15] Davies remarks, and points out that even those who defend Yhwh's behavior have resorted to specious parallels (comparing Yhwh's dual role to Saul's in judging—and then massacring—the priests at Nob).[16]

We need only look at the emotional valence given to Yhwh's enforcement of the covenant as an indicator of his lack of impartiality, his *inability* to judge fairly in his own case. The book of Micah exhibits a standard example of the "covenant lawsuit," which portrays Yhwh as prosecuting, judging, and punishing, Israel:

> Hear, you mountains, the case of Yhwh—you firm foundations of the earth! For Yhwh has a case against His people, He has a suit against Israel. "My people! What wrong have I done you? What hardship have I caused you? Testify against Me. In fact, I brought you up from the land of Egypt, I redeemed you from the house of bondage, . . . but you? Will I overlook, in the wicked man's house, the granaries of wickedness? . . . I, in turn, have beaten you sore,[17] have ravaged you for your sins." (6:2–4, 10, 13)

Yhwh, as the "plaintiff" in this case, plays up his personal connection with the "defendant," detailing all he has done for Israel, releasing her from Egypt and the oppression of slavery. But then Yhwh quickly becomes judge and punisher, in this case not indifferently imposing a sentence but venting out pent-up frustration and anger by beating the errant nation to the point of illness. It is difficult to claim that Yhwh is acting appropriately as a judge. We need not impose our modern sense of proper judicial neutrality to disapprove of Yhwh's emotional stake in judging his people; Deuteronomy instructs human judges: "you must not distort justice; you must not show partiality" (Deut. 16:19).[18] There can be no question that Yhwh is not impartial in judging his chosen people, whom he redeemed from Egypt, and whom he now ravages.

There may be as many passages in the Hebrew Bible that stress the depth of Yhwh's love, hurt, and anger as manifest in his relationship and dealings with Israel as there are declaring him a dispassionate judge. Terence Fretheim contends that "God . . . grieves because the people have rebelled, . . . [and] acts both in terms of anger and compassion."[19] However, Fretheim goes on to virtually negate the impact of his observations about God's extraordinary emotional responses by insisting that "God's grief does not entail being emotionally overwhelmed or embittered. . . . Through it all, God's faithfulness and gracious purposes remain constant and undiminished."[20] But Ellen van Wolde begs to differ. In a linguistic study of the terms for anger in the Hebrew Bible, she concludes that

> [o]ne may . . . challenge the view that YHWH (or Elohim) in the Hebrew Bible exemplifies control over his feelings, for more than 500 times he is represented as subjected to the explosive force of fury and aggression leading to violence. . . . [I]n the Hebrew Bible, it appears that the sentiment of anger is seen as "in charge": it exerts control over a person.[21]

Van Wolde's depiction of Yhwh's "explosive force of fury and aggression leading to violence" resonates with the vast feminist literature on the latter prophets which focuses on the marriage metaphor between Yhwh (male) and Israel / Judah (female) in which Yhwh is the batterer-husband. Gerlinde Baumann reviews the multifaceted images of Yhwh that emerge from the prophets' use of this metaphor, among which is a deity who "exercise[s] excessive forms of violence primarily against women."[22]

The Hebrew Bible at the very best offers mixed messages regarding Yhwh's stance toward humans, portraying him both as trustworthy judge ("for you judge the people with equity and guide the nations upon earth" [Ps. 67:4]) and fiery adversary ("Yhwh is avenging and wrathful; Yhwh takes vengeance on his adversaries and rages against his enemies" [Nah. 1:2]).[23] According to Joel Kaminsky, these discordant views of God may be explained historically; the uncontrolled nature of divine wrath represents "the more ancient ideas that are traditionally associated with this concept," while the "theological framework of Deuteronomy and the deuteronomistic historian has covenantalized the notion of divine wrath by linking it to both human sin and divine punishment."[24] In other words, early notions of an erratic and overwrought deity are contextualized by biblical authors within a juridical framework, allowing Yhwh's behavior to be viewed in light of a philosophy of justice. Yet these authors or compilers could not erase the tension between the emotional, partial, personal God lashing out at his betrayers and the covenantal judge and guarantor of justice. The Hebrew Bible's assurances of ultimate, divine justice consequently cannot help but evoke a more emotional, unpredictable God who may retaliate unfairly because of his anger; as the Psalmist paradoxically puts it, "God is a just judge, who rebukes in anger every day" (Ps. 7:12).

YHWH PUNISHES, *TALION*-STYLE

Jackson's second contention that Yhwh uses his unique "power and . . . knowledge to apply [the *lex talionis*] with perfect justice"[25] also requires closer scrutiny. Biblical *talion* ("an eye for an eye") insures that the offender receives corresponding harm for the pain he or she inflicts. It is unclear to what extent *talion* was actually carried out in ancient Israel;[26] nevertheless, the principle of equal retribution stands as a fixture of biblical jurisprudence. According to Tikva Frymer-Kensky, this principle, which "is so in accord with our own sense of justice and fair play," represents the very foundation of justice itself: it aims "to return the parties to a type of status quo, to maintain symmetry, and to preserve the balance of the forces on the 'scales of justice.'"[27]

Given *talion*'s central place in Israelite thinking about justice, one might expect it to be the cornerstone of divine justice as well; and we can in fact see that biblical narratives endeavor to portray a sense of symmetrical justice, in which Yhwh rewards or punishes according to one's just deserts.[28] One need look no further than Genesis for numerous examples of this principle demonstrated in biblical narrative: from Abraham's argument with God that the righteous of Sodom do not deserve to suffer along with the guilty, to Jacob enduring deceptions in his old age as he himself deceived others in his youth, to Joseph being divinely placed in a position of authority to inflict suffering upon his brothers as they inflicted suffering upon him.

Even the prophetic books, which offer a wealth of rationales for human suffering,[29] overwhelmingly emphasize a talionic sense of justice. Patrick Miller has shown that all of the latter prophets use rhetoric that attempts to forge a correspondence between the crimes of the people and the imminent divine punishment, which was to take the form of Israel's military defeat. According to Miller, the prophetic emphasis on this correlation between sin and punishment "sets at the center of Yahweh's judgment the affirmation of *appropriate justice*. What Yahweh requires in all human beings—*mishpat*."[30] This justice, then, is inextricably linked to the notion of *talion*.

Two examples of Miller's analysis of the prophets may be drawn from Hosea, an early prophet of divine judgment. Hosea pronounces:

> Ephraim has become like a dove, silly and without sense; they call upon Egypt, they go to Assyria. As they go, I will cast my net over them; I will bring them down like birds of the air; I will chastise them when I hear their bargaining. (Hos. 7:11–12)

The correspondence between sin and punishment, as Miller points out, here "depends entirely on figures of speech, metaphor, and simile. . . . The key clause in this regard is the beginning of verse 12, [*ka'asher yeleku*], 'as they go' referring back to [*ashur halaku*] of verse 11, 'they go to Assyria.' So even as Israel plays the fowl, then Yahweh will play the fowler."[31] This wordplay underscores the idea that God's defeat of Israel (at the hands of Assyria) corresponds in kind to Israel's sin. An equivalence in degree may also be implied, as Israel's sin of abandoning Yhwh and placing its hope in foreign powers warrants Yhwh's abandonment of them to the hands of that same foreign power. But can this punishment then be seen to fit the crime? Does entering into a treaty with a foreign empire, in a time when the tiny state of Israel was politically desperate, warrant a divine punishment of utter destruction, as promised in verse 13? Perhaps only when seen through the rhetorical "spin" of the prophet, who speaks on behalf of Yhwh.

Another verse in Hosea describes a similar type of divine judgment, only this time the priests, the very representatives of Yhwh within the community, are judged and assured of punishment:

> My people is destroyed because of your disobedience. Because you have rejected obedience, I reject you as My priest; because you have spurned the teaching of your God, I, in turn, will spurn your children. (Hos. 4:6)

Here, the priests' direct rejection of obeying Yhwh leads to God's direct rejection of the priests themselves; in the following phrase, the priests' rejection of Yhwh's issue—his teaching, or *Torah*—leads to God's rejection of the priests' issue—their children, who, metaphorically, refer to all of Israel. Miller observes that here "the prophet . . . announces a judgment against the priesthood which point for point matches the sin it has committed. The talionic emphasis is inescapable in such an extended correspondence as these verses contain."[32] Perhaps this is so—but it is a type of talion which operates through vicarious punishment, a mode of "justice" which ancient Israelites seem to have rejected. Frymer-Kensky writes:

> Talionic principles are applied very vigorously in the laws of Hammurabi, which impose talionic retribution even to vicarious punishment. Thus §H116 provides that if . . . a debtor's son dies in the hands of [an] entrepreneur, the entrepreneur's son must pay with his life. . . . Vicarious *talion* is expressly forbidden in the Bible—"If it ([an] ox) has gored a *son* or *daughter*, according to this law it shall be done unto *him* (*the owner* of the ox)." (Ex. 21:31)[33]

Frymer-Kensky notes here that the prohibition against vicarious punishment was not initially applied to Yhwh or divine punishment, given the frequent statements in the Hebrew Bible that Yhwh punishes to the third and fourth generation (see Ex. 20:5)—and it is an example of this double standard that we see here in Hosea. However, that fact only underscores the notion that Yhwh's *strictly* talionic punishment of the children of offenders in Hosea would have been seen as divine exceptionality rather than an extension of an Israelite philosophy of justice, as it violates a core principle of biblical *talion*.

Prophetic renderings of divine justice, then, seem to rely more on imagery and rhetoric than the content of the measures described to make their case for Yhwh acting according to the rules of *talion*. As Miller himself acknowledges, the prophets declare that "punishment will be according to, in some way like, or appropriate in *either a literal or a symbolic fashion* to the sin committed."[34] Michel Foucault shows how the "symbolic" correspondence between crime and punishment was evidenced in the real world of jurisprudence—punishments that precisely correspond to the nature of the crime (e.g., piercing the tongues of blasphemers), rampant in eighteenth-century France; jurisprudence, he writes, had become "an entire poetics."[35] But despite the attractiveness of such a symbolic system, few would see this kind of jurisprudence as a model of true proportional justice. Martha Nussbaum, who celebrates the capacity of the literary to guide us toward justice, nonetheless warns that "literary works can distort the world for their readers. . . . They can . . . misrepresent the importance of various types of suffering or harm."[36] The symmetry of metaphorical *talion* can thus distort the real unfairness of the punishment.

As the prophets poetically provide the comforting impression of divine fairness, other biblical texts are more explicit about divine injustice. Joel Kaminsky observes that "divine wrath . . . is sometimes stored up over a long period and then released in a *disproportionate* way upon the individual, or group, who happens to cause its release."[37] In Leviticus, this divine disproportionate response is repeatedly given normative value: "I will strike you sevenfold for your sins" (Lev. 26:18, 21, 24, 28).[38] The exilic prophets lament: "cry [for Jerusalem] that she has served her term, that her penalty is paid, that she has received from Yhwh's hand double for all her sins" (Isa. 40:2). Moreover, Gershom Scholem's observations about the covenantal promises of Deuteronomy 28 portray divine retribution as anything but specific, measured, and precisely proportional: "In place of the simple relation between disobedience to God and a specific punishment, . . . there appears here a genuine paroxysm of punishments. Nothing is left out, nothing from the whole field of ancient man's experience.

Everything rebels against him, and the paroxysm of punishment becomes a paroxysm of hopelessness."[39]

DO JUSTICE, AND WALK HUMBLY WITH YHWH

If Yhwh is indeed depicted in the Hebrew Bible as passionate—"a jealous God"—and responding to human sin disproportionately—"punishing children for the iniquity of parents . . . [and] showing steadfast love to the thousandth generation of those who love [him]" (Ex. 20:5–6), then perhaps we need to reevaluate whether Yhwh's activities in the world can ever be said to be congruent with human justice. Even though the Hebrew Bible does offer several glimpses of a just, fair, and equitable God, ultimately, as Patrick Miller writes, the rhetoric of the Hebrew Bible "suggests a multi-faceted or multi-dimensional perception of the nature and meaning of Israel's experience of [divine] judgment."[40] Human jurisprudence, however, requires consistency above all. A system of law, as has been argued by Oliver Wendell Holmes, is little else but "prophecies of what the courts will do in fact. . . . [It allows one to] know under what circumstances and how far they will run the risk of coming against what is so much stronger than themselves."[41] Even within biblical theology, there is a sense that Yhwh's justice ought to mean that "I get what I deserve, no more and no less."[42] If we are unsure whether our transgressions will provoke Yhwh's anger, his compassion, his love, his fairness, or his indifference, Yhwh cannot be understood as complying with the dictates of human jurisprudence; as John Barton wrties, "[c]ommentators have always been tempted to fudge the issue of just how unjust the God of the [Hebrew Bible] is when evaluated in human terms—and not simply in our terms (this is not mere anachronism) but in the moral terms they themselves apply to human conduct."[43] Thus, if one can say anything generally about the Hebrew Bible at all, one might suggest that Yhwh as the God of Justice always remains transcendent and variable, despite any rhetoric which would like to convince us otherwise.

The image of Yhwh's emotional intensity and inconsistency perhaps deliberately underscores the significance, above all, of obeying the commandments, which is depicted by Deuteronomy as literally "choos[ing] life" (Deut. 30:19). As Haim Cohn observes, "God's wrath could be the most potent deterrent."[44] But if transgression occurs nonetheless, we find two major methods of avoiding Yhwh's unspecified retribution: cultic atonement and the practice of law. Deliberate, known, inadvertent, or unknown sin could be purged by the priests in the temple so that Israel would not have to face divine wrath. Through a hierarchy of sacrifices, the priests are able to neutralize the evil which infects the sanctuary as a byproduct of human sin.[45] Yhwh is thus allowed to remain dwelling in the sanctuary and may favor Israel with his protection.

If a crime becomes known and can be prosecuted, however, the community can "maintain the purity of [Yhwh's] holy people"[46] by carrying out the convict's sentence; as Deuteronomy instructs, "show no pity; you shall purge the guilt of . . . Israel, so that it may go well with you" (19:13). In other words, if the people of Israel remove the stain of "moral impurity"[47] from the land through fair and equitable punishment, they will not be subject to divine retribution which may or may not be similarly just. And the *human* process of fair and equitable punishment, as we have seen, is divinely guaranteed—at the limits of human cognition, judges are given access to "oracle, oath [and] ordeal"[48] in order to pronounce a true verdict.

In the end, the Hebrew Bible may present us with a deity who is unpredictably vindictive, compassionate, and fair—a god who reflects the very variability of human existence. But biblical rhetoric forcefully argues for a certain path to peace and security, a way out of the suffering and trauma that life entails; as Jon Levenson puts it, "[i]t is through obedience to the directives of the divine master that [God's] good world comes into existence."[49]

Pursuing Justice in Rabbinic Literature

Turning to the early rabbis, Jackson's outline of the spheres of human and divine justice entail both extensions of and departures from biblical models:

> In the early rabbinic period, corresponding to the Roman principate, the respective roles of man and God in the legal process are further separated. The direct involvement of the deity in human legal procedure is rejected; cases requiring the perfection of divine cognition tend to be left to divine jurisdiction, and the problems of cognition highlighted by this division become more sophisticated. Stress is placed upon the perfection of divine justice despite appearances to the contrary; on the separate spheres of

human and divine legal interest as indicated within the Bible itself; and on the perfection of divine wisdom not only in its content but also in its revealed formulation. . . . [Furthermore, divine] judgment, it was said, [would be] on an individual basis.[50]

According to Jackson, the rabbis develop biblical notions of the distinct juridical roles given to humans and to Yhwh, further distancing human jurisprudence from divine justice. They also continue to reinforce the notion of "the perfection of divine justice," even as such a doctrine becomes more difficult to uphold, and they expand the concept of divine revelation to include the written, canonized text of the Torah. The rabbis also break with biblical precedent, in Jackson's view, by rejecting "direct" divine intervention in human adjudication (no more appeals to oracle, oath, and ordeal), and in insisting that divine judgment, as well as human judgment, would most often operate on the scale of the individual rather than the community.[51]

What chiefly distinguishes rabbinic from biblical religious jurisprudence, according to Jackson, is the relegation of divine judgment to its own sphere, in place of divine intervention in human jurisprudence. In this sphere, God's justice directly mirrors human justice in holding thieves liable for payment, marking criminals for execution, and, in a general sense, adhering to juridical impulses in inflicting suffering upon the guilty and always exonerating the innocent. Imagining such a sphere of perfect divine justice, the rabbis, according to Jackson, were free to leave uncertain cases to await divine decision: "the extent to which jurisdiction was left to God corresponded in some degree to the extent of human doubt on the matter."[52]

The problem with positing such a seamless system, however, is that the rabbis find profound uncertainty to pervade every field of the law, as we have seen. Yet, they are loath to absolve themselves of responsibility for decision making, emphasizing the dire consequences for communal life if human juridical action is not taken, even, for some, in the case of uncertain capital punishment (see chapter 3). Relying on God to effect worldly justice must have seemed unfeasible for the rabbis, and at root is the same problem with which the biblical writers struggled: although God's actions are continually described in juridical terms, the reality of God's actions as revealed in nature and history simply does not display a system of proportional, impartial justice. The rabbis, I would posit, did not have confidence in a divine justice that was consistent with human justice; parallel to the biblical tradition, they generate multiple readings of God's deeds, which at times appear congruent with human jurisprudence and at other times appear unjust, or unfathomable. Much of rabbinic literature suggests that divine justice is ontologically distinct from the human practice of law—as Peretz Segal writes, for the rabbis, "the two systems [of norms]—divine and human—are mutually exclusive."[53]

I would like to examine two aspects of the rabbinic understanding of divine justice that renders it incompatible with human justice: disproportionality and variability. While these categories are similar to the ones evoked above to analyze the Hebrew Bible's approach to divine justice, the rabbis reshape each to meet their own theological needs. Thus the disproportion of divine retribution in the Hebrew Bible is most often masked, justified by the severity of Israel's breach of the covenant; in rabbinic sources, the imbalance is instead highlighted, as the rabbis link harsh retribution to trivial sin rather than real legal transgression. The variability or partiality of God in the Hebrew Bible is related to Yhwh's emotional investment in his people; in early rabbinic sources, God is depicted not as passionate, but rather as personal—his variability derives from treating each individual uniquely. I will treat both of these aspects of rabbinic divine justice together, as they are highly intertwined.

VARYING MEASURES

Just as the biblical use of talionic rhetoric often conceals a "paroxysm" of punishment, so too the rabbinic concept of "measure for measure" presents a stylistic correspondence between sin and retribution instead of a correlation of magnitude, a measure of proportional justice. Yael Shemesh writes that:

> Measure for measure, in the narrow sense of the term, means that human beings are punished or rewarded in due proportion for their actions. In its broader sense, though, it means that there is some correlation (material or linguistic) between a deed and the reward or punishment meted out for it. The existence of such a relationship is proof of a causal link between deeds and what happens to their doers, and thus to the truth of the doctrine of reward and punishment.[54]

It is this "broader sense" that scholars of rabbinic literature seem to apply to the rabbinic (and especially tannaitic) use of the "measure for measure" principle, and they, like Shemesh, see in it an affirmation of a kind of justice, a "doctrine of reward and punishment." Both E. E. Urbach and, more recently, David Kraemer agree that the early rabbis were essentially conservative, affirming traditional, biblical notions of divine justice.[55] Though tannaitic literature is not the focus of his work, Yaakov Elman remarks that "[g]enerally speaking, the tannaim link the sufferings of the righteous to some spiritual shortcoming or to the presence of the wicked in this world, and are disinclined, at least as portrayed in the surviving material, to allow for exceptions to the rule of 'measure for measure.'"[56]

What is obscured in this broad notion of "measure for measure," however, is the radical injustice contained within this "doctrine of reward and punishment," one that clearly ventures beyond the covenantal theology of the Hebrew Bible. Ishay Rosen-Zvi confirms that scholars

> have tended . . . to read rabbinic sources as basically continuing the biblical theology of divine justice which presents the God of Israel, the supreme judge of history, as paying all men and nations back for their actions. This scholarly tendency has blurred the distinctive ways that rabbinic sources develop and implement this famous biblical notion of "poetic justice."[57]

The focus of Rosen-Zvi's work is one of the most-quoted tannaitic passages on the topic of "measure for measure," one which catalogues a litany of divine rewards and punishments as witnessed in biblical texts. It begins by explaining the ordeal prescribed for the suspected adulteress which mediates cases of alleged adultery in which there are no witnesses and no proof. In it, the suspected adulteress is brought to the Temple, exposed, and forced to drink a special water; if she remains healthy she is considered innocent, and if she is guilty she suffers an affliction that apparently involves the dropping of her uterus (see Num. 5:11–31). In examining this ordeal, the mishnah traces a pattern of divine retaliation in biblical law and narrative:

A. In the measure with which a man measures it is meted out to him. She [the suspected adulteress] adorned herself for a transgression; the Holy One, blessed be he, made her repulsive. She exposed herself for a transgression; the Holy One, blessed be he, held her up for exposure. She

began the transgression with the thigh and afterwards with the womb;
therefore she is punished first in the thigh and afterwards in the womb
...

B. Samson went after [the desire of] his eyes; therefore the Philistines
put out his eyes, as it is said, "and the Philistines laid hold on him,
and put out his eyes." Absalom gloried in his hair; therefore he was
hanged by his hair. And because he cohabited with the ten concu-
bines of his father, therefore he was stabbed with ten lances, as it is
said, "and ten young men that bare Joab's armor compassed about."
And because he stole three hearts, the heart of his father, the heart
of the court of justice, and the heart of Israel, as it is said, "so Absalom stole the hearts of the men of Israel," therefore three darts were
thrust through him, as it is said, "and he took three darts in his
hand, and thrust them through the heart of Absalom."

C. It is the same in connection with the good. Miriam waited a short
while for Moses, as it is said, "and his sister stood afar off"; therefore Israel was delayed for her seven days in the wilderness, as it is said, "and
the people journeyed not until Miriam was brought in again.". . . Moses
earned merit through the bones of Joseph and there was none in Israel
greater than he, as it is said, "and Moses took the bones of Joseph with
him." Whom have we greater than Moses since none other than the
omnipresent occupied himself [with his burial], as it is said, "and he
buried him in the valley"?

D. Not only concerning Moses did they say this, but concerning all the
righteous, as it is said, "and your righteousness shall go before you, the
glory of the Lord shall be your rear-guard [/ shall gather you up]."
(*m. Sot.* 1:7–9)

This mishnah begins by describing the *sotah* ordeal, a form of trial or punishment for the suspected adulteress which was no longer performed in
rabbinic times, and then segues into a long discussion of talionic punishment and like reward in biblical narratives. The lack of proportion in terms
of magnitude of sin and punishment has been noted by Michael Satlow—the
sotah is only *suspected* of adultery, and yet she becomes the victim of "hu-
miliation and abuse." He continues that this mishnah and the parallel tannaitic texts "go beyond the articulation of 'measure for measure.' The adul-
terous wife is punished beyond her measure."[58] Rosen-Zvi comments that
the mishnah "strives to give meaning to these unusually violent gestures by
presenting them as emanating from the crimes themselves."[59] It seems that
the rabbis here establish correlation in *kind* for deed and outcome but not
necessarily in scale.

The punishments of Samson and Absalom, detailed next in the mishnah, appear overly aggressive because of the choice of minor details the rabbis link to the gruesome torture they suffered, despite the fact that both characters are guilty of treason. The mishnah bypasses making a connection with the characters' grave crimes, instead choosing a "connection between deed and retribution [in the case of Samson] . . . based on similar *words* ('eye' and 'hair'), while the next two examples regarding Absalom's punishment are based on *numerical* similarities."[60] Once we turn to the section on rewards the mishnah clearly and candidly assigns a magnitude of recompense that overwhelms the good deeds performed: an individual waits for another, so a whole nation waits for that individual; one human showed respect to another human posthumously, and so God himself shows respect to that human posthumously. According to Rosen-Zvi, we have here a correspondence "based on a shared *theme* (lingering and burial)"[61] rather than language or measure. And lest we think that reward, as opposed to punishment, is exceptionally disproportionate, the section begins: "it is *the same* in connection with the good. . . ." As Elaine Phillips writes, "the actual matching of punishments and rewards that the rabbis discovered in the biblical text are MFM [measure for measure] in kind but not in intensity. There is characteristically a greater degree of punishment than the crime might have warranted."[62]

This mishnah's description of "measure-for-measure" reward and punishment, disproportionate as it is, still orients itself backward, toward the elucidation of biblical texts; rather than demarcating a theology of the present, the mishnah demonstrates that *biblical* narrative and law often depict a correlation between sin and punishment. The *sotah* ritual was no longer practiced in rabbinic times; the narratives the rabbis explicate are about biblical heroes rather than rabbinic sages. Rosen-Zvi, expanding upon Isaac Heinemann's insight, makes the case that the rabbis use "measure for measure" to uncover a "hidden web of divine providence"; however, this

> search for order is conducted via the discovery of links between parts of the *text*, not of the *world*. . . . The tannaitic usage of the aphorism [measure for measure] is interpretive in nature, relating only indirectly—through assumptions regarding the relationship between scripture and history—to their own present reality.[63]

Curiously, only the last phrase in the mishnah attempts to use the insight of biblical "measure for measure" didactically, to suggest that they continue to have meaning for people of their own day; it suggests that just as the righteous Moses was rewarded at death, so too all righteous people will be rewarded. The mishnah quotes a vague promise from Isaiah which offers an assurance that righteousness is not futile, that the virtuous will enjoy "the glory of the Lord." The passage in Isaiah reads:

> Is not this the fast that I choose: to loose the bonds of injustice, to undo the thongs of the yoke, to let the oppressed go free, and to break every yoke? Is it not to share your bread with the hungry, and bring the homeless poor into your house; when you see the naked, to cover them, and not to hide yourself from your own kin? Then your light shall break forth like the dawn, and your healing shall spring up quickly; your vindicator shall go before you, the glory of Yhwh shall be your rear guard. (Isa. 58:6–8)

The mishnah plays on Isaiah's poetic image that God will "gather up the rear" (while righteousness walks in front of you). The verb used is "*ya'aspeka*," and the root *'SP* is used elsewhere in the Hebrew Bible to imply a kind of "gathering in" to one's ancestors after death (e.g., Gen. 25:8, Judg. 2:10). Thus just as Moses' virtue was rewarded by God's burying him after he dies, so also, the mishnah suggests, all the righteous will be gathered in by God at their death. This rabbinic gesture toward divine care at the moment of death hardly depicts a traditional, deuteronomic sense of divine reward and punishment *in this world* contingent on observance of the commandments, and thus this statement signals a particular rabbinic departure from biblical theology.

This reading is supported by the very context from which the verse is taken. The beginning of Isaiah 58 consists of a long excursus on the necessity of human justice, above all. The promise of divine "gathering" is part of Yhwh's reply to a hypocritical people, who complain that God has abandoned them, has ignored their prayers, though they continue to oppress the poor and neglect the hungry. God insists that he will not respond to their petitions and demands until they "loose the bonds of injustice, to undo the thongs of the yoke, to let the oppressed go free . . ."—only then will they clear a path to the Lord. In this passage, God *refuses* to set things right, offering primarily divine guidance and strength (58:11) in the human pursuit of justice. By invoking this verse, the rabbis imply that direct divine recompense for one's deeds is not something one can expect in this life; instead humans must forge their own worldly justice.

In one mishnah, then, the concept of "measure for measure" is used to justify a ritual ordeal, to create a thematic connection between good deeds performed by biblical characters and their rewards, and to uncover linguistic / numerical connections between biblical sins and their punishments. When we begin to look outside of this single text, the issue becomes even more complex:

> The use of the principle of "measure for measure" in rabbinic and even Tannaitic literature is broad and . . . extremely vague. Abundant connections and analogies are drawn between deed and reward in a rich variety of contexts, causing great difficulty in defining the principle's exact contours. . . . [The] concept . . . is very broad and multi-dimensional.[64]

Other scholars analyzing divine justice in rabbinic literature confirm this conclusion. Jonathan Schofer writes:

> Rabbinic thinking about God's actions is highly flexible. The basic process is that God rewards good action and punishes bad. . . . But [t]he formal relation between act and result . . . varies tremendously. Despite the important rabbinic claim that divine justice is "measure for measure" (*middah keneged middah*), accounts of divine justice present numerous relations between act and result. Correspondence or lack thereof may appear in the nature of the two events, the literary expression in which they are formulated, or both. Correspondence may admit of degrees, with sometimes an exact fit between act and response, sometimes a more loose connection, and sometimes an explicit disjunction.[65]

In what follows, I would like to examine several tannaitic texts which undercut a notion of just divine reward and punishment; in painting God's justice as disproportionate and variable, these texts suggest that difficult cases in rabbinic courts could not simply be referred to "divine jurisdiction" with the hope that ultimate justice may be wrought. If we define justice through the lens of rabbinic jurisprudence—as requiring equity, impartiality and proportionality—then many tannaitic texts reject outright the notion of divine justice.

Several mishnayot create a parallel of sorts between human and divine justice by overtly linking divine reward and punishment with the fulfillment or transgression of *Torah* law; however, they also often present a disparity between deed and recompense:

> Anyone who fulfills one commandment, it is good with him and his days are lengthened and he inherits the land. But anyone who does not fulfill one commandment, it is not good with him and his days are not lengthened and he does not inherit the land. (*m. Qidd.* 1:10)

This mishnah sounds virtually like Deuteronomy; as quoted above, Deuteronomy states, "you must carefully observe every commandment . . . so that you live . . . and enter and occupy the land" (Deut. 8:1). But one detail has been changed; Deuteronomy bases divine reward on the keeping of "every commandment," while the mishnah only requires the observance of "one commandment." This mishnaic pronouncement poses both logical and theological problems, which are taken up in all of the classical commentaries. Does the mishnah refer to one specific commandment, or any one commandment? Does "not fulfilling one commandment" mean *refusing* to fulfill a commandment on one occasion, or never fulfilling one commandment throughout one's lifetime? As exegetes of this mishnah struggle with its implications, we can at least determine what it does *not* do—it does not reproduce Deuteronomy's traditional argument of just divine reward and punishment, for it is precisely the *measure* of the deed ("one" versus "every") that has diverged from the deuteronomic verse.

Another mishnah correlates divine retribution to items of rabbinic law, suggesting a kind of divine justice at work: "For three sins women die in childbirth: because they are not cautious in menstrual purity [*niddah*], in *hallah,* and in the lighting of the [Sabbath] candle" (*m. Shab.* 2:6). Regarding this text, David Kraemer writes: "[i]gnoring the apparent lack of proportion between the sin and the attendant punishment . . . it remains clear that suffering is punishment for sin."[66] It is precisely my point, however, that we cannot ignore this "apparent lack of proportion." Carelessness in the three areas of law mentioned in this mishnah may indeed have grave consequences, at least as far as rabbinic ritual law is concerned: if a woman is not careful with the details of menstrual impurity, she may inadvertently lead her husband to have prohibited sex; if she does not attend to the details of the required *hallah* tithe, she may accidentally allow someone to consume prohibited holy foods; if she is not sure to light a candle on the Sabbath eve, she may, somehow, cause a member of her household to inadvertently blunder into violating the Sabbath. Though the mishnah essentially sentences the woman to death, she has not actually committed any of the serious ritual sins feared; she has merely, out of inattention, created a situation in which she might lead someone to sin unknowingly. And while casualness regarding divine ritual prohibitions need not be tolerated, it is difficult to imagine that they call for capital punishment. The fundamental notion of *appropriate* divine punishment is thus undermined, perhaps in order to assure male rabbinic disciples that they need not worry about divine retribution due to their wives' neglect of ritual commandments, that God will deal with such women swiftly and directly, resorting to the severest of punishments.

A mishnah in *Abot* similarly depicts God's response to human transgression as disproportionate, essentially an enigma: "Be as careful with a light precept as with a grave one, for you know not the reward [for the fulfillment] of precepts" (2:1). In Deuteronomy, one is advised to keep the law in order to ensure a like reward, which is guaranteed by God. This mishnah urges conformity to the law precisely because of what one does *not* know: those commandments which seem most critical may merit less recompense than those that seem minor. That one can never know or anticipate God's response to human action may induce Jews into keeping *all* of the commandments precisely by depicting a God who does *not* conform to the predictability of human justice.

If the above rabbinic texts show an imbalance in divine reward and punishment, they nonetheless argue for a connection between matters of sacred law and God's recompense. But many rabbinic passages highlight the non-juridical nature of divine response to human activity by linking it not to transgression of a commandment, but rather something less identifiable—an interior state, a momentary indiscretion.[67] The following passage from the Tosefta has been understood by scholars as *confirming* the conventional piety of the rabbis, as it links historical suffering with punishment for sin; its more subversive effect is often overlooked. The text reads:

> R. Yoḥanan ben Torta said: Why was the first Temple of Jerusalem destroyed? Because there was in it idol worship and prohibited sexual relations and the shedding of blood. But in the latter Temple we know that they toiled in Torah and were careful with tithes, so why were they exiled? Because they loved money and each one hated his neighbor. This is to teach you that hatred of one man for his fellow is equal before God to idolatry, sexual misconduct, and the shedding of blood. . . . (*t. Menaḥ.* 13:22)

David Kraemer again downplays the innovation of this tosefta. He comments:

this Tosefta, while not attributing the second, more recent destruction to sin in a restricted sense (if sin = matters specifically prohibited by the Torah), nevertheless makes it clear that wrongdoing is at the root of the catastrophe. Recalling the nature of the wrongdoings described by Amos (chapter 2 and throughout), we may even say that this sort of wrongdoing has a long tradition in prophetic condemnations.[68]

Leaving aside for the moment that hating your neighbor is in fact specifically prohibited by the Torah in Leviticus 19:17, the claim that this tosefta is essentially conservative, echoing the prophetic correspondence between sin and punishment, eclipses the most piercing innovation of this text. Amos, chapter 2, reads:

> For three transgressions of Israel, and for four, I will not revoke the punishment; because they sell the righteous for silver, and the needy for a pair of sandals; they who trample the head of the poor into the dust of the earth, and push the afflicted out of the way; father and son go in to the same girl, so that my holy name is profaned; they lay themselves down beside every altar on garments taken in pledge; and in the house of their God they drink wine bought with fines they imposed. (Amos 2:6–8)

This litany of offenses can hardly be compared to the sins invoked in the tosefta; Amos decries *oppression* of the poor, even alluding to specific Torah laws (such as Deut. 24:12), whereas the tosefta targets the root *causes* of such oppression, loving money and hating one's neighbor. These are not crimes, *per se* (unlike the offenses Amos lists), but attitudes, normally unpunishable by any system of jurisprudence. In fact, the tosefta specifies that the Jews of the Second Temple era "toiled in Torah" even to the point of being exacting with tithes, indicating that they were innocent not only of the heinous crimes Amos attributes to his contemporaries, but that they could not be faulted with any formal transgression whatsoever.

The passage nonetheless draws an equivalence between the most unforgivable transgressions—idolatry, sexual immorality, and murder—and the feelings of hatred and greed.[69] The tosefta acknowledges that this parallel is not at all intuitive; it proposes that God destroyed the temple as a pedagogical act: "*to teach you* that hatred . . . is equal before God to idolatry. . . ." Here, God metes out punishment for some other purpose than strict justice—to teach Israel a lesson. But this lesson is not that evil thoughts are entirely indistinguishable from evil deeds; the passage specifies that "hatred . . . is equal *before God* to idolatry. . . ." Human jurisprudence may—and in fact must—

distinguish between act and intention, and must calibrate the punishment to the crime. According to the rabbis, however, God does not follow this model of justice.

This pedagogical theme is echoed in a midrash that continues to dissociate divine activity from proportional and predictable justice:

> R. Meir says: "Know then in your heart that as a parent disciplines a child so Yhwh your God disciplines you." (Deut. 8:5). Your heart should know the deeds that you have done and the suffering that I have brought upon you—not according to your deeds have I brought suffering upon you. (*Mek. Bahodesh* 10)

This theodical passage in the *Mekilta* asks its readers to view suffering as a kind of paternal discipline. In the biblical verse cited, this suffering refers specifically to the Israelites' trials in the wilderness after the Exodus from Egypt:

> Remember the long way that Yhwh your God has led you these forty years in the wilderness, in order to humble you, testing you to know what was in your heart, whether or not you would keep his commandments. He humbled you by letting you hunger, then by feeding you with manna, with which neither you nor your ancestors were acquainted . . . Know then in your heart that as a parent disciplines a child so Yhwh your God disciplines you. (Deut. 8:2–5)

According to Moses' speech, suffering in the wilderness had one aim: "to know what was in your heart, whether or not you would keep his commandments" (Deut. 8:3). But while Israel has been disciplined by God in her infancy in order to be prepared for the demands of the law, she is now expected to keep the commandments and receive reward; the passage begins, "This entire commandment that I command you today you must diligently observe, so that you may live and increase, and go in and occupy the land that Yhwh promised on oath to your ancestors" (Deut. 8:1). In the midrash, the idea of "discipline" is highlighted, and specifically contrasted to a proportional notion of just punishment; the midrash understands this verse as indicating that one cannot measure one's sinfulness on the basis of one's suffering: "*not* according to your deeds have I brought suffering upon you." The midrash does not emphasize the biblical idea that God's discipline is relegated to a youthful past only to be replaced by the regular proportionality of justice; instead, the notion of disciplinary suffering is iterated in the perpetual present. And the sense that suffering need not be understood as just punishment is articulated in this midrash as a simple inner calculus, a transparent intuitive knowledge that, the midrash suggests, ought to be trusted.

Finally, a deeply unsettling narrative in the *Mekilta* dramatizes God's pedagogical infliction of disciplinary suffering, illuminating the unfairness of God's retribution:

> At the time when R. Simeon and Ishmael were led out to be killed, R. Simeon said to R. Ishmael: Master, my heart fails me, for I do not know why I am to be killed. R. Ishmael said to him: Did it never happen in your life that a man came to you for a judgment or with a question and you let him wait until you had sipped your cup, or had tied your sandals, or had put on your cloak? And the Torah has said "If you abuse in any way . . ." [Ex. 22:22], whether it be a severe affliction or a light affliction. Whereupon R. Simeon said to him: You have comforted me, Master. (*Mek. Niziqin* 18, Ex. 22:20)

Unable to find meaning in his execution, R. Simeon is led to his death in a profound state of distress. It appears to him that God has abandoned any providential care, allowing an innocent, righteous, and pious man to suffer and die. R. Ishmael seems to reply brazenly, suggesting that R. Simeon has brought his unfortunate fate upon himself by being less than perfect, by having, in a moment of distraction, focused on himself while another person waited for a judgment or a reply. R. Ishmael's remark does not merely rely on an intuitive sense of justice; he lends his words the divine authority of scripture, appealing to a biblical verse to support his contention that God might repay even a minor infraction with death. The context of the verse is the judicial mistreatment of a widow or orphan: "You shall not abuse any widow or orphan. If you do abuse them, when they cry out to me, I will surely heed their cry; my wrath will burn, and I will kill you with the sword, and your wives shall become widows and your children orphans" (Ex. 22:21–24). The biblical clause, "if you do abuse" (*im ʿanneh teʿanneh*), employs a typical grammatical technique for emphasis, a doubling of the verb (infinitive absolute followed by the conjugated form). R. Ishmael interprets this emphatic doubling to mean any kind of abuse, great or small. Thus according to R. Ishmael's reading, God promises, for any mistreatment, no matter how trivial, "I will kill you with the sword."

This passage and the host of similar martyrdom narratives in rabbinic literature have been analyzed by several scholars in light of their approach to divine justice. Jonathan Schofer provides the most comprehensive study of this narrative and its variants in rabbinic literature. He argues that a trope of "trivial sin" permeates rabbinic literature; in each case,

> an apparently minor transgression brings a strikingly harsh punishment. . . . Such passages rhetorically emphasize the importance of apparently small dimensions of life. They may also convey that, at least for the great Sages, every action and inner state is spiritually and ethically significant. The life of a Sage is fragile, and even the smallest slip in attentiveness can mean disaster.[70]

Schofer asserts that when we evaluate these texts within the discourse of spiritual and ethical teaching, as opposed to that of divine justice, we find justification for God's "strikingly harsh punishment" of the sages. There is no claim, in other words, that God operates in order to right the wrongs of human jurisprudence, to provide a model of human justice, or to enforce strict obedience of the commandments. Rather, God is understood to intervene in human affairs on a case by case basis, to teach each person the lessons that he (or she) needs to learn.

In the case of R. Simeon's martyrdom narrative, Schofer maintains that we find "a strong assimilation of the martyrdom into a teaching about trivial sin":[71]

> The deaths raise deep questions concerning God's action—can the language of justice be used to describe God as acting in the world, and is God's justice at all similar to human justice? The strong warning against a delay in judgment, in contrast, is part of a pedagogical motif that presumes a strong confidence in divine justice: for aspiring Sages, apparently small actions may bring tremendous consequences.[72]

Schofer here suggests that in combining two different rabbinic motifs—the questioning of God's justice and the ethical teaching regarding trivial sin—the rabbis permit neither to exhaust the other; both linger beyond the rhetorical boundaries of the passage. However, Schofer implies, in his presumption that the text accomplishes an "assimilation of the martyrdom," that the challenge to God's justice can indeed be quelled by the solution offered. Later he concludes that "[t]o the extent that these stories assimilate strong challenges against divine justice into a pedagogy of ethical

teaching, they are among the strongest affirmations of that justice in rabbinic literature."[73] But do these ethical teachings actually manage to sub-
due the power of the profound doubts raised in relation to God's justice?
Friedrich Avemarie contends that the story of R. Simeon's martyrdom:

> offers an intentionally weak argument, one that is formally logical but
> that in content has the effect of being as unconvincing as possible. If one
> considers how convincing the argument could have been if the rabbi had
> been given clear legal guilt, then the minimization of the guilt of the rabbi
> instead can fulfill only one purpose: to prove that this seeming indication
> of guilt suggests, in reality, the innocence of the rabbi.[74]

According to Avemarie, then, the story's pedagogical conclusion does little
to vitiate the lingering injustice of the narrative, the needless suffering and
death of the righteous. In the story, R. Simeon is comforted by the spiritual
teaching which promulgates a troubling, indeed frightening, theology. He
feels that his death is somehow justified because though he has been righteous throughout his life, he, like any human being, has not been perfect.
He is comforted because no matter how unjust his death is, he need not
view it as entirely arbitrary; this injustice is inscribed into a biblical verse,
and thus he may believe that though God's standards may be exacting,
and though God may punish severely and disproportionately, God nonetheless acts meaningfully rather than capriciously—God continues to care
and has not simply abandoned his people. As such, Schofer is right to say
that "at the end divine *authority* is legitimated and order affirmed,"[75] but
perhaps divine *justice* is not.

THE DIFFERENT FACES OF GOD'S JUSTICE

Contrary to the passages cited above, in which God's ordering presence
is upheld while his fairness and justice is undermined, many rabbinic
passages affirm God's role as a guarantor of ultimate justice, in this world,
or especially in the next. One famous narrative tells a tale of a murderer
who could not be prosecuted because there were no direct witnesses to the
crime:

> R. Judah b. Tabbai entered a ruin and found a slain man still writhing,
> and a sword still dripping blood was in the hand of the slayer. Judah b.
> Tabbai said: May it come upon me if either you or I killed him! But what

can I do, since the Torah has said, "By the mouths of two witnesses shall the matter be established" (Deut. 19:15)? (*Mek. Kaspa* 3)

In this story, human jurisprudence is at an impasse—a murder has occurred, the slayer has been caught, but none of it can be established legally. At this moment, the midrash appeals to divine justice. It continues: "He who knows even thoughts will exact punishment from this man. Hardly had he come out from there when a serpent bit that man and he died." God's justice is presented as completely congruent with human jurisprudence, stepping in at the precise moment when human justice fails because of a formal legal technicality, and punishing swiftly and proportionally.

Despite the confidence in divine justice displayed by this midrash, it is presented as little more than a singular anecdote; and, as I argued with regard to the Hebrew Bible, in order for God's retribution to be seen as just from the perspective of human law, it needs to be equitable and consistent. There are many occasions in tannaitic literature in which God is called upon at the point of failure of human law; the rabbis resignedly assert that the perpetrator is free from human penalties but "his judgment is left to heaven" (or a variation on this formula). Again, while it is tempting to see in these passages an affirmation of a divine assurance of ultimate justice when true justice cannot be reached in court, these statements do not actually confirm such a position. An accused's judgment may be relegated to God, but we still cannot know with certainty how God will choose to judge him or her.[76] Indeed, many scholars view these rabbinic statements as having moral weight, but no juridical implications.[77]

One passage in *Sifre Deuteronomy* may serve as a microcosm of rabbinic attitudes towards divine justice. It is appended to a verse from an extended poem uttered by Moses shortly before his death. He proclaims: "The Rock, his work is perfect, and all his ways are just (*mishpat*). A faithful God, without deceit, just (*tsadiq*) and upright is he" (Deut. 32:4). This passage, in typical fashion, elicits a variety of interpretations for this straightforward verse—a collection of commentaries that essentially presents a multivalent definition of divine justice, one that has been shaped by a redactor, as Steven Fraade notes, "to maintain the impression that the text before us is a collective, traditional one, constituting 'words of Torah.'"[78] It is to this collective *torah* on divine justice that I would now like to turn to summarize the vast array of rabbinic theologies of divine justice.

The *Sifre* commentary on Deuteronomy 32:4 begins by interpreting God's justice on a physical, material level:

A. *The Rock (ha-Tsur)*—the Artist *(tsayyar)*, for He first designed *(tsar)* the world and then formed man in it, as it is said, *Then the Lord God formed (va-yitser) man* (Gen. 2:7)—*His work is perfect.* His workmanship in regard to all creatures of the world is perfect; there can be no complaint whatsoever about His work. None of them can look at himself and say, "If only I had three eyes, if only I had three arms, if only I had three legs, if only I walked on my head, if only my face were turned the other way, how nicely it would become me!" Hence the verse goes on to say, *For all his ways are justice*—He sits in judgment on everyone and dispenses to each that which is appropriate for him. *A God of faithfulness*—who believed in the world and created it. *And without iniquity*—for men were created not in order to be wicked but in order to be righteous, as it is said, *Behold, this only I have found, that God made man upright; but they have sought out many inventions* (Eccl. 7:29). *Just and right is He*—He conducts Himself uprightly with all the creatures of the world.

In this interpretation, God's justice begins in the act of creation, which, according to the *Sifre,* we ought not take for granted. But the midrashic questions are intriguing, because the alternatives it proposes are not all transparently outrageous. Three eyes might help us see better, or from different angles; three arms might help us accomplish more tasks at once. The midrash here might be subtly implying that perhaps we *could* imagine a more perfect, more able human body, but that nonetheless we must know with conviction that God has given us what is right and just, no more and no less; that creation *is* perfect, despite what one might imagine to the contrary.[79] Indeed, parallel texts in Genesis Rabbah and Ecclesiastes Rabbah compare this line of questioning to visitors at a king's palace who remark, "if only the columns were higher, it would be more pleasant. If only the walls were higher, it would be more pleasant. If only its ceiling were higher, it would be more pleasant" (*Gen. Rab.* 12:1; *Eccl. Rab.* 2:12). These critiques betray a kind of arrogance, as the visitor second-guesses the royal architect—but they do not rule out the notion that the criticism might be valid.

The moral implications of understanding the creation of the human as flawless are spelled out as the midrash continues; wickedness and transgression are said to be solely the responsibility of human beings, who are created "upright," but seek out mischief. God, in contrast, only conducts himself "uprightly" in relation to humans. This midrash, then, confirms a kind of conventional wisdom about God's justice—that God's act of creation and further involvement in the world are nothing but just and upright, while humans stray from God's straight and simple path. There is only a hint that God in some way could have done more for humans— made them bigger, better, more capable. This insinuation may be echoed in the verse quoted from Ecclesiastes, which states that God made men *yashar* (lit. "straight")—a word which can be and has been translated both as upright and as "plain"; and men engage in many *hishbonot*—reasonings, calculations, thoughts, devices. Does the physicality of human creation not live up to humans' mental acuity, allowing them to imagine many more perfect alternatives to the world we have?

The next section of the midrash drives further doubt into God's justice toward humans, shifting from the stage of the body to biblical history:

B. Another interpretation: *The Rock*—the powerful one. *His work is per-fect*—His actions in regard to all creatures of the world are perfect; there should be no complaint whatsoever about His work. None of them can look and say, "Why should the generation of the flood have been swept away by water? Why should the people of the tower have been scattered from one end of the earth to the other? Why should the people of Sodom have been swept away by fire and brimstone? Why should Aaron have assumed the priesthood? Why should David have assumed the kingship? Why should Korah and his followers have been swallowed up by the earth?" Therefore the verse goes on to say, *For all his ways are justice*—He sits in judgment on everyone and dispenses to each what is appropriate for him.

A God of faithfulness—who keeps His trust. *And without iniq-uity*—He collects that which is His only at the end. For the way of the Holy One . . . is not like the way of creatures of flesh and blood: if A deposits with B a purse of two hundred while owing B a *manah,* when A comes to retrieve it, B says to him, "I will subtract the *manah* you owe me, and here is the balance." Similarly, if a work-man working for B owes him a *denar,* when he comes to collect his wages, B says to him, "I will subtract the *denar* you owe me, and here is the balance." But He-who-spoke . . . is not like that; rather *He is a God of faithfulness*—who keeps His trust—and *without iniq-uity*—collecting that which is His only at the end—*just and right is*

He—as it is said, *For the Lord is righteous, He loves righteousness*[; *the upright (yashar) shall behold his face*] (Ps. 11:7).

This midrash is composed of two parts: the first explicates God's perfect justice, the second his faithfulness. In the first part, the midrash raises several penetrating theological challenges to God's rewards and punishments as revealed in scripture, albeit prefaced by the blanket statement that no one ought to consider these questions for even a moment. The biblical injustices the midrash illuminates involve the suffering of a number of innocents (the flood, Sodom), overly harsh punishment for pride (Babel, Koraḥ), and unparalleled, eternal reward of individuals who committed grave sins (Aaron, who led the Israelites into idolatry; David, who committed adultery). Because God's justice is *not* self-evident, the midrash suggests, we need a verse to *tell* us that God is, in fact, always just, giving each individual "what is appropriate for him." This midrash repudiates a human model of justice which must be transparent and universal, and posits that God's justice is instead opaque and unreadable. The emphasis on the individual alludes to a philosophy we have seen above—a sliding scale of recompense in which divine justice is highly personalized. Even biblical examples cannot be read as models and each must be understood in its own particularity.

The difference between God's justice and human justice is explicitly taken up in the latter half of this midrash. A contrast is drawn between "the way (*middah,* lit. 'measure') of the Holy One" and the "way of creatures of flesh and blood." Human justice, perhaps surprisingly, is depicted as even-handed and reasonable: parties are paid exactly what they deserve, and their debts are collected in all fairness. God, however, does not take what he is owed until "the end"; God's reckoning, in other words, comes after humans' worldly affairs. This intimation of reward and punishment being held until the afterlife is underscored by quoting Psalm 11, in which the innocent suffer, but God promises that the righteous shall "see his face," that is, as interpreted by the rabbis, shall join God in the world-to-come. The wicked, in the psalm, are avenged with fire and brimstone, an echo of the punishment of Sodom and Gomorrah referenced in the first half of the midrash. God's justice in the second half of the midrash is imagined in monetary terms; and though the balance is cleared in the end, after death, God's deferral of his own accounting creates an imbalance in the here and now.

The notion of ultimate reward and punishment occurring only in the afterlife is rendered explicit in the following midrash:

C. Another interpretation: *The Rock*—the Powerful One. *His work is perfect*—The work of all creatures of the world is complete before Him, both the dispensing of reward to the righteous and the infliction of punishment to the wicked. Neither takes anything due to them in this world. Whence do we learn that the righteous take nothing due to them in this world? From the verse, *Oh how abundant is Your goodness, which You have hidden for them that fear You!* (Ps. 31:20). And whence do we learn that the wicked take nothing due to them in this world? From the verse, *Is not this stored up with Me, sealed up in my treasuries?* (32:34). When do both of them take (that which is due to them)? *For all his ways are justice*—in the future, when He will sit upon the throne of justice, He will sit in judgment on each one and give him what is appropriate for him. *A God of faithfulness*—Just as He grants the perfectly righteous a reward in the world-to-come for performance of the commandments in this world, so does He grant the perfectly wicked a reward in this world for any minor commandment performed in this world; and just as He requites the perfectly wicked in the world-to-come for any transgression performed in this world, so does He requite the perfectly righteous in this world for any minor transgression committed in this world. *And without iniquity*—When one departs from this world, all his deeds will come before him one by one and say to him, "Thus did you do on such-and-such a day, and thus did you do on such-and-such other day—do you acknowledge these matters?" And he will reply, "Yes." He will be told, "Sign!" as it is said, *The hand of every man shall seal it, so that all men may know his deeds* (Job 37:7). *Just and right is He*—the man thereupon will justify the verdict and say, "Well was I judged," as it is said, *That You may justify [the judgment] when you speak.* (Ps. 51:6)

This midrash not only invokes the afterlife, or world-to-come, as the location of God's true justice, but it positions this world as a complete *reversal* of justice—a way station in which individuals receive the opposite of their deserved recompense. The wicked are rewarded in this world for any good deed they may have done so that they can be punished exclusively in the world-to-come; the righteous are punished for every minor transgression so that their future reward will be untainted. Whereas the previous commentaries circumvent the details of divine jurisprudence repeating a proclamation of God's perfect justice as a refrain ("He sits in judgment on everyone and gives him what is appropriate for him"), this midrash exploits the shift in setting to the hereafter by fantasizing a divine judgment which is perfectly itemized to every last human deed; which gives humans a voice in their own ultimate judgment by requiring their signatures (!) on their eternal verdict; and which reconciles each human being with God, as every individual is able to say, "I was judged well."

The latter two human elements in the rabbinic vision of God's final judgment are constructed out of grammatical ambiguities in two biblical verses. The first verse from Job refers to Yhwh's control of the snow and rainfall, stating that "it is a sign (*yaḥtom*) on every man's hand (*beyad*), that all men may know His deeds." The midrash reads the prefix *be* in a standard, though acontextual, way, as an instrumental prefix—thus, "every man shall sign *by* hand." It then views the pronoun "his"—which contextually points to Yhwh— as referring to "every man," producing the phrase, "every man will know his [own] deeds." Hence, the verse is rendered: "every man shall sign by hand, so that he shall know his deeds." The verse in Psalms is interpreted similarly by the rabbis: the pronoun is reread in the word *bedebareka*, converting the phrase "You [God] are justified in Your [God's] words" into "you [human being] will justify [it] with your words." In addition to the pronouns, the rabbis adjust the tense of both verses. The biblical Hebrew imperfect is flexible, but both verses are most often translated in the present: the snow and rain *are* signs of God's mastery of nature, and God *is* justified in his judgments. The rabbis, however, pointedly choose to gloss these verses in the future tense rather than the present, thus supporting their assertions about the future orientation of divine justice. They subtly but significantly employ the same technique with regard to Deuteronomy 32:4 as well; whereas the previous midrashim gloss the phrase "all his ways are justice" with "He sits in judgment of everyone . . . ," this midrash adds a significant prelude: "*In the future [lemaḥar],* when He sits upon the throne of justice. . . ." The reader is then forced to read the proceeding midrashic refrain in the future tense: "He *will sit* in judgment on everyone and *will give* him what is appropriate for him."

In stark contrast to the midrashic depiction of divine justice in the previous midrashim, the rabbinic vision of perfect *future* justice stresses the transparency of God's judgments, the participation of humans in sealing their own fate, and humans' full understanding of God's ways. These three elements can be understood to comprise a rabbinic manifesto of ideal justice, and they are all essential elements in rabbinic jurisprudence—transparency of process, the importance of testimony instead of casting lots or initiating an ordeal, and the recognition of the "good judgment" of the rabbis. This midrash thus argues most forcefully for the correlation between human and divine justice; it must do so, however, at the expense of divine involvement in the present world, in which these features of divine justice are markedly absent.

In sharp contrast to the fantasy of God's perfect justice in the world-to-come, the midrash continues with a tragic narrative of martyrdom:

> D. Another interpretation: *The Rock, His work is perfect*—When they apprehended R. Haninah ben Teradion, he was condemned to be burned together with his Torah scroll. When he was told of it, he recited this verse, *The Rock, His work is perfect*. When his wife was told, "Your husband has been condemned to be burned, and you to be executed," she recited the verse, *A God of faithfulness and without iniquity*. And when his daughter was told, "Your father has been condemned to be burned, your mother to be executed, and you yourself to be assigned to hard labor," she recited the verse, *Great in counsel, and mighty in work, whose eyes are open [upon all the ways of the sons of men, to give everyone according to his ways]* (Jer. 32:19). Rabbi said: How great were these righteous people, in that at the time of their trouble they invoked three verses justifying [God's] judgment, similar to which there is nothing else in all of Scripture. The three directed their hearts and accepted the justice of God's judgment.
>
> A philosopher protested to the prefect, saying, "My master, do not boast that you have burned the Torah, for it has now returned to the place whence it had come—its Father's house." The prefect replied, "Tomorrow your fate will be the same as theirs," whereupon the philosopher said to him, "You have conveyed good tidings to me, that tomorrow my portion will be with them in the world to come."

Much like the story of R. Simeon and R. Ishmael, the tale of the martyrdom of R. Hanina ben Teradion and his family establishes God as the primary authority behind the course of events, instead of the Roman prefect. By reciting our verse in Deuteronomy as well as Jeremiah 32:19, the characters in the story confirm their righteousness by accepting their horrible fate as part of God's justice. But, as Zachary Braiterman observes, this narrative also differs from the account of R. Simeon's martyrdom:

> R. Hanina b. Teradion and his family neither search for nor discover any mitigating sin that could explain why they suffer. They eschew any ex-

planatory scheme based on this-worldly or otherworldly retribution. They simply justify God, accepting death and degradation.[80]

There is a kind of divine mystery suggested here, a remote, unfathomable quality to God's decisions and deeds that is highlighted in this midrash. The family accepts its suffering by *declaring* God's justice, even while that justice cannot be *demonstrated*. And the two verses they proclaim, the midrash tells us, stand alone in scripture; out of the entire Torah,[81] only two verses, apparently, can unequivocally testify to God's perfect justice.

Contrary to the silent submission of R. Hanina ben Teradion's family to the divine decree, a philosopher speaks out—not to God, but to the Roman prefect, the authority who is historically most directly responsible for these unjust sentences. As Christine Hayes has argued in reference to the Babylonian Talmud, "rabbinic authors introduce or exploit the presence of *minim* (i.e., heretics or sectarians) and Romans . . . in order to voice and thus grapple with their own ambivalence and radical doubt."[82] Do the rabbis have misgivings about assigning these wrongful deaths to God? Do they wish to accuse the Romans but feel constrained by a biblical tradition which insists on God's sole control of history? A philosopher thus becomes the mouthpiece for the rabbis, protesting against the prefect, and invoking a truly compassionate God, who lavishes reward in the world-to-come upon those who suffer the cruelty of tyrants on earth. The God of R. Hanina ben Teradion and his family appears aloof and uncaring, though he is said to be just; the God of the philosopher appears to have lost control of the wickedness of his human creation, but he compensates for it by effecting true justice in the heavens. The rabbis waver between these two portraits of God, offering both as flawed models of divine justice.

A final midrash concludes with what Braiterman understands as the "epistemological modesty [which can] characterize [the] rabbinic response to suffering":[83]

> E. Another interpretation: *The Rock, His work is perfect*—When Moses descended from Mt. Sinai, all Israel gathered together around him and said to him, "Our master Moses, what is the measure [*middah*] of judgment on high?" He said to them, "I cannot tell you that he justifies the innocent and punishes the guilty but even when he reverses the matter, *a God of faithfulness and without iniquity*."[84]

This succinct midrash dispenses with any attempt to justify God's actions in the world in terms of justice. God's judgments are portrayed as inconsistent (he does not always justify the innocent or punish the guilty) and even the reverse of what one might deserve. As the rabbis appeal to Moses, the ultimate sacred authority who conversed with God face to face and transcribed the Torah, we are teased with the possibility of direct insight into the divine mind; instead, Moses seems as bewildered as anyone when it comes to divine reward and punishment. Perhaps the rabbis here allude to the Hebrew Bible's own mixed messages when it comes to defining divine justice—the Torah, the embodiment of revelation, offers no guidance, and even confuses us further. Abraham Joshua Heschel calls Moses' response here "cryptic" and claims that it represents a thread in rabbinic literature which holds the belief that "mortals can neither see nor comprehend the nature of the Divine Presence."[85] In this Jobean turn, the midrash seems to give up entirely on divine justice—the phrases *"For all his ways are justice"* and *"just and right is he"* are notably absent from the commentary on the verse. Instead we get a perfect God [*tamim*], a faithful God [*'el 'emunah*], without iniquity [*'eyn 'avel*]. God may not be just but we may have faith in his faithfulness and perfect devotion to his people, however it is manifest.

And thus the section on divine justice concludes in the *Sifre*. The understandings of divine justice run the gamut from perfect justice in the physical world to complete arbitrariness and unfathomability in this world and the next; and yet, instead of hopeless mystification, we may sense a deliberate shaping of this pericope into a *torah* on God's judgment. The redactor(s) of the *Sifre* offer(s) us five midrashim; the midrash placed at the center is the longest, daring to imagine the contours of divine justice in vivid detail, shaped by biblical verses into a full realization of a scene in the heavenly beyond. Echoing the balanced scales of justice, this central midrash is perfectly balanced itself, first expounding upon the measure of divine justice in this world, in which each individual receives the opposite of what they deserve, and then illuminating the justice of the hereafter, in which all is made right.

Surrounding this fantastical midrash are commentaries which invoke lived experience instead of idealized speculation. The opening two midrashim point backward, the first to creation and the second to biblical narrative. Tackling both the physicality of the human body and the vicissitudes of human history, both midrashim declare—but cannot demonstrate—

God's unfathomable justice. Following the center midrash are two commentaries that relate to the present, a rabbi's story of martyrdom and a text of Mosaic revelation about the enduring nature of divine justice. Neither of these midrashim asserts God's justice: in the martyrdom story, it is the family of R. Hanina ben Teradion that proclaims God's justice, while the author of the midrash remains silent; in the final midrash, divine justice is not affirmed at all.

Steven Fraade argues in relation to *Sifre Deuteronomy* that within each section,

> [e]ach discrete interpretation can stand quite well on its own—as implied in the linking phrase, *another interpretation*. Nonetheless, such interpretations have been combined and juxtaposed in such a way as to encourage and enable the student of the text to make some sense of them in relation to one another.[86]

I would like to suggest that our passage at once prioritizes and undermines the central midrash which lays out the full spectacle of divine justice, holding it up as an item of faith and fantasy that is undercut by the reality of human existence. As much as our passage is arranged around a stable center, it also exhibits a linear progression which advances on both an individual and collective scale. The passage mirrors the progress of a human life, from the creation of the body, to the vagaries of life experience, to the moment of death (here through martyrdom). Collectively, we witness the movement from the moment of creation, to biblical history, to the rabbinic era, to the eschatological future in which direct divine revelation is once again possible. The last midrash, evoking the imagined experience of the End, provides the denouement, a direct encounter with Moses in which the question which has haunted our entire passage is finally asked outright: "what is the measure of judgment on high?" The answer, a kind of Jobean inscrutability, an affirmation of God but not of his justice, forces us to give up our quest for final answers in ascertaining God's ways, to focus on other things, to move on to the next verse in Deuteronomy.

EVICTING GOD FROM THE COURTROOM

While the Hebrew Bible presents a God that deals with humans on his own terms instead of adhering to the contours of human justice, biblical

rhetoric positions this jealous God at the head of the courtroom, prosecuting and persecuting those who would brazenly violate his commandments
and break his covenant. Tannaitic rabbinic literature also depicts a God
whose justice does not follow the dictates of human jurisprudence, but it
so exaggerates the imbalance between human deeds and divine recompense that no adherence to a code of behavior could reliably secure God's
favor. Surely, promises and threats about divine retribution were used
extensively by the rabbis to shape ethical behavior or forms of rabbinic
piety. But the notions of divine justice and judgment were ironically seen
as a juridical by the rabbis, separate from the sphere of human jurisprudence and the practice of rabbinic law. As the rabbis banished divine decision making from human courts, they also relegated God's involvement
with humans and the world—divine reward and punishment—to a sphere
beyond the law in which God could be encountered personally and
individually.

If the martyrdom stories we saw above affirm God's providence by
stretching the language of justice, a famous amoraic martyrdom narrative
approaches God from a perspective that eschews the language of justice
altogether. Daniel Boyarin observes that many rabbinic martyrdom narratives differ from those of the earlier, Hasmonean period in the kind of
religious fulfillment they entail: "Now we find martyrs fulfilling through
their deaths a positive [commandment]—to love God."[87] R. Aqiba, the sage
who is portrayed in rabbinic sources as continually adopting a stance of
epistemological doubt while wrestling with the law, dies a famous martyr's
death in rabbinic texts; he proclaims his unqualified love for God at the
moment of his execution in the most absolute terms: "until now, I did not
know how to love God with all my soul" (*y. Ber.* 9:5). The very sage who,
in the Mishnah, declares his refusal to implement capital punishment
because of doubts about guilt gladly accepts his own execution without
any reference to guilt or innocence; the wrongful punishment that he
viewed as an injustice that he could himself never perpetrate becomes, in
his own personal circumstance, a sign of intimacy with God. He is said to
interpret a verse in the Song of Songs by pre-empting the biblical poem
and answering its rhetorical question himself: "'*How is your beloved more
than any other beloved?*' For His sake you die, for His sake you are slain,
as it is said, 'We have loved you unto death.'" (*Song Rab.* 2:16). Again, here,
it is love of God alone that calls for the martyr's death. R. Aqiba devotes

his life to studying, interpreting, and implementing God's law, but the moment of his death is unique and personal, a positive fulfillment of the most extreme Torah commandment of divine love. Instead of a juridical event, we find an affirmation of a singular relationship. In the figure of R. Aqiba, then, we are offered the embodiment of the dual avenues of rabbinic truth-seeking: the ambivalent construction of *legal* truth and the unequivocal devotion to the *felt* truth of divine love.

FIVE

Objects of Narrative

As for conscience, it is nothing other than the inner, heartfelt
conviction that inhabits the soul of the judge or the jury,
equitably pronouncing the judgment. In this regard, we
can say that the equity of a judgment is the objective face
for which this inner conviction constitutes the subjective
guarantor. The tie between inner conviction and the speech
act consisting in stating the law in a particular circumstance
removes the judgment in situation from pure arbitrariness.

In imagining God's role in implementing justice both the Hebrew Bible
and rabbinic literature depart from their focus on punishment that fits
the crime, allowing God to operate emotionally and personally in his
dealings with humans. In this chapter, I would like to return to our subject
of evidence and beliefs about the capacity of humans to access truth; this
time, we will approach the subject not just through the lens of human
jurisprudence but as it is refracted through the full religious world-view
of the Bible and ancient Judaism. In order to locate the kinds of knowledge
obscured by legal discourse, I turn to biblical narrative and *aggadic*
midrash.[1] Within the anecdotal sphere of the personal that narrative depicts, the interpretation of evidence is viewed from multiple perspectives
which include both the minutia of human activity and the omniscience
of the divine—and authorial—point of view. Biblical narratives abandon
the exhortatory rhetoric of the law, exposing a confused and hazardous
path to divine truth in which humans are easily led astray. The rabbis also
expose the flaws in legal procedure, but they discover divine truth and
inner conviction along the way.

Physical objects tend to be read in two different ways in biblical and rabbinic narratives. The American philosopher Charles Peirce (1839–1914) made a distinction between the index, or natural sign, which is causally correlated with its referent, and a symbol, or conventional sign, which stands for its referent by virtue of a rule or custom of interpretation. Physical objects which function as evidence would be considered indices, as they would be causally linked to what they intend to prove; for example, a bloody knife proves a murder because it was caused to become bloodied through the act of killing. For symbols, however, there is only a conventional connection between the object and the interpretation; for example, a bloody knife could symbolize violence in the abstract rather than prove a particular murder. Objects in the Hebrew Bible and rabbinic midrash are used as channels through which guilt and responsibility are designated, but they do not always act as indices; rather, they are often cast as symbols, and woven into real or internal monologues that prompt a normative response.

The Perils of Deduction in Biblical Narrative

Biblical narratives depict human beings struggling to assign responsibility when situations are ambiguous or out of balance. From the very first story of Adam and Eve in the Garden of Eden, human beings are told by the deity that they cannot hide their transgression, that they have betrayed their guilt by trying to hide their nakedness. In this story, Yhwh does not simply tell Adam and Eve that through his divine omniscience he knows what they did; instead, he proves his case by pointing to the evidence of their crime, the fig leaf which is in itself a tangible trace of an awareness of their nakedness: "Who told you that you were naked?" Yhwh asks. "Have you eaten of the tree of which I commanded you not to eat?" (Gen. 3:11). On the strength of this evidence, Adam and Eve are forced to admit at least partial guilt, to confess that they did in fact eat of that very tree.

The story of Judah and Tamar in Genesis 38 offers a paradigmatic example of evidence that is proffered to prove a case and elicit an admission of responsibility. The story involves Judah's failure to meet his obligations relating to levirate marriage. According to Israelite law (Deut. 25:5), if a man dies childless, his brother (or, in the absence of a brother, close male kin) is obligated to provide offspring to continue the dead man's name and the family line by impregnating the dead man's widow. In Genesis 38, Judah fails to give his daughter-in-law, Tamar, to his last living son after two other sons who joined with her die. Tamar decides to take matters into her own hands, and to continue the family line herself: she dresses as a prostitute, seduces Judah, and secures some of his personal items as a pledge: his signet, cord, and staff. When Judah hears that his daughter-in-law Tamar has become pregnant through prostitution, he (as the paterfamilias, the patriarch with the authority to keep order in the family) immediately orders her burned at the stake. But Tamar has kept Judah's personal items, which she produces just in the nick of time, and says, "Recognize, please, whose these are, the signet and the cord and the staff!" (Gen. 38:25). Through these physical objects, which Judah recognizes as his own, Judah confesses that he has failed to meet his legal obligation, and that Tamar, albeit through unorthodox methods, has ensured its fulfillment. The verse reads, "Judah recognized and said, 'She is more righteous than I, because I did not give her to Shelah my son . . .'" (Gen. 38:26).

There is a quasi-legal feel to this entire narrative, conveying a sense of how law may have operated in a small, tribal society. When a transgression was reported to a paterfamilias, it is quite possible that he would have had the authority to call for punishment without formal trial proceedings. Tamar's only recourse was to produce some kind of evidence on her own behalf. However, it is not only her showing Judah the evidence but Judah's acceptance of the evidence that enabled guilt to be assigned properly. Tamar, in fact, is said to "send" the signet, cord, and staff to Judah—she has relinquished control of these objects, staking her life upon the effect this evidence will have upon Judah's conscience. The verse emphasizes, "Judah *recognized* and said, 'she is more righteous than I.'" David Daube discusses the legal background to this term "recognize," the Hebrew term *haker:*

> There can be little doubt that this word was technical of the formal finding out of, and making a statement to the other party about, a fact of legal relevance; be it one on which a claim might be based, or one on account of which a claim must be abandoned, or one on account of which the other party's claim must be admitted. . . . In the story of Judah and Tamar, the term is [thus] employed . . . : there is a submission of formal evidence with a request to acknowledge it, and the acknowledgement.[2]

The narrative thus depicts the relationship between the presentation of evidence and the truth it signifies—that Judah himself is the one Tamar seduced—in a fairly straightforward way. The reader knows that Tamar is telling the truth; the narrator presents her story unambiguously, showing how she came by Judah's signet, cord, and staff—all that needs to happen is for Judah to realize what the reader already knows. As Esther Menn writes in her book on the Judah and Tamar story, "Judah illustrates both the limitations of human perception and the possibility of movement from partial to more complete knowledge. . . . The fact that Judah accuses himself in Genesis 38 emphasizes his personal progress from irresponsibility and ignorance to self-knowledge and responsibility."[3] Little question is left in the mind of the reader that Judah's final conclusion is the correct one. Judah's personal items, in the hands of Tamar, function as evidentiary *indices* par excellence: Tamar could have them only because Judah has given them to her.

Nevertheless, the "natural" correlation between the signet, cord, and staff and Judah's complicity in Tamar's crime need not necessarily have led to Tamar's exoneration. The tensest moment in the story may not be fully resolved by the story's end. Tamar, the woman accused of prostitution and summarily sentenced to death, was, within the narrative, forced to rely on Judah's willingness to recognize and confess. The evidence did not "speak for itself": while it demonstrated a connection between Judah and Tamar, Judah easily could have offered alternative interpretations as to how Tamar came by his possessions; some later rabbinic interpretations of this passage actually supply precisely such hypothetical scenarios, as we will see below. Judah could also have simply destroyed the evidence now in his possession, or he could have walked away. Judah has mistreated Tamar throughout the story; it is only through physical evidence that the shamefulness of his deeds finally strikes him. The transformation from meaningless object into evidence capable of exonerating Tamar is only achieved by Judah's voluntary recognition. Yet this possibility—that telling objects might fail to convey the true story—is glossed over in this narrative. First, the story's satisfying resolution does not have the effect of prodding the reader to think further about alternative possibilities. Second, the omniscient position of the narrator creates the sense of the "true facts" of the story, which Judah's confession matches: the reader is never led to doubt that the signet, cord, and staff in Tamar's possession are evidence of Judah's wrongdoing.

Objects, in the Judah and Tamar story, are presented as relatively stable signifiers of events, and a reliable means of provoking the acceptance of responsibility for a wrong committed. Their evidentiary power is portrayed as direct, immediate, and accurate. The alternative scenario, in which objects fail to convey the facts as they happened, is never negated in this narrative; it is simply ignored.

In the book of Genesis, the Judah and Tamar episode is embedded within a larger narrative, the familiar story of Joseph and his brothers. Much has been written about the structure and subtleties of this narrative, including the various objects that appear throughout the story as evidence of events and signifiers of guilt. In every instance that evidentiary objects are used in the Joseph story, they are used deceptively in that they are presented by characters in the narrative to corroborate a lie. Much as in the Judah and Tamar story, the facts of the narrative are presented plainly; the reader of the Joseph story is told the true story by the narrator, only then to discover how various characters hide the truth by producing false evidence. Such evidence traps the characters into accepting as fact stories which are fabricated, creating tension in the plot until the final denouement, when the real facts—along with a higher truth—are revealed.

Three pivotal episodes within the larger narrative arc of the Joseph story center on the planting of false physical evidence. Two instances occur early in the narrative: as the story begins, Joseph's brothers, jealous of their father's favoritism towards Joseph, sell their brother as a slave to the Midianites. They then bloody his coat, and show it to their father as proof that Joseph is dead (Gen. 37:32). In Egypt, working as a slave in the house of Potiphar, Joseph is accosted by Potiphar's wife, who attempts to seduce him. He runs from her, leaving his tunic in her hands. As vengeance for being spurned, Potiphar's wife cries attempted rape against Joseph, and substantiates her false claim by brandishing his abandoned tunic. Later in the narrative, Joseph, through a series of fortuitous events, rises to a position of power in the Egyptian court. His brothers approach him for assistance, but do not recognize him. Joseph then creates a climactic confrontation between himself and his brothers by planting his divining cup in Benjamin's sack of grain, framing him for theft (Gen. 44:2), and taking him back to Egypt as a slave.

Nelly Furman analyzes the use of garments in this story and offers a gendered reading: the garment functions as a "symbolic marker of filial love and recognition" for men, and as "the expression of women's resentment and rebellion."[4] Moreover, she makes the significant point that these objects are "items whose function and referential meaning can easily be changed," but she genders as female this flexibility in interpretation, con-

trasting it with a male "fixed, precise meaning." While it is true that
women do exploit the significance of the garment to their own ends, as we
have seen in the example of Tamar and Potiphar's wife, men do as well:
Joseph's brothers seek to reinscribe themselves as favored sons of Jacob by
leading Jacob to believe—by showing him Joseph's bloody coat—that Joseph, the real favored son, is dead. Moreover, it is difficult to find any fixed
or precise meaning attached to any object in the Joseph story; in no incident in the narrative does physical evidence directly represent something
given as fact. The flexibility in attaching referent to sign is exploited
throughout the entire Joseph narrative, and it contributes to one of the
main themes of the story—a point which I will take up below.

Writing with an anthropological approach, Victor Matthews also investigates the significance of clothes in the Joseph narrative. He explores the
acts of both robing and disrobing—giving the gift of clothing and taking it
away—as representative of a deeper status change.[5] Matthews convincingly
argues that clothes function as narratological markers of a change in fortune,
but he does not do justice to the *deceptive* way clothes are used in the Joseph
story. He states that "[Joseph's cloak] is used as evidence of his demise, the
corpus dilecti, convincing Jacob that his son has been killed and eaten by wild
animals," but then goes on to argue that "the loss of the garment, like the
stripping away of insignia from a soldier who is being 'drummed out' of the
military, transforms Joseph from honorable person to a shamed person."[6]
But in fact, the stripping of Joseph occurred much earlier in the story; and
while Joseph does fall from favored son to enslaved outcast, the bloodying
of his coat and the use of it as "evidence of his demise" also suggests the
failure of the coat to symbolize Joseph's true position: it implies that he is
dead, though in reality he is not. Finally, it is not clear that garments hold a
unique position as signifiers of status change. For example, Benjamin's status
changes from free man to slave not by way of a garment, but by the damning
discovery of the divining cup in his bag.

While the examination of the significance of particular objects, such as
garments, illuminates many aspects of the Joseph story, the legal concept of
evidence may help us understand more broadly how the significance of
physical objects is manipulated in this narrative. Physical objects are repeatedly brought to the fore in response to juridical crises. The cup is produced
from Benjamin's sack of grain after Joseph has accused the brothers of theft.
Potiphar's wife produces Joseph's coat in order to support her claim of at-

tempted rape. And, as David Daube contends, the brothers' presentation of Joseph's bloody coat to Jacob served to absolve them of responsibility for Joseph's disappearance.[7]

I believe that these crises are "juridical" not because they take place in a court of law, but because they center on legal, criminal issues: theft, rape, murder. In each case, the evidence proffered is deliberately misleading, the conclusions drawn are false, and guilt (or lack thereof) is wrongly allocated. The Joseph story uses the trope of the presentation of irrefutable, tangible evidence, employed to great effect in the Judah and Tamar story, and destabilizes it, showing over and over again that as simple as the conclusion seems, one cannot trust what the eye sees. Joseph's torn coat seems to represent the fact of his death, but instead it represents only the fact of the brothers' story of his death; the item's "natural" significance has been exploited by deliberate artifice. As a result, there is a miscarriage of justice: responsibility for Joseph's disappearance has been assigned to a wild animal, to happenstance, when it ought to be assigned to the brothers themselves.

In an ironic twist, the brothers do, at the end of the story, accept a displaced guilt: they take communal responsibility for an act they did not commit. They were guilty of selling Joseph, but they were exonerated; they were not guilty of the theft of Joseph's divining cup, but they accept responsibility in an effort to save Benjamin. But just when the scales of justice seem balanced at last, the juridical paradigm radically shifts. We suddenly find out that the brothers are not in fact responsible for the crime they perpetrated after all: Yhwh is. Joseph says to his brothers, "do not be distressed, or angry with yourselves, because you sold me here, for God sent me before you to preserve life. . . . It was not you who sent me here, but God" (Gen. 45: 5, 8). Gerhard Von Rad remarks that in this verse, "the narrator indicates clearly for the first time what is of paramount importance to him in the entire Joseph story: God's hand which directs all the confusion of human guilt ultimately toward a gracious goal."[8]

There is a double deception in this narrative: It is not only the fabricated physical evidence presented by the characters in the narrative that leads other characters to assign responsibility mistakenly, but also the narrative evidence of the story that leads us, the readers, astray. The details of the story lead the reader to believe that certain characters are guilty, that they bear responsibility for their actions: the brothers, Potiphar's wife, and Joseph. We, the readers, are told at the end that we too have been misled—the real responsibility for all the events relayed in the story is God's alone. As allies of the omniscient narrator, this can only unsettle our complacency.

The Joseph story forces the reader to second-guess his or her logical assumption that truth can be gleaned from objective evidence, and to reassess normative biblical discourse in which facts are found and legal cases are easily solved. It forces the reader to confront the troubling idea that the truth, once uncovered, still may not point toward the one who is responsible. The conclusion of this narrative calls the efficacy of evidence into question; it asks whether an easy causal connection may be reliably drawn between sign and referent. It allows for objects to still function as *indices,* as "natural signs," but immediate causes are discarded in favor of the one ultimate cause: the will of Yhwh. Thus the Joseph story paves the way for the beginning of the Exodus narrative, and the signs and wonders that Yhwh performs as proof of his deliverance of the people of Israel. In the exodus narrative, physical objects continue to act as evidence, but they all signify one thing: the mighty hand of the Lord. Judah's staff, which signified his own responsibility in the seduction of Tamar, has been replaced with Moses' staff, which is held up as a sign of God's providence.

I turn now to two stories in the book of Samuel, which thematically parallel the two Genesis stories discussed above, and which center upon the interpretation of evidence and the assigning of responsibility. In the first, truth is hopelessly indeterminate, and the verdict pronounced and the punishment carried out remain open to question; in the second, one finds a return to the acceptance of true guilt and responsibility, but now through different means— not through the presentation of evidence, but through the relating of a narrative.

The book of 2 Samuel begins with an eyewitness report of the deaths of King Saul and his son Jonathan on the battlefield. A nameless Amalekite, claiming to be one who "escaped from the Israelite camp" (2 Sam. 1:3) comes before David, Saul's successor, and tells him the news of Saul's and Jonathan's demise. David does not simply accept this man's version of events; he asks the Amalekite, "How do you know that Saul and Jonathan are dead?" David asks this evidentiary question, and receives a more detailed story from the Amalekite as well as physical proof. The Amalekite answers that he was closer to the events of Saul's death than he first let on; he tells David,

[Saul] said to me, "Come, stand over me and kill me; for convulsions have seized me, and yet my life still lingers." So I stood over him, and killed him, for I knew that he could not live after he had fallen. I took the crown that was on his head and the armlet that was on his arm, and I have brought them here to my lord. (2 Sam. 1:9–10)

After hearing this story, and seeing physical proof of Saul's death, David rhetorically asks the Amalekite, "Were you not afraid to lift your hand to destroy Yhwh's anointed?" (2 Sam. 1:14). Before the Amalekite can defend himself, David has him executed, and justifies his swift judgment by explaining, "Your blood be on your head; for your own mouth has testified against you, saying, 'I have killed Yhwh's anointed'" (2 Sam. 1:16).

The many problems with this narrative have been noticed by ancient and modern readers alike. The most glaring difficulty is the incongruity of the Amalekite's report with the narrator's version of the death scene in the previous chapter, in 1 Samuel 31. Here, the story of Saul's death is told differently:

The battle pressed hard upon Saul; the archers found him, and he was badly wounded by them. Then Saul said to his armor-bearer, "Draw your sword and thrust me through with it, so that these uncircumcised may not come and thrust me through, and make sport of me." But his armor-bearer was unwilling; for he was terrified. So Saul took his own sword and fell upon it. When his armor-bearer saw that Saul was dead, he also fell upon his sword and died with him. So Saul and his three sons and his armor-bearer and all his men died together on the same day. (1 Sam. 31:3–6)

Ancient writers such as Josephus try to harmonize these stories, delineating how the Amalekite could have entered the scene after the armor-bearer refused to kill Saul, and after Saul had attempted suicide unsuccessfully.[9] Many modern scholars seek to reconcile these stories differently, by positing either different writers, each with a different tradition of the story of Saul's death at Mount Gilboa, or only one author who wanted to convey that the Amalekite was a liar.[10] Neither theory is completely satisfactory. The documentary solution is contradicted by some textual evidence which has been fully itemized.[11] The other theory, that the Amalekite was simply a liar, is difficult in two respects. First, it fails to do justice to the details of the text, as there is little intrinsic to this narrative that implies that the Amalekite is being dishonest; in fact, the story includes details that seem to verify the Amalekite's story. Much like David, the reader wonders how, if the Amalekite was innocent of Saul's murder, he came by Saul's crown and armlet. Second, if the Amalekite were a liar, and had not harmed the king, the story leaves us with a glaring injustice: an innocent man has just been executed before he was able to utter any words in his own defense. This is not a problem of the text, per se, but it would drastically alter the meaning of the story: rather than being left with the sense of David's complete fidelity to God's anointed, one reads this story as indicative of David's failure to allow for due process, to let the truth come to light, before implementing a swift and final punishment.

If these theories of the narrative leave us at an impasse, a different approach may be illuminating. Some literary critics of the Bible have allowed the two versions of this narrative to stand side by side, without neutralizing either. Adele Berlin writes:

> We seem to have Saul's death from the narrator's objective point of view, concluding the story of Saul's life, followed by Saul's death from David's point of view, who now deals with Saul in death as he did in life. . . . These viewpoints are combined into a unified, multi-dimensional narrative. The resulting narrative is one with depth and sophistication; one in which conflicting viewpoints may vie for validity. It is this that gives biblical narrative interest and ambiguity.[12]

For Berlin, the narrative of Saul's death, presented in two different ways, is intriguing to the reader because it is not easily harmonized. Hugh Pyper offers another literary interpretation which allows the narrative to remain multi-faceted and unresolved, as Berlin suggests. For Pyper, the story is not about David's fidelity to the king, nor is it about Saul's death; rather, the story is about David as a reader and interpreter.[13] He argues that we know so little about which version of the story is true because "the narrator has no interest in enlightening us. All we know is that the Amalekite's own account lies under a cloud—and that is all we need to know. The important aspect of the story is not what happened, but how it is interpreted."[14] In other words, for Pyper, the facts of the story are never resolved because they are immaterial; he writes that "it is not what the Amalekite *did*, but what he *said*, that becomes his condemnation." Because the Amalekite uttered the fateful words, "*and I killed him,*" David sees fit to administer punishment. As Pyper sees it:

> David is revealed as a skilled practitioner of the art of *anacrisis,* of the eliciting of a response which can be turned against the speaker. This text

offers a model of reading which calls into question the appropriateness of a methodology that seeks to recover the irrecoverable events or sources behind the text, and to assess their reliability and accuracy. Instead it offers a model where an utterance is elicited and the responsibility for the utterance can be turned against a speaker with no regard for his intentions or deeds. The words themselves are enough.[15]

According to Pyper, David is not in this story playing the detective, asking for evidence in order to deduce the truth, the accurate version of events. Rather, he is seeking to place responsibility and does so by eliciting a statement from the Amalekite that may be used as proof of his guilt. It is the Amalekite's words, and not the evidence that he produces, that leads David to have him executed. It is enough for him to have uttered the treasonous "I have killed Yhwh's anointed" to elicit the death penalty. As David himself justifies his actions at the end of the story, "Your blood be on your head; for *your own mouth* has testified against you, saying, 'I have killed Yhwh's anointed'" (2 Sam. 1:16).

Pyper persuasively demonstrates that there is no truth in this episode, only interpretation. David's understanding is the one that ultimately wins, but only because in killing the Amalekite, "David makes sure his own interpretation of these words sticks in the most direct way."[16] But what of the proof? What lingers after the Amalekite's hasty death are the crown and the armlet, the objects that attempted to bring some forensic objectivity into the chaos of the dueling narrative accounts and value-laden interpretations. Much like Joseph's torn and bloody coat, the crown and the armlet are produced as "irrefutable" evidence that Saul is dead, and that the Amalekite's story is corroborated. To serve as evidence, these items must testify to the causal link between a previous event and their now being in the possession of the Amalekite; the Amalekite supplies this link with his words "and I killed him." But this version of events is called into question by the alternate narrative of Saul's death provided in 1 Samuel 31. Furthermore, we do not even find out how David understands the significance of these objects. Unlike the story of Judah and Tamar, in which we are told that Judah "recognized" the evidence, in this narrative we are merely told that "David took hold of his clothes and tore them; and all the men who were with him did the same" (2 Sam. 1:11). It is never made clear in the narrative whether this gesture of mourning is a reaction to seeing the physical evidence of Saul's death, or a reaction to the Amalekite's confession of having killed him. And

David's remarks after having killed the Amalekite, that it was his words that condemned him, indicate that it was not the physical proof that elicited David's judgment. Saul's crown and armlet completely fail as evidence, as they literally have no referent. We have no idea how they wound up in the hands of the Amalekite—the causal connection between them and any real event has been hopelessly obscured.

Nonetheless, as Pyper notes, these items do not fail to signify entirely:

> How [the crown and armlet] arrived in Ziklag is not the point. The very fact that they are there signifies the loss of Saul's power and that it lies within David's grasp. Saul without these signs of power and manifestly without the power to keep them in his possession is dead as a king, whatever his physical state.[17]

In other words, the "natural" correspondence between these items and the event that caused them to be in the hands of the Amalekite is lost, but the "conventional" correspondence between these items and the authority they stand for is vividly present. The handing over of these physical objects thus *symbolizes* the transfer of royal power. In this story, we witness a shift in meaning between the Amalekite's presentation of these items as evidence, and David's acceptance of them as symbol. The Amalekite hopes that David will accept the truth of his claim when he hands over Saul's crown and armlet, but David instead invests himself with all of the royal and judicial authority these items symbolize, and turns around and renders swift judgment.

The story of the Amalekite is left entirely indeterminate as far as the assigning of guilt and responsibility. Who was ultimately responsible for the death of "the Lord's anointed" and the transfer of royal power from Saul to David? Only when we look to the larger narrative of the book of Samuel does a fuller picture emerge. In 1 Samuel 15, the prophet Samuel admonishes Saul for not obeying the precise orders of Yhwh and not destroying all of the spoils after a battle with the Amalekites. With full divine authority behind him, Samuel informs Saul that he has been judged guilty, and as punishment, the monarchy will be wrested away from him and given to another. Samuel pronounces: "rebellion is no less a sin than divination, and stubbornness is like iniquity and idolatry. Because you have rejected the word of Yhwh, he has also rejected you from being king" (1 Sam. 15:23). Acknowledging his guilt, Saul responds, "I have sinned; for I have transgressed the commandment of Yhwh and your words. . . . Now therefore, I pray, pardon my sin, and return with me, so that I may worship Yhwh" (1 Sam. 15:24–25). Samuel, though, is unrelenting, and he turns from Saul, who grasps Samuel's robe and tears it. The striking image of this torn robe becomes a symbol of Saul's irredeemable guilt: Samuel tells Saul, "Yhwh has torn the kingdom of Israel from you this very day, and has given it to a neighbor of yours, who is better than you. Moreover [he] will not recant nor change his mind; for he is not a mortal, that he should change his mind" (1 Sam. 15:28–29). According to this narrative, ultimate responsibility for the death of Saul, along with his sons, and the transfer of the monarchy to David, lies only in Saul himself. The assignment of guilt is unequivocal, as it comes from Yhwh himself, and the interpretation is never challenged, even by Saul, who seeks only to repent. The physical object at the center of this story—Samuel's robe—has no evidentiary power whatsoever, since no facts are called into question. It functions only as a powerful symbol of a kingdom torn away, and which will never be restored.

Nevertheless, the verdict issued by Yhwh through Samuel seems arbitrary and overly severe. Saul never disputes the facts, but he remarks repeatedly that his actions were never intended for evil, only for good. Saul destroyed all the spoil of the defeated Amalekites according to the commandment, but, he says, "the people spared the best of the sheep and the cattle, to sacrifice to Yhwh your God" (1 Sam. 15:15). While Saul's deflecting of responsibility onto "the people" seems patently desperate, his contention that only the best spoils were kept so they could be used to worship the Lord may constitute a legitimate defense. Why does Samuel nonetheless insist that the punishment must stand? Samuel simply does not allow for the possibility of an alternate interpretation of events, a stance which is echoed in his repetition of the very same words after Saul begs him for mercy. Samuel responds by simply reiterating: "you have rejected the word of Yhwh, and Yhwh has rejected you from being king over Israel" (1 Sam. 15:26). In the face of divine judgment, human perspective is deemed fruitless. Saul could not posit an alternate reading of the symbol of Samuel's torn robe, as the interpretation uttered in the prophetic voice obliterates all other possibilities.

If the physical object in biblical literature can serve as the prophetic symbol with one divinely-sanctioned and authoritative meaning, as indeed it does throughout the prophetic books of the Hebrew Bible,[18] how are people meant to interpret the world around them? The legal codes of the Hebrew Bible instruct the people of Israel to appoint judges, listen to testimony, assess evidence, and punish the guilty, but biblical narrative undercuts the sense that such juridical procedures are anything more than provisional. How, then, can true guilt be assigned? The story of David's encounter with Nathan the prophet, after having committed the sins of adultery and murder, provides a model of assigning and accepting responsibility that echoes the Judah and Tamar narrative, though the assigning of guilt comes through the medium of a narrative, a parable, rather than through evidence.

The story of David's sin with Bathsheba is a familiar one. While the Israelites are at war, David, the king, remains in his palace, and seduces the married woman Bathsheba, and impregnates her. When David cannot tempt her husband, Uriah, to return from the front and sleep with his wife, thus covering up Bathsheba's illegitimate pregnancy, he sends word to his general to have Uriah placed in a particularly vulnerable position among the troops, insuring that he would be killed in battle. The plan works, and David then takes Bathsheba as his wife. Shortly afterward, Nathan, a prophet, comes before David, but not immediately with words of divine condemnation, the way Samuel confronted Saul. Rather, Nathan tells David a story:

> There were two men in a certain city, the one rich and the other poor. The rich man had very many flocks and herds; but the poor man had nothing but one little ewe lamb, which he had bought. He brought it up, and it grew up with him and with his children; it used to eat of his meager fare, and drink from his cup, and lie in his bosom, and it was like a daughter to him. Now there came a traveler to the rich man, and he was loath to take one of his own flock or herd to prepare for the wayfarer who had come to him, but he took the poor man's lamb, and prepared that for the guest who had come to him. (2 Sam. 12:1–4)

This narrative provokes an immediate response from David in the form of a judgment: he says, "As Yhwh lives, the man who has done this deserves to die; he shall restore the lamb fourfold, because he did this thing, and because he had no pity" (2 Sam. 12:5–6). Nathan then tells David the true meaning of his story; as Robert Alter puts it, "Nathan's rhetorical trap . . . now snap[s] shut."[19] Nathan tells David, "You are the man!" and then continues by spelling out the divine judgment upon him. David responds by acknowledging his guilt:

"I have sinned against Yhwh" (12:13), he utters, without adding any words in his own defense.

Nathan's parable achieves much the same goal as Judah's signet, cord, and staff did in the Judah and Tamar story—it compels a character to recognize his responsibility to which he was previously blind. In fact, in commenting on Tamar's words "recognize, please," Alter employs the same metaphor he uses to explain Nathan's parable: Tamar's presentation of the evidence, he writes, is "like a trap suddenly springing closed. . . . "[20] A strong parallel can be drawn between these two stories not only because they both end with the acknowledgment of sin, but also because their respective confessions are elicited in functionally similar ways. In both cases, the guilty party is confronted with something that would most readily be interpreted, by the accused and by any third party character or reader, as revealing where true responsibility lies. This may be said to be an evidentiary function, as it lends weight to one particular interpretation of events. Nathan's parable does not create David's guilt, but rather it helps build a case for it. (This would stretch the meaning of evidence, certainly, as even in law it would be considered an analogy or a precedent; but one could easily say that the correctness of a verdict in an easier, analogous case is evidence of the correctness of the same verdict in the more difficult-to-define case).

Uriel Simon, in an article on this biblical passage, identifies the genre of which Nathan's parable is paradigmatic as the "juridical parable." Simon defines the juridical parable as "a realistic story about a violation of the law, related to someone who had committed a similar offence with the purpose of leading the unsuspecting hearer to pass judgment on himself."[21] Simon has been taken to task by other scholars for his classification of Nathan's narrative. George Coats argues that the term "juridical parable" confuses genre, or form, with function. He argues that Nathan's story is a fable, and as such, it is the fable's moral which instructs David. Leaving out any legal or ethical terminology, Coats interprets Nathan's story as follows:

> The rich man had many animals and should have used one of them. He would hardly have missed it. But instead, he used the one lamb of the poor man's family. The irony serves to reduce the rich man to the ridiculous not because the rich man broke a law, but because his act was so extreme. The connection with the application comes not by having David establish a legal precedent for the case involving the rich man, but rather by showing

that the rich man and the man at the point of the comparison in the application are both ridiculous in the eyes of the audience. David confesses, then, not because he has convicted himself legally. That connection does not really fit the context. He confesses because in the eyes of the audience, the witnesses to the parabolic story, he no longer has power to do otherwise. He has been exposed. [22]

Coats' use of the terms "irony" and "ridiculous" serve the interpretation of a fable, but can the rich man in this story really be seen as "ridiculous" rather than hideously unjust? Do the rich man's actions in the story produce a sense of irony rather than a sense of horror? David's reaction to the story is instructive—he reacts by noting the rich man's criminal and civil responsibility: the man must die for his crime; he must pay back fourfold for his theft. In the eyes of the audience, David, like the rich man, is not ridiculous: he is guilty.

Coats' final point, that David has "no power" but to confess because he has been "exposed," implies that only one possible moral may be drawn from Nathan's parable, that only one interpretation may be adduced. Many scholars have pointed out the glaring incongruities between Nathan's parable and David's sin, prompting some even to claim that the parable was derived from a wholly different context. [23] Could David himself not have pointed out similar discrepancies had he wished to defend himself? Could he not have simply exercised his royal authority and cast Nathan from his presence? Much as Judah "recognized" the evidence presented before him, David actively recognizes himself in the parable, and accepts his guilt. Both David and Judah were free not to accept responsibility, but they do so nonetheless.

In order to rescue this narrative from its critical impasse, I would like to recast Simon's definition of the "juridical parable." The story is not "juridical" because it describes a violation of the law or because it leads to a judgment being rendered. It is juridical, rather, because it describes one reality in order to urge the listener to imagine an alternative and to act accordingly. And this may be described as the function of law. Robert Cover, in his seminal essay "Nomos and Narrative," writes, "law may be viewed as a system of tension or a bridge linking a concept of a reality to an imagined alternative—that is, as a connective between two states of affairs." [24] Nathan's parable does not seek to depict "what is" for its own sake; rather, its purpose is to spur a vision of what could be, an effect which is evidenced in David's response to the parable: the rich man deserves punishment "because he had no compassion." The rich man, in the story, clearly has the power to do what he wills, but the parable impels one to imagine a world in which those with power have compassion and act ethically. And, as Cover reveals, the bridge between these two states of affairs is law, is the acceptance of responsibility and paying back what is owed.

Some of Simon's other examples of "juridical parables" do not even fit his own criteria, but they do meet the criteria established here. He refers to the song of the vineyard in Isaiah:

> Let me sing for my beloved my love-song concerning his
> vineyard:
> My beloved had a vineyard on a very fertile hill.
> He dug it and cleared it of stones,
> and planted it with choice vines;
> he built a watchtower in the midst of it,
> and hewed out a wine vat in it;
> he expected it to yield grapes,
> but it yielded wild grapes.
> And now, inhabitants of Jerusalem and people of Judah,
> judge between me and my vineyard.
> What more was there to do for my vineyard that I have not done in
> it?
> When I expected it to yield grapes, why did it yield wild grapes?
> (Isa. 5:1–4)

Simon includes this passage in his study because, as he remarks, "Isaiah . . . sets his audience up as judges."[25] But this parable does not describe a "violation of the law," unless one widens one's category to include a law of nature. Rather, this parable seeks to accomplish precisely what Nathan's parable does: to enjoin the reader to imagine an alternative to the bleak scenario described, and to judge—to accept responsibility for an injustice and to seek to correct it. In this case, the people of Judah are urged to see themselves in the wild grapes, tended to and cared for by God, and, in thus recognizing the injustice of their ways, to reform themselves.

In these biblical passages, the "juridical parable," at times accompanied by the physical symbol, reliably leads to divine truth; conventional evidentiary means of assessing the truth and assigning responsibility are presented as risky and even faulty. The direct appeal to the conscience of the offender intends to provoke a confession of wrongdoing, and this confession is elicited by one with special insight into the truth of the matter—in Genesis, characters intimately connected to the crime and in 2 Samuel and other prophetic literature, a prophet with access to the divine voice. Such an approach assumes a system of justice in which ultimate, divine judgment is the only true arbiter, and divine truth is always eventually available. As biblical narrative undermines standard legal practices, such as reading physical evidence as an index of a crime committed, it supplies us with access to divine omniscience in its stead. Despite vehemently advocating for human jurisprudence, the Hebrew Bible suggests in the end that Yhwh himself is the only reliable path to truth.

Recognizing God in Rabbinic Midrash

How do the rabbis approach biblical narratives which undermine the efficacy of seemingly reliable evidence for drawing conclusions about guilt and responsibility? On the one hand, rabbinic legal literature consistently acknowledges the uncertainty inherent in each judicial decision, as we have seen, but on the other hand, biblical narratives go much farther than the rabbis generally do in utterly undermining human fact finding and decision making in favor of the direct divine voice. Rabbinic commentaries on these stories actually amplify the idea suggested in the biblical text: that physical signs are not reliably connected to the events they purport to signify. But the rabbis suggest that biblical characters have at their disposal other avenues to truth, such as divine inspiration or personal knowledge, that allow them to redress wrongs and admit culpability.

As mentioned above, the Judah and Tamar story in Genesis 38 presents a relatively stable connection between physical evidence and circumstances of the crime: Judah recognizes the staff, cord, and signet that Tamar holds as his own, realizes that he himself is at fault, and admits his wrongdoing. The evidence that Tamar produces appears to reliably connect Judah to the sin of which she is accused. Many rabbinic midrashim that comment on this narrative fill out the juridical aspects of this incident, some even depicting a fully realized courtroom with a panel of judges. Nevertheless, these same midrashim, and others as well, highlight the unreliability of Tamar's evidence, stressing instead the righteousness of Judah's unnecessary confession or the presence of the divine hand working to insure justice.

Christine Hayes examines the midrashic treatment of the Judah and Tamar story, dividing the various midrashim into two categories: "positive portrayals" of Judah and "less positive portrayals."[26] The "positive portrayals" tend to praise Judah for his confession, emphasizing that he saves Tamar's life by admitting his sin. As such, they downplay the role that Tamar's strategic production of hard evidence played in her exoneration. Two of these midrashim typify this understanding of Judah's confession.

> "God has made himself known in Judah" (Ps. 76: 12). This is what is meant in the verse "that which wise men have told and have not withheld from their fathers" (Job 15:18). This refers to Judah, since he confessed and said, "She is more righteous than I" (Gen. 38:26) and did not withhold it from Jacob and Shem who were the judges. And since he saved Tamar and her two sons from the fire, as it is written: "Judah said, 'Take her out and burn her'" (Gen. 38:24), therefore Hananiah, Mishael, and Azariah were saved from the fiery furnace as it is written "Nebuchadnezzar answered saying, 'Blessed be the God of Shadrach, Meshach, and Abednego'" (Dan. 3:28). (*Num. Rab.* 13:4)[27]

This midrash imagines a scene in which judges preside over the dispute between Judah and Tamar, and the judges are understood to be Jacob and Shem, the fathers of Judah and Tamar, as "fathers" are mentioned in the verse from Job. Though the setting is described as a kind of legal tribunal, Judah alone is credited with "saving Tamar . . . from the fire" because he did not withhold the facts of his own involvement in the crime. As Hayes points out, "Judah is praised as wise for confessing his sexual misconduct before his fathers."[28] Indeed, the reward he reaps is twofold: his descendants are saved from the fiery furnace as a kind of measure-for-measure recompense, and "God's name is made known through Judah. This is a reference to Nebuchadnezzar's acknowledgement of the God of Heaven as a result of the miracle wrought for Mishael, Azariah and Hananiah on the basis of Judah's merit."[29]

By so greatly praising Judah's decision to confess, such that the rewards for this act of confession reverberate through generations, this midrash emphasizes two aspects of the narrative which are ambiguous at best in the original biblical narrative: that Judah's confession is entirely voluntary, and that it is only Judah's righteousness that prevents Tamar's execution.[30] The main thrust of the midrash may be to elevate the status of Judah the patriarch, but alongside this interpretive move comes the devaluation of Tamar's trap—the physical evidence of Judah's identity that Tamar made certain to procure. The narrative never makes clear whether the items Tamar produces would only be recognizable to Judah himself, or whether they would have indicted him in the eyes of all those who saw them. In the midrash, this would include even the judges, individuals who themselves may have been able to ascertain the identity of the owner of the signet, cord, and staff. But the midrash does not entertain that possibility; instead, Judah is praised for "not withholding" the facts from Jacob and Shem. These items, in the eyes of the rabbinic authors of this midrash, are significant only in that they prod Judah's conscience and cause him, a virtuous man, to confess.

Another midrash which expresses the same ideas as the one above provides even more of a legal context for Judah's confrontation with Tamar.

> Why did God give the crown [of kingship referring to the Davidic kings and the Davidic Messiah] to Judah? Was he, alone among his brothers, a hero? Were not Simeon and Levi heroes? And the others too? Rather, it was because he judged with true justice in the case of Tamar; hence, he was made the judge of the world [i.e., the King Messiah who will be of Judah's line will be the judge of the world]. It can be likened to the case of a judge before whom was brought the case of an orphan girl and he decided the case in her favor. Similarly with Judah: the case of Tamar came before him that she should be burned, but he decided it in her favor because he found her innocent. How? Isaac and Jacob were sitting there as well as his brothers, condemning her. But Judah recognized his God and spoke the truth of the matter saying, "she is more righteous than I." And [for this] God made him a prince. (*Exod. Rab.* 30:19)[31]

This midrash, like the previous one, takes place in a courtroom, but Judah's function has shifted. Hayes observes that "Judah is portrayed not as the key witness for the defense but as the judge himself. He is (and his progeny are) rewarded with the 'crown of kingship' because he demonstrated in the Tamar incident his ability to 'judge with true justice.'"[32] Judah's praiseworthy act as a judge is not simply strict application of the law to reach the truth; rather,

> Judah is praised for taking the extra effort to seek out some way to acquit Tamar, and he is likened to a judge who labors to acquit the orphan. The passage makes less of the fact that Tamar is indeed innocent of harlotry

and that Judah was the very one to imperil her than it does of the claim that Judah went to extraordinary lengths to declare her innocence, despite the urgings of his 'advisors' (Isaac and Jacob!) to condemn her.[33]

The midrash is able to turn Judah's contrition before Tamar's incriminating evidence into a heroic legal act of acquittal by rereading one key phrase: "and Judah recognized and said . . ." (Gen. 38:26). In the context of the biblical narrative, Judah recognizes his personal items which Tamar has produced; in the midrash, no mention of these items is made—Judah recognizes "*lamaqom*," his God, and thus discerns the truth. Whereas in the biblical narrative Judah is trapped by the physical evidence presented before him into admitting his complicity, in the midrash Judah's greatness is precisely in seeing a truth that lies hidden behind all appearances to the contrary. Judah's involvement in Tamar's crime—as well as the evidence of this involvement—is curiously missing from this account of events. The only access to "true justice" lies in recognizing the divine truth instead of relying upon what appearances suggest—a message that is hardly present in the biblical account of Judah and Tamar.

The above midrashim downplay the role of Tamar's production of evidence as a trap for Judah in order to more greatly elevate Judah's virtue. However, even the "less positive" portrayals of Judah diminish the importance of Tamar's evidence in provoking Judah's admission. One midrash, which has many textual variants, relates that Judah's confession was provoked primarily by divine revelation:

> R. Jeremiah said in the name of R. Samuel b. R. Isaac: The Holy One, blessed be He, revealed Himself in three places: in the courts of Shem, Samuel, and Solomon. In the court of Shem: *and Judah acknowledged them, and said: she is more righteous than I* (*mimmeni*), which R. Jeremiah interpreted in the name of R. Samuel b. R. Isaac: It was the Holy Spirit that exclaimed, From Me (*mimmeni*) did these things occur. . . . (*Gen. Rab.* 85:12)[34]

This midrash reinterprets the word "*mimmeni*" which occurs in Judah's admission. Hayes explains the grammatical ambiguity exploited by this midrash in the context of clarifying the translation choices of the ancient Targums:

> There is no comparative adjective in Hebrew. . . . Instead the comparative is expressed by the regular adjective or verb form plus the comparative

preposition *mn*-(lit. "from," also "than"). The lack of a grammatical form for the comparative adjective provides an opportunity for a radically different comprehension of the phrase *ṣdqh mmny*, as exemplified in the Aramaic translation of Onkelos. Rather than grasping the two words as integral units in a comparative construction ("she is more right[eous] than I"), Onkelos assumes a break between the two words. The result is a speech consisting of two sentences: first, the verb denominative *ṣdqh*, "She is right[eous]/innocent," followed by the prepositional phrase *mmny*, "from me. . . ."[35]

Onkelos understands both of these phrases as spoken by Judah, each representing a different element of his confession: (1) she is innocent (2) from me [she conceived]. The midrash, however, understands at least the latter phrase, as spoken by the divine voice, the holy spirit, who declares "from me did these things occur," showing Judah that there was a higher purpose to all of the confusion of responsibility and sin between Judah and Tamar, and that Tamar is innocent of wrongdoing. Again, the emphasis is placed on the special divine insight offered to Judah which makes him see Tamar's righteousness, rather than the evidence presented before his eyes.

A version of this midrash found in the Babylonian Talmud explicitly addresses the discrepancy between the biblical version of how Judah recognizes Tamar's righteousness and the version in the midrash:

> R. Eleazar said: In three places the Holy Spirit [more commonly, *bat qol*] appeared—in the court of Shem, in the court of Samuel, and in the court of Solomon. In the court of Shem as it is written, "Judah recognized and said, 'She is more righteous than I.' How did he know? Perhaps the woman who was with him gave her [the signet, cord, and staff] and another man had been with her [Tamar]. But a *bat qol* came forth and said, 'From me come forth secrets.'" (*b. Mak.* 23b)[36]

This midrash explicitly questions the reliability of the evidence presented by Tamar, arguing that a divine pronouncement was necessary. The signet, cord, and staff in Tamar's possession may belong to Judah, but that is no proof that he was her partner in sexual misconduct. The midrash shows that there is room for reasonable doubt: perhaps one prostitute traded pledges with another. Thus, as Hayes explains, "the *bat qol* has a specific function in the court proceedings. It is the *bat qol* and not the evidence of the three pledge objects that convinces Judah that he is the father of the children and that Tamar is innocent of the charge of harlotry."[37] Indeed, the gap between the unreliable physical evidence produced by Tamar and the incontrovertible truth of the divine revelation is highlighted in one of the variants of the *Genesis Rabbah* text; here, the *bat qol* differentiates its own evidence from Tamar's by stating, "you testify as to what is apparent but I will testify concerning him as to what is hidden."[38]

This midrash does not portray Judah as heroically confessing to save Tamar from the fire; instead,

> [d]espite excellent evidence of Tamar's innocence (the three pledges) Judah apparently still finds it possible to suspect his daughter-in-law of harlotry and is not willing to "shame" himself publicly and save her life until he has it on higher authority that he is indeed the responsible party.[39]

In other words, Judah is presented as a typical defendant who seeks alternative interpretations of evidence which tends to condemn him. This same idea is expressed in another midrash in *Genesis Rabbah*:

> *She sent to her father-in-law, saying: by the man whose these are am I with child.* He wished to deny it, whereupon she said to him: "Recognize your creator in these, for they are yours and your creator's." (*Gen. Rab.* 85:11)

Here, Judah is again portrayed as a defendant who "wishes to deny" his complicity until Tamar forces him to look beyond the evidence itself. The midrash reinterprets her words "recognize, please . . ." to mean not only "recognize these items as your own" (which may be redundant, considering she has already stated that she is pregnant by the owner of these items which Judah would surely identify), but also "recognize your God through these items and know the moral truth."

How the signet, cord, and staff are evidence of God's hand in these events may be understood in the same sense as the *bat qol* which announces "from me did these things occur"—Tamar may be urging Judah to understand that her possession of his personal items should be taken as a sign that God had orchestrated the entire scenario, and therefore Judah should not be ashamed to admit the truth. Alternatively, this midrash may refer to the one immediately preceding it in Gen. Rabbah which demonstrates divine providence in this narrative by once again severing the link between the pledges Tamar produces and Judah's complicity:

When she was brought forth (38:25). R. Judan said: They [the signet, cord, and staff] had been lost, and the Holy One, blessed be He, provided others in their place, the word having the same meaning as in the verse, "Or have found that which was lost" (Lev. 5:22). (*Gen. Rab.* 85:11)

R. Judan's interpretation is based on his reading of the word "*mwṣʾt*," which is usually understood as a passive participle: "she was found / brought forth." In the midrash, however, R. Judan vocalizes this verb as an active participle (*moṣʾet* instead of *muṣʾet*), and reads the verse "When she found [the pledges] she sent to her father-in-law, saying, by the man to whom these belong I am with child. . . . " This is actually a rather fluid reading of the verse, considering that the pledges are the subject of Tamar's subsequent statement, but if she is said to "find" the pledges one may infer that they had been lost; this implication allows R. Judan to imagine a scenario in which Tamar had lost her key evidence, but God, in his divine benevolence, provided her with identical copies. Thus Tamar is able to say to Judah "recognize your creator in these" literally, because these are not the same objects which Judah had left behind, but instead replicas fashioned by the divine hand.

These midrashim in *Genesis Rabbah* strongly suggest a juridical proceeding as the context for the confrontation between Judah and Tamar: the setting is said to be "the court of Shem"; Judah "wishes to deny" his involvement in the crime; and Tamar's evidence serves as a rebuttal. Each facet of the incident, however, is shifted away from human control and authority (implied in the biblical text) and towards a more active divine providence and intervention. First, the causal link between Judah's act and the evidence Tamar presents is severed: the pledges are lost, and thus no longer bear witness as *indices* to Judah's deed; in contemporary legal parlance, we might say that the chain of custody is broken. To make up for this failure of physical evidence (it is lost), God intervenes and supplies exact replicas of Judah's pledges. Second, Judah still attempts to deny his involvement in Tamar's misconduct because the evidence may be interpreted differently: she could have obtained them from another prostitute. Physical evidence fails yet again, because even if chain of custody is presumed and the actual objects are present, one may interpret their presence in a variety of ways. This problem is overcome again by divine assistance: either Tamar's urging Judah to recognize God's hand as the "creator" of the identical signet, cord, and staff, or as a divine voice itself telling Judah the truth. Finally, the connection between Judah's pledges in Tamar's possession and Judah's moral or legal culpability is lessened as well—"she is more righteous than I" is changed from a comparative, which suggests Judah's guilt, to a statement about Tamar's culpability only (that she is innocent) and another statement that all of these events have proceeded from God. Judah is no longer trapped by evidence into admitting his guilt, but instead is rendered a mere pawn in a divine plan to grant Tamar offspring. Humans' ability to assess the facts and assign responsibility is hopelessly flawed in these midrashim, but divine providence is clear and manifest, and it paves the way for a just and right outcome.

This midrashic approach to the Judah and Tamar story echoes the biblical conclusion to the Joseph story—specifically, Joseph's words to his brothers that they are not responsible for the sequence of events that has occurred ("do not be distressed, or angry with yourselves, because you sold me here, for God sent me before you to preserve life. . . . It was not you who sent me here, but God," Gen. 45: 5, 8). But the rabbis insist that though God has orchestrated all of these events for the greater good, the characters are still judged by their actions, and need to accept responsibility and admit culpability.

The midrashim that comment on the Joseph story still recognize that the human players require divine assistance to perceive truth, and they are not so easily led astray by false evidence as they are in the biblical narrative. Nevertheless, the midrash does not gloss over the characters' moral failings by allowing God's providence to stand as the final word, but rather see divine insight as a means to a juridical end.

The first presentation of physical evidence occurs when Joseph's brothers attempt to convince their father, by showing him Joseph's bloody coat, that Joseph has been killed by a wild animal. The midrash in *Genesis Rabbah* reads:

> *And he recognized it, and said: it is my son's coat* (37:33). He said to him [Judah]: "I do not know what I see: *It is my son's coat; an evil beast has devoured him.*"—R. Huna said: The holy spirit was enkindled in him: *an evil beast has devoured him*—this is Potiphar's wife. (*Gen. Rab.* 84:19)[40]

According to this midrash, Jacob is not easily duped by Joseph's bloody coat before him; he is momentarily confused before the holy spirit is enkindled in him and he is able to see through the false evidence into the truth. In the biblical story, Jacob's words testify to the success of the brothers' ruse; he states precisely what the brothers would have him believe, that "it is my son's coat; a wild beast has devoured him." In the midrash, however, this moment is completely inverted: Jacob's immediate recognition is converted into complete bewilderment ("I do not know what I see"),[41] and his false conclusions are replaced with a prophetic insight into the future (that Potiphar's wife will "devour" Joseph, will cause his downfall). What is telling about this midrash is that Jacob never arrives at a false conclusion about Joseph; the holy spirit does not reveal to Jacob that the evidence is unreliable, but rather verifies his instinctive sense that something is not right with an insight into the truth. In other words, Jacob does not see through the brothers' ruse because he has divine assistance—the holy spirit is not with him but "enkindled" in him (the Hebrew word used is "*niṣneṣah*," the root *NṢṢ* signifying "to blossom" or "to germinate," denoting the emergence of something new which had not been there before). In the biblical story the brothers' evidence is conclusive, but in the midrash it provokes uncertainty. In the biblical story God's plan is not revealed until the end; in the midrash divine truth is linked to fatherly intuition and alerts Jacob to Joseph's endangerment.

The next pivotal episode in the Joseph narrative in which physical evidence plays a key role, referenced in the previous midrash, is the story of Joseph and Potiphar's wife. As described above, the wife of Potiphar accuses Joseph of attempted rape, and she tells her husband (Joseph's master) her version of events while still in possession of Joseph's tunic. In fact, the text highlights the importance of this evidence by specifically remarking that "she laid his garment by her, until his lord came home" (Gen. 38:16). In the biblical story, Potiphar appears to easily believe his wife's story, reacting quickly and emotionally: "When his master heard the words that his wife spoke to him, saying, 'This is what your servant did to me,' he became enraged. And Joseph's master took him, and put him in prison" (Gen. 39:19–20). These verses appear to further a rather simple story: Potiphar's wife attempts to seduce Joseph; she is rebuffed but grabs hold of his tunic; she manufactures a story in which Joseph is the attempted seducer rather than herself; her story is believed and Joseph, the slave, is sent to prison. The language of the text, however, is laconic. Nowhere does the narrator state explicitly that the men of the house, or even her own husband, believe her story. The text does not even specify that Potiphar's anger is directed at Joseph; we are told that Potiphar "becomes enraged" after hearing his wife's claim, and then that Joseph is put in prison. The midrash exploits these ambiguities and shifts the sense of the narrative:

> *And Joseph's master took him, and put him into the prison* (39:20). "I know that this is not your [fault]," he assured him, "but [I must do this] lest a stigma fall upon my children." (*Gen. Rab.* 87:9)

The midrash accounts for two incongruities in the line "Joseph's master *took him* and put him in *prison*": (1) that Joseph is apparently personally escorted by his master (a man of stature) to prison and (2) that Joseph, a lowly slave, believed to have attempted to violate the honor of his master's wife, is merely put in prison instead of being executed. The midrash creates a scenario in which Joseph's master Potiphar personally escorts him to prison in order to confide in him that he holds no ill will toward him, that he does not believe that he is at fault, and that his motivations for incarcerating Joseph are different from what he might have assumed. Potiphar opts for a lenient punishment because he does not believe that Joseph is a malefactor. According to this midrash's version of events, Potiphar immediately sees through his wife's charade, but he publicly goes along with her story so that his children will not be stigmatized when they discover that their mother is both a liar and a would-be adulterer.

The midrash does not reveal how Potiphar is able to see through his wife's manipulations—why he trusts Joseph's innocence more than his wife's report and the evidence she wields. One gets the sense that Potiphar knows his wife's character and does not trust her, which is the best explanation for why he could be certain of a slave's innocence. This knowledge (the Aramaic reads *yeda°ana°*) trumps his wife's report and even the evidence of Joseph's tunic; he does not seem to give this evidence a second thought. Joseph's tunic, which appears in the biblical story as the instrument of Joseph's undoing, the "objective" proof that Potiphar's wife's story was true, now appears in the midrash as immaterial compared to past personal experience. The "legal" truth that evidence is meant to establish is outdone by personal knowledge, a sensibility that persists despite the proof presented.

One midrash directly points out the fallacy of relying upon physical evidence in reaching conclusions about events and guilt, pointing out the importance of personal character knowledge instead. When Joseph's planted divining cup is discovered in Benjamin's sack, the biblical story continues, "they [the brothers] tore their clothes, and loaded every man his ass, and returned to the city" (Gen. 44:13). The brothers rend their clothes because they realize that they will lose their younger brother; once the incriminating evidence is found, it becomes clear that Benjamin will be taken into servitude in Egypt. But does the divining cup ever actually serve as evidence? Does it lead anyone to believe that Benjamin actually stole it, or does it function merely as a token in a game in which everyone is forced to participate? The servant whom Joseph sends to plant the cup is in on the deception; the brothers' previous experience of finding silver in their sacks might lead them to recognize a pattern of things being planted among their possessions. On the other hand, perhaps the brothers do perceive the divining cup as evidence of a crime—perhaps they tear their clothes not only because Benjamin must now become a slave, but because they are led to believe that their brother is a thief. The midrash comments:

> *And the goblet was found in Benjamin's sack.* When it was thus found they exclaimed to him: "What! You are the thief and the son of a thief!" [alluding to Rachel's theft of her father's household idols, cf. Gen. 31:34]. To which he retorted, "Have we a he-goat here? We have here brothers who sold their brother." (*Gen. Rab.* 92:8)

This midrash pointedly demonstrates that those who bear sin should not throw stones—those of questionable character ought not to be quick to defame the character of others. Most significant for our purposes, however, is that the midrash conveys this lesson through the focus on the fallibility of evidence. The midrash comments not on the verse in which the brothers tear their clothes as they realize what has occurred, but rather on the passage in which the evidence of the cup is found—the brothers' accusation represents their immediate reaction to the evidence, a kind of legal deduction, as it precedes their mournful gesture. Moreover, Benjamin begins his response to the brothers' accusation with "have we a he-goat here?" This remark overtly connects not the machinations of deception but the objects themselves—the evidence of the cup and the evidence of Joseph's coat. Thus Benjamin urges the brothers to recognize the inherent spuriousness of this evidence by relating it to their own first-hand experience with misleading evidence. Benjamin's assertion stands as the last word in the midrash.

The rabbinic interpreters comment on every pivotal juridical moment in the Joseph story in which physical evidence is manipulated, and they underscore the biblical narrative's message that one cannot trust what the eye sees. The biblical story presents characters who assign responsibility to the wrong people because they are misled by fabricated evidence; later, they discover that God alone bears ultimate responsibility for the course of events. In the midrash, the characters never wrongly assign blame— they are caught in the confusion of different sources of knowledge and, at times, personal guilt that they would rather not recall. God's role in the biblical narrative is ultimately to absolve all the characters of culpability, as he appears as the invisible hand behind the humans' missteps, guiding them toward a hidden goal. But in the midrash, God's role is to help the characters see the complete truth in the moment: to clear up confusion, to reveal deeper significances of events, and to stir the conscience of those who are in the wrong so that they recognize their own accountability.

A midrashic interpretation of the confrontation between the brothers and Joseph after the discovery of the divining cup seizes upon this moment of reckoning to account for the real guilt of the brothers which is unrelated to Joseph's evidentiary ruse. When the brothers are brought before Joseph to account for stealing the divining cup, Judah speaks for them: "What shall we say to my lord? What shall we speak? How shall we justify ourselves? God has found out the iniquity of your servants . . ." (Gen. 44:16). Judah essentially grovels before Joseph, humbling himself and admitting guilt in order to appeal for clemency in an impossible situation. The midrash utilizes the redundancy of Judah's rhetorical questions and the ambiguity of the term "my lord" to develop a three-fold interpretation of this passage:

> And Judah said: what shall we say unto my lord in respect of the first money; what shall we speak in respect of the second money; how shall we clear ourselves in the matter of the cup. What shall we say unto the Lord in the matter of Tamar; what shall we speak in the matter of Bilhah; how shall we clear ourselves in the matter of Dinah. What shall we say to our father in Canaan in respect of Joseph; what shall we speak in respect of Simeon; how shall we clear ourselves in respect of Benjamin. We shall not say that we have sinned, for behold it is known and manifest that we did not sin. [And if we say that we did not sin,] God has found out the iniquity of your servants. (Gen. Rab. 92:9)[42]

Judah's questions, in the biblical text, are rhetorical, and tantamount to an acknowledgment of guilt before Joseph. In the midrash, these questions are genuine and represent the quandary in which the brothers find themselves; they have been trapped by their past misdeeds into a confusing puzzle of guilt and innocence. Each of the three questions, according to the midrash, addresses a different act of one or more of the brothers, and the full set of questions may be understood on three distinct levels. The first attends to the brothers' immediate situation before Joseph and addresses the three crimes of which they were suspected: the first money found in their sacks, the second money, and the divining cup. Of these crimes, the brothers are innocent—Joseph had planted the evidence. The second level of meaning takes Judah's words "my lord" to imply the divine Lord; the sins before God all involve sexual misconduct, and of these the brothers are guilty. The third way in which "my lord" may be understood is as their father, Jacob; here, the brothers have deprived Jacob of three of his sons, and they are to blame for his emotional anguish. Although the brothers collectively are responsible for six different sins, none has suffered penalty or been brought to justice. Thus the brothers, with Judah as their spokesperson, are stymied when they are forced to account for their deeds. If they say they are guilty, it will be clear to all in the room that they are not telling the truth, since the servants of Joseph are the very ones who planted the evidence. If they say they are innocent, since they are in fact innocent of the present charges, they are exposed as liars before God because of their past misconduct; the verse continues: "God has found out the iniquity of your servants."

The quandary the brothers face reveals that according to this midrash, justice is complex, and guilt and innocence are neither binary nor limited to immediate circumstances. The responsibility assigned by fellow humans is shown to be flawed because of both the unreliability of evidence and individuals' various motivations for lying, deceiving, or misdirecting punishment. But personal guilt may nonetheless be recognized through the eye of the divine, as well as from the perspective of loved ones who have been hurt by our conduct. In this sense, the midrashic interpretation of the Joseph story differs quite significantly from the biblical moral: rather than God taking responsibility and directing the course of human events "to a gracious goal," human characters are allowed to flounder and deceive while truth becomes manifest through the conscience, through sincere introspection, through personal knowledge that cannot be proved or demonstrated. This private knowledge, this inner conviction, is linked with divine inspiration and ultimate, substantive truth.

The midrashic interpretations of these narratives in Genesis echo the stories about Saul and David, discussed above, in which crimes are recognized not by listening to testimony and sorting through physical evidence but by a confrontation with divine truth. The difference, however, is that for rabbinic midrashim there is no prophet and no "juridical parable"— there is only the individual will to recognize the creator by introspecting and inquiring into one's deeds. What is consistent throughout these midrashim is that the divine presence always is manifest in the realm of the *personal*—it jogs Judah's conscience rather than directly acquitting Tamar; it deals Jacob special foreknowledge rather than accusing the brothers outright. In the midrashim there is no confrontation with a judging prophet, no intermediary—the divine truth appears to directly suffuse the human mind. Moreover, unlike in the Saul and David stories, in which divine insight into responsibility leads directly to divine punishment, in the rabbinic midrashim guilt is not immediately rectified by divinely imposed penance. Thus the midrash does recognize a realm of divine truth that surpasses all human discernment, and it is a juridically encoded truth: the truth of guilt or innocence, liability or exemption. But these divine verdicts do not necessarily imply the attainment of perfect justice. Individuals are left to struggle with their culpability on their own.

Divine Providence and Inner Conviction

After having inflicted nine plagues upon the people of Egypt, Yhwh announces the final anguish the Egyptians will endure, a measure-for-measure retribution for the monstrous policy of drowning newborn Hebrew boys in the Nile:

> About midnight I will go out through Egypt. Every firstborn in the land of Egypt shall die, from the firstborn of Pharaoh who sits on his throne to the firstborn of the female slave who is behind the handmill. . . . Then there will be a loud cry throughout the whole land of Egypt, such as has never been or will ever be again. (Ex. 11:4–6)

In the Babylonian Talmud, the rabbis are vexed by a trivial detail in this story:

> It is written: *About midnight I will go out into the midst of Egypt.* Why "about midnight"? Shall we say that the Holy One, blessed be He, said to [Moses]: "About midnight"? Can there be any doubt in the mind of God? Hence we must say that God told him "at midnight," and [Moses] came and said: "About midnight." (*b. Ber.* 3b)

The rabbis insist that God's truth must be perfect—it cannot be at all imprecise. But the moment God's impending, exacting retaliation is conveyed to Moses, uncertainty is transmitted as well. Moses simply cannot replicate God's unyielding truth, his "*at* midnight." For Moses, the justice imposed on the Egyptians can only be approximate; he hears, and repeats, "*about* midnight."

We have seen that in legal texts, the Hebrew Bible exhibits confidence in human decision making, allowing the appeal to divine omniscience for help with implementing perfectly proportional justice in alignment with absolute, substantive truth. Including narrative in our assessment of the Hebrew Bible's rhetoric of human judgment, however, reveals a deep skepticism about the human ability to discern the truth, and the sense that God's perfect plan for the world triumphs regardless of human contrivances.

Rabbinic literature, on the other hand, utilizes the language of law to authorize the truth of judicial decisions, and admits to perpetual uncertainty regarding substantive reality. Nevertheless, through the meticulous elaboration of evidence law, the rabbis strive to apply divine law appropriately if provisionally. When we turn to rabbinic *aggadah*, we find that though evidence and interpretation remain central concerns, they do not provide the language through which God is encountered or truth is represented. Rabbinic law elicits heated debate, strong conviction, and authoritative pronouncements; legal truth is determined. But the substantive, absolute truth is accessed ultimately through a less procedural, more intimate encounter with God. This divine truth is felt and experienced, not demonstrated or proven. What the rabbis ultimately recognize—and what gives shape to their juridical landscape—is that they were confined to a world that would always yield a paler, more decidedly earth-bound version of the more exalted and elusive divine truth. In the tension between feeling and verification, experience and proof, the rabbis authoritatively shape Jewish law and religion by negotiating between human limitations and the divine standards. The fallible system of law they construct stands beside the call for the individual encounter with a deeply felt divine truth.

NOTES

Introduction

The epigraph is from Charles Nesson, "Theories of Inference and Adjudication: Agent Orange Meets the Blue Bus: Factfinding at the Frontier of Knowledge," *Boston University Law Review* 66 (1986): 521.

1. All translations of the Hebrew Bible are based on the New Revised Standard version, with some modifications for consistency of terminology or a more literal sense of the Hebrew.

2. Robert R. Wilson, "Israel's Judicial System in the Preexilic Period," *Jewish Quarterly Review* 74 (1983): 229–248.

3. See Steven D. Fraade, "Priests, Kings, and Patriarchs: Yerushalmi Sanhedrin in its Exegetical and Cultural Settings," in *The Talmud Yerushalmi in Graeco-Roman Culture*, ed. Peter Schäfer and Catherine Hezser (Tubingen: Mohr Siebeck, 1998), 332 where Fraade suggests that the rabbis saw the priests as rivals to their and the Patriarch's authority. Also see his n. 53 which contains a valuable bibliography on priests as leaders after the destruction of the Temple.

4. Steven D. Fraade, *From Tradition to Commentary: Torah and Its Interpretation in the Midrash Sifre to Deuteronomy* (Albany: State University of New York Press, 1991): 148, 156.

5. This verse from Psalms is both challenging to translate and nearly impossible to make sense of in a monotheistic context because of the various uses and permutations of the term "god," or "*el*." Originally, this verse probably described the polytheistic court of El, the supreme god, who was enthroned among the other gods. But the rabbis, as strict monotheists, understood, in this case and others, the word "*elohim*" to mean "judges," while taking the singular El to mean God. They interpret this verse, then, not as a description of the heavens but as a depiction of a human court over which the one God presides.

6. Though too complex to be taken up in these pages, Paul's attitude toward the law (especially as discussed in Romans) may be similar—or perhaps even be a precedent—to this rabbinic sentiment, echoing the idea that as "no human being will be justified in His sight by deeds prescribed by the law" (Romans 3:20), one therefore desires to live apart from the law.

7. The full passage reads as follows:

[Jehoshaphat] appointed judges in the land in all the fortified cities of Judah, city by city, and said to the judges, "Consider what you are doing, for you judge not on behalf of human beings but on Yhwh's behalf; he is with you in giving judgment. Now, let the fear of Yhwh be upon you; take care what you do, for there is no perversion of justice with Yhwh our God, or partiality, or taking of bribes." (2 Chronicles 19:5–7)

8. The use of masculine pronouns, throughout this book, for judges, witnesses, and subjects of the law simply reflects a rabbinically imagined society in which women could not have served as judges or witnesses, and would not generally have been owners of property or possessors of rights. To use more gender-neutral language is to obscure the patriarchal attitudes of rabbinic culture.

9. To be sure, rabbinic literature does not provide us with any case law—in fact, rabbinic law may never have been enforced as a legal system in the fullest sense. Seth Schwartz has shown that:

It is . . . counterintuitive to think that the Romans granted official status to the patriarchs and their rabbinic protégés after 70 or 135. To be sure, the government did nothing to prevent Jews from patronizing their native legal experts for advice and arbitration. Yet by failing to recognize their jurisdiction, they made them effectively powerless to compete with the Roman courts and the arbitration of Jewish city councilors and landowners for most purposes (Seth Schwartz, *Imperialism and Jewish Society: 200 B.C.E. to 640 C.E.* [Princeton, N.J.: Princeton University Press, 2001], 111).

Nonetheless, the rabbis certainly put into practice much of Jewish law they propounded, regardless of how limited their jurisdiction as far as the Jewish community in general; and they certainly approached the law they studied as an intended social practice, a means to live by one's convictions. And therefore we find moments in rabbinic literature which are not necessarily integrated into a systematic historical record which depict or anticipate acts of judgment, which attempt to contend with the exigencies of the real world and which illuminate the practical commitments of rabbinic jurisprudence.

10. Peter Brooks, *Troubling Confessions: Speaking Guilt in Law and Literature* (Chicago: University of Chicago Press, 2000), 4.

11. Pierre Bourdieu, "The Force of Law: Toward a Sociology of the Juridical Field," *Hastings Law Journal* 38.5 (1987): 805–853.

12. Daniel Boyarin, *Carnal Israel: Reading Sex in Talmudic Culture* (Berkeley: University of California Press, 1993), 10–18. On the profound influence of Boyarin's work on the field of rabbinic literature, see Charlotte Fonrobert, "On *Carnal Israel* and the Consequences: Talmudic Studies Since Foucault," *Jewish Quarterly Review* 95.3 (2005): 462–469.

13. Boyarin, *Carnal Israel*, 15. Other recent works which have used a similar approach to rabbinic legal texts include Aryeh Cohen, *Rereading Talmud: Gender, Law, and the Poetics of Sugyot* (Atlanta, Ga.: Scholars Press, 1998); Judith Hauptman, *Rereading the Rabbis: A Woman's Voice* (Boulder, Colo.: Westview, 1998) and Charlotte

Fonrobert, *Menstrual Purity: Rabbinic and Christian Reconstructions of Biblical Gender* (Stanford, Calif.: Stanford University Press, 2000).

14. Jeffrey Rubenstein, *Talmudic Stories: Narrative Art, Composition, and Culture* (Baltimore, Md.: Johns Hopkins University Press, 1999); Rubenstein cites Ofra Meir as a predecessor in this work.

15. Steven Fraade, "Navigating the Anomalous: Non-Jews at the Intersection of Early Rabbinic Law and Narrative" in *The Other in Jewish Thought and History: Constructions of Jewish Culture and Identity*, ed. Laurence J. Silberstein and Robert L. Cohn (New York: New York University Press, 1994): 145–165 and "'The Torah of the King' (Deut. 17:14–20) in the Temple Scroll and Early Rabbinic Law" in *The Dead Sea Scrolls as Background to Postbiblical Judaism and Early Christianity*, ed. James R. Davila. Studies on the Texts of the Desert of Judah (Leiden: Brill, 2003): 25–62. Moshe Simon-Shoshan's recent dissertation also takes on the interconnections between law and narrative in the Mishnah: Moshe Simon-Shoshan, "Halachah LeMa'aseh: Narrative and Legal Discourse in the Mishnah" (Ph.D. diss., University of Pennsylvania, 2005).

16. Christine Hayes examines both the authority of the rabbis—and the anxiety they experienced over wielding it—in "Authority and Anxiety in the Talmuds: From Legal Fiction to Fact" in *Jewish Religious Leadership: Image and Reality* v.1, ed. Jack Wertheimer (New York: Jewish Theological Seminary, 2004), 127–154, and "Rabbinic Contestations of Authority," *Cardozo Law Review* 28.1 (2006): 123–141. Beth Berkowitz reads death penalty discourse in Tractate *Sanhedrin* as instrumental in the rabbinic construction of authority: Beth A. Berkowitz, *Execution and Invention: Death Penalty Discourse in Early Rabbinic and Christian Cultures* (New York: Oxford University Press, 2006). Ishay Rosen-Zvi's recent dissertation does the same with regard to the issue of the suspected adulteress, or *Sotah;* Ishai Rosen-Zvi, "The Ritual of the Suspected Adulteress (Sotah) in the Tannaitic Literature: Textual and Theoretical Perspectives," (Ph.D. diss., Tel-Aviv University, 2004). Both Elizabeth Alexander and Natalie Dohrman discuss legal rhetoric in terms of rabbinic ideology and authority: Elizabeth Shanks Alexander, *Transmitting Mishnah: The Shaping Influence of Oral Tradition* (New York: Cambridge University Press, 2006); Natalie Dorhmann, "The Boundaries of the Law and the Problem of Jurisdiction in Early Palestinian Midrash," in *Rabbinic Law in its Roman and Near Eastern Context*, ed. Catherine Hezser (Tübingen: Mohr Siebeck, 2003), 83–104.

17. Jonathan Wyn Schofer, *The Making of a Sage: A Study in Rabbinic Ethics* (Madison: University of Wisconsin Press, 2005), 180, n. 19. Along these lines we must also include the important work of Yair Lorberbaum, *Image of God: Halakha and Aggadah* (Tel Aviv: Schocken Publishing House, 2004).

18. As Steven Fraade comments, "after the cessation of prophecy and the canonization of Torah, collective access to the . . . word of God continues through the redacted texts and social institutions of rabbinic Torah study." Fraade, *From Tradition to Commentary*, 65.

19. Fraade, *From Tradition to Commentary*, 162.

20. Ibid., 115.

21. Along such lines, David Stern notes that in face of the polysemy of the biblical text, the rabbis uphold "a principle of jurisprudence . . . justif[ied] midrashically through an interpretation of Ex[odus] 23:2, 'after the majority incline.' . . . [T]he

halakha is decided by following the opinion of the majority of sages." David Stern, *Midrash and Theory: Ancient Jewish Exegesis and Contemporary Literary Studies* (Evanston, Ill.: Northwestern University Press, 1996), 25.

22. Moshe Halbertal, *People of the Book: Canon, Meaning, and Authority* (Cambridge, Mass.: Harvard University Press, 1997), 54. This perspective has persisted and has possibly intensified throughout the medieval and modern periods so much so that it has become somewhat of a contemporary orthodoxy; one recent scholar of Jewish law laments, "the divinity of the law would, one should think, presuppose its certainty" [Haim Cohn, *Jewish Law in Ancient and Modern Israel* (New York: Ktav, 1971), x].

23. Steven Fraade convincingly argues, contra Boyarin, that the rabbinic stance of polysemy with regard to scripture and a pragmatic decision to follow the majority are evidenced in tannaitic texts as well as the Babylonian Talmud. See Steven Fraade, "Rabbinic Polysemy and Pluralism Revisited: Between Praxis and Thematization," *AJS Review* 31.1 (2007): 1–40.

24. Joel Roth notes that the rabbis find a way to overrule "objective truth" by "interpret[ing a] Deuteronomic passage to mean that, as . . . empowered authorities . . . , they have the right to interpret the Torah normatively, even to the point of an apparently erroneous interpretation." Joel Roth, *The Halakhic Process: A Systematic Analysis* (New York: Jewish Theological Seminary, 1986), 122. The passage Roth refers to is Deut 17:9–11: "When they have announced to you the verdict in the case, you shall carry out the verdict that is announced to you from that place that Yhwh chose, observing scrupulously all their instructions to you. You shall act in accordance with the instructions given you and the ruling handed down to you; you must not deviate from the verdict that they announce to you either to the right or to the left."

David Kraemer goes so far as to claim that polysemous, polyphonous reading practices are a product of a rabbinic bid for authority: "they *want* to show that the meaning of scripture—and the desire of its Author—is subject to doubt and that the law will ultimately follow the [rabbinic] tradition . . . regardless of the simple meaning of the Written text." David Kraemer, *Reading the Rabbis: The Talmud as Literature* (New York: Oxford University Press, 1996), 48.

This characterization of rabbinic utter fidelity to their own legal procedures to the extent of rejecting an "objectively true" interpretation in favor of one agreed upon by the majority is found most notably in the well-known "Oven of Akhani" story in the Babylonian Talmud (*Bava Metsia* 59a–59b), and it is thematized most often in the Babylonian Talmud. As this book concerns itself primarily with the work of the earliest generations of rabbis in Roman Palestine, the tannaim, it will not include a discussion of this late Babylonian story. For some recent treatments of the story that consider it in its full narrative and legal context, see Jeffrey Rubenstein, *Talmudic Stories;* Suzanne Last Stone, "In Pursuit of the Counter-Text: The Jewish Legal Model in Contemporary American Legal Theory," *Harvard Law Review* 106 (1993): 813–896. See also Chaya Halberstam, "Encircling the Law: The Legal Boundaries of Rabbinic Judaism," *Jewish Studies Quarterly* (forthcoming). According to Christine Hayes, however, the attitude expressed better characterizes the activities of the tannaim than it does the Babylonian rabbis. See Christine Hayes, "Rabbinic Contestations of Authority," 123–141.

25. Fraade, *From Tradition to Commentary*, 115.

26. Stern, 25.

27. See Daniel Boyarin, *Border Lines: The Partition of Judaeo-Christianity* (Philadelphia: University of Pennsylvania Press, 2004), 151–160 for the tannaitic "hope for 'certain knowledge'" (151) and the invention of plural notions of truth only in the Babylonian Talmud.

28. See Susan Handelman, *The Slayers of Moses: The Emergence of Rabbinic Interpretation in Modern Literary Theory* (Albany: State University of New York Press, 1983).

29. Plato, *The Laws,* trans. Trevor R. Saunders (Baltimore, Md.: Penguin Books, 1972), 171.

30. Halivni writes, "There is a double standard of religious verity or, if you prefer, doubled-tiered religious verity, one prevailing in the world of behavior and one in the world of the intellect. Minority opinion is wrong in the world of behavior but could be right in the world of intellect." David Weiss Halivni, *Peshat and Derash: Plain and Applied Meaning in Rabbinic Exegesis* (New York: Oxford University Press, 1991), 110.

31. Halivni, 121, emphasis mine.

32. See Halivni: "Majority decision does not make its rule inherently true. It is merely a practical necessity, so that whenever feasible, plurality is preferable" (121). Halivni's understanding of rabbinic thought regarding truth and practice conflicts with the general consensus of midrash scholars (such as Fraade, Stern, and Kraemer), which concludes that the rabbis construct a notion of divine truth which is *inherently* multi-vocal; believe in a revelation which continues through human exegesis of the holy scriptures; and downplay the role of divine, authorial intent.

33. Halbertal, 87. The latter view most accurately represents Halivni's understanding of the rabbis.

34. Halbertal, 88.

35. In regard to this question, see Halbertal's discussion of the conflicting interpretations of the verse "you must not deviate from the verdict that they announce to you either to the right or to the left" (Deut 17:11) in the early Midrash and Mishnah (Halbertal, 82–85).

36. Daniel R. Schwartz, "Law and Truth: On Qumran-Sadducean and Rabbinic Views of Law" in *The Dead Sea Scrolls: Forty Years of Research,* ed. Devorah Dimant and Uriel Rappaport (Leiden: E. J. Brill, 1992), 230.

37. Schwartz writes, "The rabbis held that God, in order to preserve the system on the whole . . . preferred authoritative rabbis who erred now and then to rabbis whose authority was always in doubt. Thus, in the well-known rabbinic account of the time they locked God out of their deliberations and insisted, despite priestly opposition, on enforcing a decision which He complained was wrong, He is said to have chuckled and agreed, saying, 'my sons have defeated me'" (238).

38. See the famous Mishnah regarding this dispute, *M. R. ha-Sh.* 2:8–9.

39. Jeffrey Rubenstein, "Nominalism and Realism in Qumranic and Rabbinic Law: A Reassessment," *Dead Sea Discoveries* 6.2 (1999): 177. Rubenstein here draws from an earlier article cited by Schwartz, Yohanan Silman, "Halakhic Determinations of a Nominalistic and Realistic Nature: Legal and Philosophical Considerations," *Dine Israel* 12 (1984–1985). The uses of the *philosophical* terms "realism" and "nominalism" by Schwartz, Silman, and others are terribly confusing to those used to working in legal theory, in which "realism" (adhering to political, sociological, even psychological realities) means almost exactly the opposite of that in the context of philosophy (grounded

in a notion of "objective reality"). See Rubenstein's excellent, concise clarification of these terms (n.5, pp. 157–158).

40. Rubenstein, "Nominalism and Realism," 175.

41. Rubenstein, "Nominalism and Realism," 180. He writes,

> in societies where laws are more or less fixed, where the laws operative at a certain point in time become canonized, . . . the legal system cannot easily change to keep in step with changes in beliefs. Laws will therefore not always reflect and express a society's worldview, its beliefs about reality. . . . In such cases, law will begin to exhibit nominalist tendencies. Some acts will be prohibited (called wrong) by law, even though society no longer believes that they really have pernicious effects. . . . Members of society will still insist that the acts prohibited by laws are wrong, because they are enshrined in their sacred tradition, but they will not necessarily be able to explain why they are wrong, other than the fact that they are prohibited. This is tantamount to a nominalist perspective, and when pressed to interpret or apply such laws, legislators will adopt nominalist attitudes. (180–181)

42. Hans Kelsen, "The Principle of Sovereign Equality of States as a Basis for International Organization," *Yale Law Journal* 53.2 (1944): 218. From a humanities perspective, Stanley Fish discusses the law's propensity for defining its own reality; see Stanley Fish, "The Law Wishes to Have a Formal Existence," in *The Fate of Law,* ed. Austin Sarat and Thomas Kearns (Ann Arbor: University of Michigan Press, 1991): 159–208. On this issue see also the recently published volume: Austin Sarat, Lawrence Douglas, Martha Umphrey, eds., *How Law Knows* (Stanford, Calif.: Stanford University Press, 2007).

43. Robert Summers, "Formal Legal Truth and Substantive Truth in Judicial Fact-Finding: Their Justified Divergence in Some Particular Cases," *Law and Philosophy* 18.5 (1999): 498–499.

44. While there are some extensive treatments of evidence law as a topic unto itself (see especially *m. Makkot,* chapter 1), in general, rules of evidence are provided alongside legal stipulations as a prerequisite for their implementation. It is this systematic presentation that has received the small amount of scholarly interest in evidence law in rabbinic literature, though still little attention is paid to what it reveals about rabbinic legal thought or culture. Boaz Cohen writes only about stipulations for witness testimony as discussed by the rabbis in tractate *Makkot* alongside some parallel texts; see Boaz Cohen, "Evidence in Jewish Law," in *La Preuve: Recueils de la Société Jean Bodin pour l'histoire comparative des institutions* vol. 16 (Brussels: Éditions de la Librairie Encyclopédique, 1964), 103–115. Shalom Albeck devotes an entire book to talmudic laws of evidence, which essentially systematizes and catalogues rabbinic discussions of evidence law, emphasizing the rules for witnesses and testimony, documentary evidence, and oaths; see Shalom Albeck, *Evidence in Talmudic Law* (Hebrew) (Ramat Gan, Israel: Bar-Ilan University Press, 1987). Ze'ev Falk also collects (in an unsystematic way) rabbinic texts in which the rabbis grapple with evidence in his article "Forensic Medicine in Jewish Law," *Dine Israel* 1 (1990): 20–30. His topic is specifically the use of *medicine* in Jewish law, both within early rabbinic literature (both tannaitic and talmudic) and later medieval Jewish legal works. Nonetheless, he brings some significant rabbinic texts to light which struggle with the interpretation of evidence that had not been previously

systematized, with discussions on such diverse subjects as menstrual blood, autopsies, murder weapons, and physical signs of puberty. Falk's examples suggest the importance of the rabbinic interpretation of the real world on a case-by-case basis, even as his treatment of these illustrations places them solely within a medical science context.

1. Stains of Impurity

The epigraph is from Richard A. Posner, "The Jurisprudence of Skepticism," *Michigan Law Review* 86 (1988): 828.

1. Mary Douglas, *Purity and Danger: An Analysis of the Concepts of Pollution and Taboo* (1966; New York: Routledge, 1992), 51–52.

2. Compare, for example, 13:2 and 15:2; 13:8, 46 and 15:3; 13:8–11 and 15:13–15.

3. Jacob Milgrom, *Leviticus 1–16,* Anchor Bible Series (New York: Doubleday, 1991), 906.

4. John E. Hartley, *Leviticus,* Word Biblical Commentary 4 (Dallas: Word Books, 1992), 209. It is difficult to determine whether the unspecific nature of the genital-flux impurity laws made it possible to circumvent the inspection of the priests, or whether the private nature of genital discharges suggested that they not be subject to inspection, and therefore the laws had to be broad and uncomplicated. While the evolution of these laws is an interesting subject, for the purposes of this chapter it is unnecessary to reconstruct this evolution. What is important is the distinction between the model presented for scale-disease impurity, in which priestly inspection is required to recognize a relatively rare subset of skin diseases, and the model presented for genital-flux impurity, in which individuals were simply instructed to ascertain the presence of discharge and would thus be rendered impure.

5. Milgrom, 945.

6. Ibid.

7. Hartley, 208.

8. Ibid.

9. For a summary of scholarly understandings of Israel's ritual purity system, see Jonathan Klawans, *Impurity and Sin in Ancient Judaism* (New York: Oxford University Press, 2000), 3–20.

10. Michael Fishbane, *Biblical Interpretation in Ancient Israel* (New York: Oxford University Press, 1985), 95.

11. Translations of the *Sifra* are my own.

12. As Michael Fishbane writes, "frequent lacunae or ambiguities in [the biblical laws'] legal formulation tend to render such laws exceedingly problematic—if not functionally inoperative—*without interpretation*" (Fishbane, 91).

13. Adriana Destro, "The Witness of Times: An Anthropological Reading of *Niddah*" in *Reading Leviticus: A Conversation with Mary Douglas,* ed. John F. A. Sawyer (Sheffield, England: Sheffield Academic Press, 1996), 125.

14. Destro, 125.

15. Destro, 127–128, emphasis mine.

16. Destro, 128.

17. Destro, 136.

18. Fonrobert, *Menstrual Purity,* 109.

19. The closest parallel to the stories of rabbinic inspection of blood found in the

Talmud is related in Tosefta *Niddah* 4:1, in which two women miscarry various irregular substances. They do not know whether they have miscarried a fetus or not, so they inquire of rabbis who then inquire of doctors. This tosefta, while indicating direct inspection of genital discharges, also distinctly implies that rabbis were not yet installed as experts on reading menstrual blood, since they defer to the authority of non-rabbinic, medical experts.

20. Bourdieu, "The Force of Law," 831–832, 819–820.

21. In no way do I wish to minimize the objectifying effect that rabbinic legal language has upon women, in particular in this mishnah and in Tractate *Niddah* as a whole, as Fonrobert and other scholars point out. But I do suggest that this unfortunate consequence of the rabbinic discourse on women is not particular to the early rabbis or an especially "androcentric" society. Legal language continues to be troublesome in this regard to this very day. Alan Hyde writes of contemporary American law: "Law's language of the body is typically . . . cold, . . . clinical, . . . and self-consciously metaphorical. . . . In legal texts there is simply nothing that may be described as reflecting the speaker's direct, unmediated knowledge of his or her own body" [Alan Hyde, *Bodies of Law* (Princeton, N.J.: Princeton University Press, 1997), 5, 8]. One example Hyde brings from contemporary legal texts to illustrate his point is a recent (1991) issuance of a search warrant "for appellant's apartment and vagina" (Hyde, 4). The objectification of the woman's body in Tractate *Niddah* is no more extreme than that produced by this search warrant, and thus it can be more convincingly attributed to the work of legal discourse than the ideology of early rabbis.

22. Bourdieu, 834.

23. Hartley, 208.

24. Destro 132, emphasis added.

25. Curiously, the word ʿ*ed* is used for "test cloth" in the Mishnah—a word found in Isaiah 64:5 in the context of menstruation and a stained cloth. Identical to the word for witness/testimony (ʿ*ed*), it may derive from a different root (ʿ*dd* vs. ʿ*wd*). Nonetheless, the words seem philologically, as well as conceptually, related. The "test cloths" are used as the primary witness to the fact of menstruation.

26. Translations of the Mishnah have been based upon H. Danby, *The Mishnah* (Oxford, 1933); they are emended as necessary.

27. I would like to note that even here, in a story in which a woman requires an expert decision about whether her flux is ritually impure, there is no *physical* inspection of blood by the rabbi.

28. Although the issue of defiling the Temple does not concern the rabbis, rabbinic law follows biblical law in forbidding a man to have sex with a woman who is ritually impure, which is listed as one of the sexual abominations.

29. Christine Hayes notes this trope in rabbinic literature in which an objection to a rabbinic legal maneuver is presented within the text ("Rabbinic Contestations of Authority," 132). She writes,

> the contrived and counterintuitive interpretations of the overzealous sage are depicted as evoking incomprehension or incredulity among non-rabbis and rabbis alike. These texts give voice to the anxiety that one can carry midrashic exegesis too far and in the process undermine rabbinic credibility and by extension rabbinic authority. Nevertheless, these expressions of doubt and

anxiety appear alongside hyperbolic praise of the great midrashic masters ... and their extreme methods—indicating a basic rabbinic ambivalence.

30. Fonrobert 114, emphasis mine.

31. Fonrobert 115, emphasis mine.

32. The idea that the sensation of menstruation—rather than the appearance of blood—determines the woman's ritual purity status is actually suggested by Samuel, a first generation Amora, in the Babylonian Talmud (*Niddah* 57a), but his position is marginal. For a thorough discussion of Samuel's stance and the taming of it by the talmudic *sugya,* see Fonrobert, 70–83.

33. Fonrobert, 114.

34. Bourdieu, 828–829.

2. Signs of Ownership

The epigraph is from Thomas C. Grey, "The Disintegration of Property" in *Property,* ed. J. Roland Pennock and John W. Chapman (New York: New York University Press, 1980), 74, n. 22.

1. See Carol M. Rose, "Possession as the Origin of Property," in *Perspectives on Property Law,* ed. Robert C. Ellickson, Carol M. Rose, and Bruce A. Ackerman (New York: Little, Brown, 1995), 181–190.

2. David Hume, *Treatise on Human Nature,* Book 3, Part 2, Section 3, quoted in Robert Sugden, "The Economics of Rights, Cooperation and Welfare," in Ellickson, Rose, and Ackerman, *Perspectives on Property Law* 176, emphasis mine.

3. Sugden, 174.

4. Brevard Childs, *The Book of Exodus: A Critical, Theological Commentary* (Louisville, Ky.: Westminster Press, 1974), 480.

5. Childs, 480–481.

6. Martin Noth, *Exodus: A Commentary* (Philadelphia: Westminster Press, 1962), 189. Emphasis mine.

7. Gerhard Von Rad, *Deuteronomy: A Commentary* (Philadelphia: Westminster Press, 1966), 141.

8. This rewording may not in fact be a generalization, but a limitation; whereas Exodus might envision the return of lost property to *all* individuals, *even including* one's enemy, Deuteronomy may only require the return of lost property to one's "brother," or a fellow Israelite.

9. Biblical law is not oblivious of matters of enforcement and adjudication. Just a few verses after the lost property law, the text considers a case in which an allegation has been made regarding a woman's virginity; though this is clearly a private matter, a procedure is outlined in which physical evidence (a bloody sheet) must be produced to adjudicate the case (Deut. 22:17).

10. Moshe Greenberg, "Some Postulates of Biblical Criminal Law," *The Jewish Expression,* ed. Judah Goldin (1970; New Haven: Yale University Press, 1976), 22.

11. This divergence between biblical ideas of ownership and rabbinic ones have not been explored in scholarly literature. In general, Jewish property law is treated as a seamless whole. See, e.g., Michael J. Broyde and Michael Hecht, "The Return of Lost

Property according to Jewish and Common Law: A Comparison" *Journal of Law and Religion* 12.1 (1995–1996): 225–253.

12. Rose, 184.

13. All translations of the *Mekilta* are from J. Z. Lauterbach, *Mekilta de-Rabbi Ishmael* (Philadelphia: Jewish Publication Society of America, 1976).

14. It occurs to me that we might be able to see in this rabbinic inversion of subject and object a parallel to rabbinic exegetical practice regarding scripture: the finder, or reader, becomes the active one, trying to make sense of an enigmatic text which cannot simply "speak for itself."

15. As M. Fishbane writes, "[Deut. 22:3] closes a perceived gap in the law as it expands its scope to embrace movables in general—not just livestock or work animals." Fishbane, *Biblical Interpretation in Ancient Israel*, 178.

16. This phrase appears in the Kaufmann edition of the Mishnah but not in Parma; it appears to be a mere scribal error, an example of dittography, but it is curious. Is there equivocation here about whether signs are necessary for an item to be considered owned?

17. This idea of mental abandonment (*ye'ush*), adumbrated in the Mishnah, is fully fleshed out in the Talmuds. See below.

18. Jeremy Bentham actually understands the entire basis of property law accordingly: "Property is nothing but a basis of expectation; the expectation of deriving certain advantages from a thing which we are said to possess, in consequence of the relation in which we stand towards it." Jeremy Bentham, *The Theory of Legislation*, ed. C. K. Ogden (1802; Littleton, Colo.: Fred B. Rothman and Co., 1987), 112.

19. In exploring these divergent approaches to evidence and decision making in the Bavli and Yerushalmi, I do not wish to generalize about the natures or characters of these Talmuds. In other words, I am not trying to argue that the Bavli is more legally inclined while the Yerushalmi is more exhortatory—instead, I am simply attempting to explore two divergent approaches to decision making in the face of legal uncertainty, which here happen to be enacted by the Bavli and the Yerushalmi.

20. Translations of the Yerushalmi are my own.

21. The distinction between the legal requirement and the extra-legal "requirement" become harder to discern here. See Fraade, "Navigating the Anomalous," 145–65, for some discussion of the issue of legal and other boundaries.

22. The beginning of this text appears corrupt; the setting of the story has been reconstructed based on the clues in the text and the end of the narrative.

23. See Jacob Neusner, *The Theology of the Oral Torah: Revealing the Justice of God* (Kingston and Montreal, Canada: McGill-Queens Press, 1999), 440.

24. Louis Jacobs, *The Talmudic Argument: A Study in Talmudic Reasoning and Methodology* (New York: Cambridge University Press, 1984), 35. See 34–49 for a thorough study of this *sugya*.

25. Jacobs, 35.

26. In fact, later developments in Jewish law so enshrine the concept that *ye'ush* is "presumed from the circumstances" that it may overrule, in some cases, the clear expression of the owner that he has despaired of recovering the object. See Isaac Herzog, *The Main Institutions of Jewish Law: Volume 1: Property* (New York: Soncino Press, 1965), 281.

27. An extended and thorough analysis of this long *sugya* is beyond the scope of

this chapter; I will instead highlight and explore those elements of the *sugya* which are relevant to the Bavli's concept of "signs" as legal proof. For an elucidation of the entirety of the *sugya*, see Jacobs, 91–100.

The full text of the *sugya* reads as follows:

Mishnah: A garment was also included among all these; why was it mentioned separately? To compare it [to other lost objects] to tell you that just as a garment is distinguished in that it bears signs and has claimants, so also anything that bears signs and has claimants must be proclaimed [when found].

Gemara:

A. The scholars propounded: are signs authorized by biblical or rabbinic law?
B. What is the practical difference?
C. In respect of returning a woman's divorce decree on the strength of identification marks: should you say that they are biblically valid, we return it; but if they are only rabbinically valid—the rabbis enacted this measure for civil matters only, not for ritual prohibitions.
D. Come and hear: A garment was also included among all these; why was it mentioned separately? To compare it [to other lost objects] to tell you that just as a garment is distinguished in that it bears signs and has claimants, so also anything that bears signs and has claimants must be proclaimed [when found].
E. The Tanna really desires to teach that there must be a claimant; signs are mentioned only incidentally.
F. Come and hear: [Therefore Scripture wrote 'ass,' to show that even] the ass [too is returned] by virtue of the signs on its saddle!
G. Read: by virtue of the witnesses [attesting to the ownership] of the saddle.
H. Come and hear: "And it shall be with you until your brother's inquiry." Would it have occurred to you that he should return it to him before he inquired after it? But it means this: examine him [the claimant], whether or not he is a deceiver. Surely that is by means of signs!
I. No: by means of witnesses.
J. Come and hear: Testimony may be given only on proof of the face with the nose, even if the body and the garment bear signs. This proves that signs are biblically valid.
K. Let us say: in respect of the body, [the signs were]: it was short or long, while [the signs] of the garments [are rejected] because we suspect they might be borrowed.
L. But if we suspect borrowing, why is an ass returned because of the signs on the saddle?
M. Let us say: people do not borrow a saddle, because it chafes the ass['s back].
N. Alternatively, the garments [were identified merely] through being white or red.

O. Then what of that which was taught: If he found it tied up in a purse, money bag, or to a ring, or if he found it amongst his utensils, even a long time afterwards, it is valid. If you think that we suspect borrowing, if he found it tied up in his purse [etc.], why is it valid? We ought to suspect that it was borrowed!

P. Let us say: A purse, wallet, and signet ring are not lent; a purse and money bag, because people are superstitious about it; a signet ring, because anyone can commit forgery with it.

Q. Shall we say that this [whether signs are biblically or rabbinically valid] was disputed by the Tannaim? [For it was taught]: Testimony may not be given on the strength of a mole; but Eleazar b. Mahabai said: Testimony may be given on the strength of a mole. Surely they differ in this: the first Tanna holds that signs are rabbinically valid, while Eleazar b. Mahabai holds that they are biblically valid.

R. Raba said: all agree that they are biblically valid: they differ here as to whether a mole is common to one's [zodiacal time of] birth; one says that a mole is generally common to one's [zodiacal time of] birth, while the other holds that it is not.

S. Alternatively, all agree that a mole is not common to one's [zodiacal time of] birth; they differ here as to whether signs are liable to change after death. One maintains that signs are liable to change after death, the other maintains that they are not.

T. Alternatively, all agree that a mole is not liable to change after death, and that signs are only rabbinically valid; they differ here as to whether a mole is a distinctive sign. One holds that a mole is a distinctive sign, while the other holds that it is not.

U. Raba said: If you should resolve that signs are not biblically valid, why do we return a lost article relying on signs?

V. Because one who finds a lost article is pleased that it should be returned on the strength of signs, because if he should lose anything, it will likewise be returned to him through signs.

W. R. Safra said to Raba: Can one confer benefit upon himself with money that is not his? Instead, [the reason is this]: the loser himself is pleased to offer signs and take it back. He knows full well that he has no witnesses, and therefore he argues to himself, "Everyone does not know its distinctive signs, but I can state its distinctive signs, and take it back."

X. But what of that which we learned: R. Simeon b. Gamaliel said: If it was one man who had borrowed from three, [the finder] must return [them] to the debtor; if three had borrowed from one, he must return them to the creditor. Is the debtor pleased that it [the promissory note] is returned to the creditor?

Y. He said to him: In that instance it is a matter of logic. If it was one man who had borrowed from three, he must return [them] to the debtor, because they are to be found [together only] in the debtor's possession, and not in the creditor's. Hence the debtor must have dropped it. If three had to borrow from one, it must be returned to the creditor, because they are to be found in the creditor's possession, but not in the debtor's.

Z. But what of that which we learned: If one finds a roll of notes or a bundle of notes he must surrender [them]! Here too, [is the reason] that the debtor is pleased that they should be returned to the creditor?!

AA. Rather Raba said: signs are biblically valid, because it is written, "And it shall be with you until your brother's inquiry." Would it have occurred to you that he should return it to him before he inquired after it? Instead, [it means this]: examine [the claimant] to find out whether he is a deceiver or not. Surely that means by means of signs! Conclude.

BB. Raba said: Should you resolve that identification marks are biblically valid...

CC. ("Should you resolve"? But he has proved that they are biblically valid! That is because it can be explained as it was above.)

DD. If two sets of signs [are offered by disputing claimants], [the lost object] must be left [in custody]. If [one claimant] states signs and one [produces] witnesses, it must be surrendered to him who has witnesses. If [one claimant] states signs and another also states signs and [produces] one witness, one witness is as though non-existent, so it must be left [in custody]. [If one claimant produces] witnesses of weaving, and another witnesses of losing, it must be given to the latter, because we argue: [the first] may have sold it, and another lost it. If [one claimant] states length, and another its breadth, it must be given to [him who states its] length, because it is possible to conjecture the breadth when its owner is standing and wearing it, whereas the length cannot be well conjectured. [If one claimant] states its length and breadth, and another its square area, it must be surrendered to the former. If the length, breadth, and weight [are stated by different claimants], it must be given to [him who states] its weight.

28. Jacobs, 91.

29. All translations of the Bavli in this book are based on the translation by I. Epstein in the Soncino Press edition of the Babylonian Talmud. Emendations have been made as needed.

30. The word "distinctive," (*mubhaq*) may imply "distinguished" or different from the general lot of signs. It may also merely imply that the mole is an "actual" sign, according to some, and according to others, is simply not distinctive enough to function as a sign (in other words, it would be equivalent to the "mere sign" from the mishnah in *Yebamot* quoted above). I would like to thank Professor Christine Hayes for bringing this point to my attention. Rashi's commentary puts forward the interpretation which I follow.

31. The dispute over benefit here emerges from the question of whether the law of returning lost property based on "signs" is biblical or rabbinic. If it is biblical, it need only be accepted and followed. If it is rabbinic, however, it must be justified by a tangible benefit to society.

32. It is difficult to ascertain whether this phrase is present in another version of this *baraita*, or whether it has been added by the *stam*; the origin of this text does not affect the argument here.

33. See Jacobs, 99: "This seems to show that this whole section has been added later, after the previous *sugya* has been completed."

34. Without a full-scale study of the function of the *stam* in the Babylonian Talmud, a task which cannot be achieved in these pages, it is difficult to ascertain why the *stam* imbues doubt into Raba's pronouncements, backing away from Raba's strong conclusions. This may, in fact, represent a trend in the *stam*. For a fuller discussion of the *stam*'s role in the Bavli, see Shamma Friedman, "Pereq ha'isha Rabbah babavli" in *Mehqarim umeqorot*, ed. H. Dimitrovski (New York: Jewish Theological Seminary, 1977), 277–441.

35. The distinction between the misgivings aired about the creation of "legal facts" in the sphere of ritual impurity as compared to property may be attributed to the differing "realities" experienced in each realm; perhaps ritual purity decisions could be made more arbitrarily, or did not need to match any personally experienced reality. I do not, however, wish to make this argument for two reasons. First, it betrays a modern bias against the "unreality" of ritual purity and impurity—it is quite possible that there was much non-juridical discernment of ritual impurity in the second and third centuries which would have posed significant challenges to R. Aqiba's brazen legal decision making. Second, I am examining particular texts from different spheres of law in order to show the spectrum of the discourse of doubt and the creation of legal facts, and not in order to generalize about each of these legal subjects. R. Aqiba's willingness in one Mishnah to do away with any worries about the connection to lived reality is not necessarily representative of all of ritual impurity law; in fact, unlike in the realm of property law, the Bavli on *niddah* is mainly interested in approaching near scientific precision on the objective reality of menstruation. In the above texts on lost property law, the concern for a connection to lived reality is preserved, but by no means as the centerpiece of the discussion.

3. The Impossibility of Judgment

The epigraph is from Jacques Derrida, "Force of Law: The 'Mystical Foundation of Authority,'" trans. Mary Quaintance, in *Deconstruction and the Possibility of Justice*, ed. Drucilla Cornell, Michel Rosenfeld, and David Gray Carlson (New York: Routledge, 1992), 24.

1. Fishbane, 164.

2. The Bible does present a case of lying witnesses, but they are caught before a mistaken judgment is rendered. See below for a fuller discussion of this case.

3. This point will be elaborated below.

4. One need only consider contemporary rhetoric surrounding the death penalty in the United States to fully appreciate the weight of uncertainty in capital proceedings. Those who support the death penalty are typically pressed to adopt a discourse of complete epistemological certainty; President George W. Bush, for example, who presided over hundreds of executions in the state of Texas, stated on "Larry King Live" that "there is *no doubt* in my mind that each person who has been executed in our state was guilty of the crime committed" [http://transcripts.cnn.com/TRANSCRIPTS/0002/23/bp.00.html, emphasis mine; accessed May 20, 2009]. Opening the door to doubt about guilt provides too much space, one might surmise, for opposing the death penalty.

5. Elie Spitz, "The Jewish Tradition and Capital Punishment," in *Contemporary Jewish Ethics and Morality: A Reader,* ed. Elliot N. Dorff and Louis E. Newman (New York: Oxford University Press, 1995), 345.

6. See Baruch A. Levine, *Numbers 21–36: A New Translation with Introduction and Commentary,* Anchor Bible Series (New York: Doubleday, 2000), 548.

7. Philip J. Budd, *Numbers,* Word Bible Commentary, v. 5 (Waco, Tex.: Word Books, 1984), 382.

8. Jacob Milgrom, *Numbers,* JPS Torah Commentary (New York: Jewish Publication Society, 1990), 291.

9. Milgrom, 509.

10. Levine, 566.

11. Presumably, these diligent inquiries are made *of the witnesses,* i.e., the witnesses are interrogated. However, this is not specified in the biblical text, which seems to leave open other avenues judges might take in order to confirm or disprove the witnesses' testimony.

12. Bernard M. Levinson, *Deuteronomy and the Hermeneutics of Legal Innovation* (New York: Oxford University Press, 1997), 121.

13. Calum Carmichael, *Biblical Laws of Talion,* Oxford Center Papers (Oxford: Oxford Centre for Postgraduate Hebrew Studies, 1986), 36.

14. Thus Tikva Frymer-Kensky's contention that "here, the literal meaning of 'eye for eye' makes no sense. . . . The sanction 'eye for eye' in the provisions for the treatment of the false witness clearly is intended as a formulaic statement of the philosophical principle of equal retribution" ("Tit for Tat: The Principle of Equal Retribution in Near Eastern and Biblical Law," *Biblical Archaeologist* 43.3 [1980]: 232).

15. Biblical narrative sources, as we will see in Chapter 5, admit and even depend on the unreliability of evidence for the stories' dramatic power. Successful, lying witnesses are at the center of the tragedy of Naboth's vineyard in 1 Kings. In fact, Calum Carmichael argues that the deuteronomic law of false witnesses was the reformulation of "an existing rule about false testimony [Exod 23:1] in light of the incident about Naboth." Carmichael, 21.

16. Gerald Blidstein, "Capital Punishment: The Classic Jewish Discussion," in *Contemporary Jewish Ethics,* ed. M. Kellner (New York: Hebrew Publishing Co., 1978), 317.

17. David De Sola Pool, "Capital Punishment Among the Jews," in *Jewish Eugenics, and Other Essays,* ed. Max Reichler (New York: Bloch, 1916), 53–103.

18. Richard Block, "Death, Thou Shalt Die: Reform Judaism and Capital Punishment," *Journal of Reform Judaism* 30.2 (1983): 4.

19. Block, 6.

20. Aaron Kirschenbaum, "The Role of Punishment in Jewish Criminal Law: A Chapter in Rabbinic Penological Thought," *Jewish Law Annual* 9 (1991): 125.

21. Kirschenbaum, 124.

22. Kirschenbaum, 129.

23. Kirschenbaum, 139.

24. Ibid.

25. Kirschenbaum, 138–139.

26. See chapter 4 for a discussion of God's role in the rabbinic system of jurisprudence.

27. For a comprehensive review of how this mishnah has been used in death penalty scholarship, as well as the most thorough review of rabbinic death-penalty scholarship to date, see Berkowitz, *Execution and Invention*, 25–64.

28. Berkowtiz, 61.

29. Berkowitz, 64.

30. Berkowitz, 63.

31. Ibid.

32. Ibid.

33. Although one may argue that a legal decision is also a statement about fact, it is clear from Mishnah *Sanhedrin* that people who have, in reality, committed crimes will nonetheless be acquitted due to legal "technicalities." For example, during the judges' deliberations, a judge who has previously argued for acquittal cannot change his mind and argue for conviction, even if his opinion has in fact changed.

34. This reliance on witnesses alone was not simply a rabbinic rehearsal of popular evidentiary beliefs of the time. Roman law admitted virtually anything into evidence, and in fact divided evidence into three categories: witnesses, documents, and signs. See Russ VerSteeg, *Law in the Ancient World* (Durham, N.C.: Carolina Academic Press, 2002), 297–298, and James Franklin, *The Science of Conjecture: Evidence and Probability before Pascal* (Baltimore, Md.: Johns Hopkins University Press, 2001), 6.

35. The continuation of the verse presents a case in which a person does not die, but merely falls ill. Simeon the Temanite, through his interpretation, may be extending the verse to the case of murder, by applying this phrase not only to this verse, but the talionic punishment required for murder presented directly following. Or, he may be arguing that the apodosis of this verse applies not only to its immediate context, but to all of judicial procedure.

36. Gerald Blidstein raises, and dismisses, this explanation for the rabbinic reluctance to convict in capital cases, but I do not find his reasons for dismissal satisfactory. He writes that if the rabbis often or always acquitted because "the Sanhedrin . . . must never arrogantly assume a certainty it cannot truly possess," then any arguments against such acquittals, such as R. Gamaliel's in Mishnah *Makkot* 1:10 ("they multiply murderers in Israel"), would be a "*non sequitur*. For once the possible innocence of the man in the docket is admitted, one cannot have his head merely to insure public safety" [Blidstein, 315]. This assertion, however, does not represent the outlook of the tannaim. The Mishnah openly entertains the notion of wrongful conviction, as we have seen above, and does not see it as a perversion of justice. And a tosefta in *Sanhedrin* which will be discussed below explicitly addresses the tension between executing an innocent and unraveling the legal system, and chooses the former over the latter. Blidstein's argument presumes a philosophical/theological stance about the taking of a human life that the early rabbis simply did not seem to possess.

37. Did the majority of tannaitic rabbis, or R. Aqiba specifically, subscribe to a real philosophy of skepticism, as some Hellenistic schools did? To answer the question of why R. Aqiba and the redactors of the Mishnah, among other rabbis, were wary of inspecting physical evidence requires a fuller historical study than can be achieved in these pages. It is also an argument I am hesitant to make because of the problem of the reliability of named tradents, the lack of much corroborative historical evidence, and the influence of later redactors upon these texts. The argument I *am* making, however, is a discursive one—that rabbinic legal texts are framed by the language

of skepticism, and by noting this we might reveal a great deal about how rabbinic legal authority is envisaged, structured, and undercut.

38. I see this biblical mandate as an advantage, rather than as the sole reason behind the rabbis' exclusive reliance on witnesses, because the rabbis are rarely, if ever, limited in their legislation by the explicit, plain-sense meaning of the biblical text. It would have been easy for the rabbis to require inspection of the murder weapon in addition to eyewitness testimony, especially considering the attention given to the weapon in the biblical texts. Blu Greenberg has noted that "where there was a rabbinic will, there was a halakhic way" (Blu Greenberg, *On Women and Judaism: A View from Tradition* [New York: Jewish Publication Society, 1981], 44). Clearly, there was no rabbinic will here to include inspection of the murder weapon in the rules of criminal procedure.

39. Berkowitz, 142.

40. Berkowitz, 126.

41. Ibid.

42. It is intriguing that the mishnah relies on this verse from Proverbs to justify capital punishment when so many passages of this sort can be found in the Pentateuch, directly appended to judicial procedure for capital crimes. One example of such a verse is quoted above: "you shall purge the guilt of innocent blood from Israel, that it may go well with you" (Deut. 19:13). I speculate that, as I shall argue in the next chapter, the rabbis wished to avoid any sense of divine retribution within the sphere of human jurisprudence—all the Pentateuchal passages would have overtones of such a theology. The verse in Proverbs, however, rationalizes the death of the wicked solely in terms of what maximizes happiness within human society (a very utilitarian position!) which supports the rabbinic structure of human justice for its own sake, regardless of ultimate divine truths.

43. I contend that this prospect of "blood-guilt" applies not only to witnesses who deliberately lie but also to witnesses who believe they are telling the truth but are, in objective fact, mistaken. The exhortatory tone of the mishnah would hardly be necessary to caution those bent on perjury; they would be guilty of a clear-cut capital crime, as set forth in Deuteronomy. But those who approach witnessing cavalierly, who would testify to the truth of an event about which they are uncertain, are capable of incurring blood-guilt, and would therefore need to be forewarned about the gravity of their undertaking.

44. This tosefta, as explored in the introduction, does bring God into the courtroom in a way that the Mishnah does not. See the introduction of this book for a fuller discussion of this text.

45. Berkowitz, 150.

46. In Berkowitz's words, "weeping marks a condition of tragedy" (149).

47. I would like to thank Ravit Reichman for helping me see this point. See Ravit Reichman, *The Affective Life of Law: Legal Modernism and the Literary Imagination* (Stanford, Calif.: Stanford University Press, 2009).

48. Derrida, 16.

4. Theologies of Justice

1. Bernard Jackson, "Religious Law in Judaism," *Aufstieg und Niedergang der römischen Welt* 2.19.1 (1979): 33–52.

198 · NOTES TO PAGES 111–115

2. B. Jackson, 39.

3. J. G. Griffiths, *The Divine Verdict: A Study of Divine Judgment in the Ancient Religions* (Leiden: E. J. Brill, 1991), 24.

5. Griffiths, 12, emphasis mine.

6. B. Jackson, 40.

7. B. Jackson, 41.

9. B. Jackson, 43.

10. James Crenshaw, *Defending God: Biblical Responses to the Problem of Evil* (New York: Oxford University Press, 2005), 127.

11. See Kirsten Nielsen, *Yahweh as Prosecutor and Judge: An Investigation of the Prophetic Lawsuit (Rib-Pattern)* (Sheffield, England: University of Sheffield Press, 1978).

12. Alan E. Bernstein, *The Formation of Hell: Death and Retribution in the Ancient and Early Christian Worlds* (Ithaca, N.Y.: Cornell University Press, 1993), 150.

13. Andrew Davies, *Double Standards in Isaiah: Re-Evaluating Prophetic Ethics and Divine Justice* (Leiden: E. J. Brill, 2000), 123.

17. I have chosen the JPS translation here which follows the ancient versions in translating *heḥeleti* as "made sick" rather than "begun" and which brings more emotional resonance to the passage.

18. Ironically, Deuteronomy also declares that "Yhwh your God is God of gods and Lord of lords, the great God, mighty and awesome, who is not partial" (Deut. 10:17)—but this is precisely one of those statements that under scrutiny does not hold up, even within the book of Deuteronomy itself (see Deut. 4:37, for example, which states "because he loved your ancestors, he chose their descendants after them" coupled with 6:15, for instance: "Yhwh your God, who is present with you, is a jealous God. The anger of Yhwh your God would be kindled against you and he would destroy you from the face of the earth.") Deuteronomy 10:17 could be referring to Yhwh not being partial to particular *individuals* within the nation of Israel, even though he is partial to (and against) Israel as a whole, but as a judge Yhwh is found most often judging Israel collectively.

19. Terence E. Fretheim, *The Suffering of God: An Old Testament Perspective* (Philadelphia: Fortress Press, 1984), 111.

20. Fretheim, 111.

21. Ellen J. van Wolde, "Sentiments as Culturally Constructed Emotions: Anger and Love in the Hebrew Bible," *Biblical Interpretation* 16.1 (2008): 14, 17.

22. Gerlinde Baumann, *Love and Violence: Marriage as Metaphor for the Relationship between Yhwh and Israel in the Prophetic Books* (Collegeville, Minn.: Liturgical Press, 2003), 134.

23. I would like to note that vengeance and anger in and of themselves are not foreign to biblical justice—more so than in the other ancient Near Eastern law codes, the laws of homicide in the Hebrew Bible are founded upon blood-feud among clans and a patriarch's right to avenge the murder of his kin. Nevertheless, such vengeance

was controlled so that only murderers were punished—see Pamela Barmash, "Blood Feud and State Control: Differing Legal Institutions for the Remedy of Homicide During the Second and First Millennia B.C.E." *Journal of Near Eastern Studies* 63.3 (2004): 183–199. What is violated in Yhwh's wrathful vengeance upon Israel is (1) that Yhwh is acting as judge as well as blood-avenger, a dual role which would not have been acceptable in Israelite jurisprudence and (2) the uncontrolled nature of Yhwh's wrath which does not inflict suffering upon only proven criminals.

24. Joel S. Kaminsky, *Corporate Responsibility in the Hebrew Bible,* Journal for the Study of the Old Testament Supplement; 196. [S.l.] (Sheffield, England: Sheffield Academic Press, 1995), 56.

25. B. Jackson, 41.

26. Jackson argues that *talion* was not really implemented within the human administration of justice (41), but others disagree. For an overview of scholarly opinion see Daniella Piattelli, "*Zedaqa:* Pursuit of Justice and the Instrument of '*Ius Talionis,*'" *Israel Law Review* 29 (1995): 65–78.

27. Tikva Frymer-Kensky, 230, 232.

28. For a full discussion of this idea, see R. Adamiak, *Justice and History in the Old Testament: The Evolution of Divine Retribution in the Historiographies of the Wilderness Generation* (Cleveland, Ohio: Zubal, 1982) and Hans J. Boecker, *Law and the Administration of Justice in the Old Testament and Ancient Near East* (Minneapolis, Minn.: Augsberg Publishing House, 1980).

29. Among the models of non-juridical suffering found in the prophets are the striking ideas that suffering serves to refine and purify the people; that Israel suffers more than she deserves; and that Israel reflexively brings suffering upon herself. On this last point see Klaus Koch's famous essay, "Is There a Doctrine of Retribution in the Old Testament?" trans. Thomas H. Trapp, in *Theodicy in the Old Testament,* ed. James L. Crenshaw (Philadelphia: Fortress Press, 1983), 57–87.

30. Patrick D. Miller, Jr., *Sin and Judgment in the Prophets: A Stylistic and Theological Analysis* (Chico, Calif.: Scholars Press, 1982), 111.

31. Miller, 16–17.

32. Miller, 14.

33. Frymer-Kensky 232–233, emphasis mine.

34. Miller, 1, emphasis mine.

35. Michel Foucault, *Discipline and Punish: The Birth of the Prison* (1977; New York: Vintage, 1995), 45.

36. Martha Nussbaum, *Poetic Justice: The Literary Imagination and Public Life* (Boston: Beacon Press, 1995), 75.

37. Kaminsky, 56.

38. "Sevenfold" is most probably not meant to be taken literally here, but rather it means "manifold." See Jacob Milgrom, *Leviticus 23–27,* Anchor Bible Series (New York: Doubleday, 2001), 2306.

39. Gershom Scholem, "On Sin and Punishment: Some Remarks Concerning Biblical and Rabbinic Ethics," in *Myths and Symbols: Studies in Honor of Mircia Eliade,* ed. J. M. Kitagawa and C. H. Long (Chicago: University of Chicago Press, 1969), 168.

40. Miller, 121.

41. Oliver Wendell Holmes, "The Path of the Law," *Harvard Law Review* 10 (1897): 461, 457.

42. Crenshaw, 3. The possibility of getting "less" than what I deserve, i.e., the issue of God's mercy, is not as problematic when perceived through the lens of human justice as the possibility of getting "more" punishment than I deserve. Human justice systems include the instrument of pardon, and it would not necessarily be seen as inappropriate for a divine judge to wield that power as well.

43. John Barton, "Imitation of God in the Old Testament," in *The God of Israel: Studies of an Inimitable Deity,* ed. R. P. Gordon (New York: Cambridge University Press, 2007), 45.

44. Haim Cohn, "The Secularization of Divine Law," in *Jewish Law in Ancient and Modern Israel* (New York: Ktav, 1971), 24.

45. See Jacob Milgrom, "Israel's Sanctuary: The Priestly 'Picture of Dorian Gray,'" *Revue Biblique* 83.3 (1976): 390–399.

46. Patrick Miller, *Deuteronomy* (Louisville, Ky.: Westminster John Knox Press, 1990), 161.

47. On this notion see Jonathan Klawans, "Idolatry, Incest, and Impurity: Moral Defilement in Ancient Judaism," *Journal for the Study of Judaism* 29.4 (1998): 397–398.

48. Jackson, 41. See also Cohn, 19.

49. Jon D. Levenson, *Creation and the Persistence of Evil: The Jewish Drama of Divine Omnipotence* (New York: Harper and Row, 1988), 127.

50. Jackson, 44–45.

51. This last point is confirmed in Raʾanan Boustan's study of rabbinic martyrology; see R. Boustan, *From Martyr to Mystic: Rabbinic Martyrology and the Making of Merkavah Mysticism* (Tubingen: Mohr Siebeck, 2005), 58–70.

52. Jackson, 48.

53. Peretz Segal, "Post-Biblical Jewish Criminal Law and Theology," *Jewish Law Annual* 9 (1991): 108.

54. Yael Shemesh, "Measure for Measure in the David Stories," *Scandinavian Journal of the Old Testament* 17.1 (2003): 90.

55. E. E. Urbach, *The Sages: Their Concepts and Beliefs* (Jerusalem: Magnes Press, 1975), 268–270 (he notes, though, that as opposed to biblical notions of justice, the rabbis believed in reward and punishment in the afterlife), and David Kraemer, *Responses to Suffering in Classical Rabbinic Literature* (New York: Oxford University Press, 1995), 51–98.

56. Yaakov Elman, "The Suffering of the Righteous in Palestinian and Babylonian Sources," *The Jewish Quarterly Review* 80.3/4 (1990): 316.

57. Ishay Rosen-Zvi, "Measure for Measure as a Hermeneutical Tool in Early Rabbinic Literature: The Case of Tosefta Sotah," *Journal of Jewish Studies* 57.2 (2006): 269. See notes 1 and 2 for a good bibliography of scholarly literature on this subject.

58. Michael Satlow, "'Texts of Terror': Rabbinic Texts, Speech Acts, and the Control of Mores," *AJS Review* 21.2 (1996): 278, 280.

59. Rosen-Zvi, 286.

60. Rosen-Zvi, 279, n. 33.

61. Rosen-Zvi, 279.

62. Elaine Phillips, "The Tilted Balance: Early Rabbinic Perspectives of God's Justice," *Bulletin for Biblical Research* 14.2 (2004): 235.

63. Rosen-Zvi, 279, 282.

64. Rosen-Zvi, 277.

65. Jonathan Wyn Schofer, "Protest or Pedagogy? Trivial Sin and Divine Justice in Rabbinic Narrative," *Hebrew Union College Annual* 74 (2003): 248.

66. Kraemer, 56.

67. Second Temple texts, for the most part, continue the tradition of the Hebrew Bible in viewing divine reward and punishment as contingent specifically on the observance of the commandments. See Chaya Halberstam, "Negotiating Law and Religion in Ancient Jewish Texts," *Law, Culture and the Humanities* 3 (2007): 189–204.

68. Kraemer, 74.

69. The resonance of this rabbinic text with some New Testament notions of sin must be noted. The early rabbis were forming their communities and traditions at approximately the same time as the early Christians. The idea that sinful attitudes are as serious as sin itself, and that God punishes these inner feelings severely, is similar to the statements attributed to Jesus by the gospels. For example, in Matthew, Jesus says: "You have heard that it was said to the men of old, 'You shall not kill; and whoever kills shall be liable to judgment.' But I say to you that everyone who is angry with his brother shall be liable to judgment; whoever insults his brother shall be liable to the council, and whoever says, 'You fool!' shall be liable to the hellfire" (Matthew 5:21–22).

70. Schofer, 251.

71. Schofer, 254, 268.

72. Schofer, 267.

73. Schofer, 278.

74. Friedrich Avemarie, "Aporien Der Theodizee: Zu Einem Schlusselthema Fruher Rabbinischer Martyrererzahlungen," *Journal for the Study of Judaism in the Persian, Hellenistic and Roman Period* 34.2 (2003): 208.

75. Schofer, 278, emphasis mine.

76. See Segal 107–121 for a full discussion of the motif of heavenly judgment in tannaitic literature. Segal's position is that these statements do not invoke God at all in the juridical sphere, but rather imply the involvement of priestly authorities.

77. Bernard Jackson glosses the concept of "liability before the heavenly court" with the phrase "moral obligation." Jackson, 49.

78. Fraade, *From Tradition to Commentary*, 17.

79. Gnostic and later rabbinic literatures in fact do envisage an outsize human Adam, created to be more god-like, before he needed to be "reduced in size" due to the jealousy of the angels. See Alexander Altmann, "The Gnostic Background of the Rabbinic Adam Legends" *Jewish Quarterly Review* 35 (1945): 380–384. The myth of the "primal androgyne" may also be relevant here as it posits the creation of an original androgynous human with four legs, two backs, two faces, etc. which was then split into two entities; see Daniel Boyarin, *Carnal Israel*, 35–46. I would like to thank Beth Berkowitz and Jonathan Schofer for these insights and references.

80. Zachary Braiterman, *(God) after Auschwitz: Tradition and Change in Post-Holocaust Jewish Thought* (Princeton, N.J.: Princeton University Press, 1998), 44.

81. The term used here is *ketubim* ("writings") which is ambiguous: does it mean all of scripture, or just the Ketubim, the third section of the Tanakh?

82. Christine Elizabeth Hayes, "Displaced Self-Perceptions: The Deployment of

Minim and Romans in Bavli Sanhedrin 90b–91a" in *Religious and Ethnic Communities in Later Roman Palestine* (Bethesda, Md.: University Press of Maryland, 1998), 250.

83. Braiterman, 55.

84. The wording in this midrash is clipped and concise; that, along with its troubling theology, led medieval commentators and translators to invert some words or add negatives, shifting the meaning of this midrash to something far more traditional. I am choosing to read the text as it appears, as others have done as well.

85. Abraham Joshua Heschel, *Heavenly Torah: As Refracted through the Generations*, trans. Gordon Tucker (New York: Continuum International, 2005), 302. Heschel maintains that it was the school of R. Ishmael, as opposed to that of R. Aqiba, who consistently present the view of the unfathomable God.

86. Fraade, 161.

87. Daniel Boyarin, *Dying for God: Martyrdom and the Making of Christianity and Judaism* (Stanford, Calif.: Stanford University Press, 1999), 114.

5. Objects of Narrative

The epigraph is from Paul Ricoeur, *The Just*, trans. David Pellauer (Chicago: University of Chicago Press, 2000), 153–154.

1. The midrash I analyze in this chapter is primarily amoraic (*Genesis Rabbah*) because of the wealth of aggadic midrash extant, especially in relation to Genesis. Though my conclusions will pertain to a slightly later time period than my conclusions in the earlier chapters, I do not believe they are irrelevant as they echo many of the ideas we have seen already in tannaitic literature.

2. David Daube, "Law in the Narratives," in *Studies in Biblical Law* (Cambridge: Cambridge University Press, 1947), 5.

3. Esther Marie Menn, *Judah and Tamar (Genesis 38) in Ancient Jewish Exegesis* (New York: Brill, 1997), 45.

4. Nelly Furman, "His Story Versus Her Story: Male Genealogy and Female Strategy in the Jacob Cycle," *Semeia* 46 (1989): 147.

5. Victor H. Matthews, "The Anthropology of Clothing in the Joseph Narrative," *Journal for the Study of the Old Testament* 65 (1995): 25–36.

6. Matthews, 31.

7. Daube, 8. The same formal words of the submission of evidence in the Judah and Tamar story are used here, and the brothers lead Jacob to believe that Joseph was attacked by a wild animal because legally, a shepherd would not be responsible were such an "act of God" to occur.

8. Gerhard Von Rad, *Genesis: A Commentary* (Philadelphia: Westminster Press, 1972), 398.

9. *Antiquities* 6.14.7, quoted in Hugh S. Pyper, *David as Reader: 2 Samuel 12:1–15 and the Poetics of Fatherhood* (Leiden: Brill, 1996), 17.

10. See P. Kyle McCarter, Jr., *II Samuel: A New Translation with Introduction, Notes, and Commentary.* Anchor Bible Series (Garden City, N.Y.: Doubleday, 1984), 62–64.

11. See McCarter, 62.

12. Adele Berlin, *Poetics and Interpretation of Biblical Narrative* (Sheffield, England: Almond Press, 1983), 82.

13. Pyper, 24–26.

14. Pyper, 24.

15. Pyper, 27.

16. Pyper, 26.

17. Pyper, 24.

18. One example of such a prophetic symbol occurs in Amos: God shows Amos a physical object in a vision and asks him "What do you see?" Amos replies, "A basket of summer fruit [*kluv qaits*]." God interprets, "The end [*qets*] has come for my people, Israel" (Amos 8:1–2). Amos's simple identification of the object ("a basket of summer fruit") is thus supplanted by its divine symbolic meaning reached not through any kind of causal connection between object and significance but rather through divine world-play.

19. Robert Alter, *The David Story: A Translation and Commentary of 1 and 2 Samuel* (New York: Norton, 1999), 258.

20. Robert Alter, *Genesis: Translation and Commentary* (New York: Norton, 1996), 222.

21. Uriel Simon, "The Poor Man's Ewe-Lamb: An Example of a Juridical Parable," *Biblica* 48 (1967): 220.

22. George W. Coats, "Parable, Fable, and Anecdote: Storytelling in the Succession Narrative," *Interpretation* 35.4 (1981): 371.

23. See, especially, Hermann Gunkel, *The Folktale in the Old Testament*, trans. M. D. Rutter (Sheffield, England: Almond Press, 1987), 55, and David Daube, "Nathan's Parable," *Novum Testamentum* 24 (1982): 275–288.

24. Robert Cover, "Nomos and Narrative," in *Narrative, Violence, and the Law: The Essays of Robert Cover,* ed. Martha Minow, Michael Ryan, and Austin Sarat (Ann Arbor: University of Michigan Press, 1993), 101.

25. Simon, 222.

26. Christine E. Hayes, "The Midrashic Career of the Confession of Judah (Genesis 38:26), Part II: The Rabbinic Midrashim," *Vetus Testamentum* 45.1 (1995): 174–187.

27. Quoted in Hayes, 178. Though this is a rather late midrash, it is based on a core idea found in Genesis Rabbah and even in the *Mekilta* (*Beshalaḥ* 5).

28. Hayes, 178.

29. Ibid.

30. The version in the *Mekilta* also presumes Judah's righteousness in his recognition of Tamar's innocence. This good deed, according to the *Mekilta,* is not enough to merit Judah the kingship, as it serves to cancel out his sexual sin with Tamar.

31. Quoted in Hayes, 180.

32. Hayes, 180.

33. Hayes, 181.

34. There are several manuscript variants of this midrash; an alternative version has God say in the court of Shem: "you testify to what is out in the open, and I testify to what is kept secret." They all have the same sense, in any case: that the events experienced by Judah were authored by God. Translations of *Genesis Rabbah* are based on H. Freedman and M. Simon, *Midrash Rabbah,* and they are emended when necessary.

35. Christine E. Hayes, "The Midrashic Career of the Confession of Judah (Genesis 38:26), Part I: The Extra-Canonical Texts, Targums, and Other Versions," *Vetus Testamentum* 45:1 (1995): 62–81, quote on 70.

36. Quoted in Hayes, 182.

37. Hayes, 183.

38. Quoted in Hayes 182, n.14.

39. Hayes, 183.

40. This version represents the majority of manuscripts, including *MS Vat. Ebr. 30*, Oxford (1 and 2) and *MS British Museum*. It also appears in the Venice printed edition. Other versions express less confusion on Jacob's part and more fatherly insight: "I know what a father sees" (*'ana' yeda' mah 'abba' ḥamy*) is found in the Venice printed edition of the *Yalkut Shim'oni*). But even other versions which preserve the reading of *'abba'* (father) preserve the initial confusion by including the *lyt* (not) in the beginning. The confusion seems to have arisen over the similarity between the ת and the ה: it can be read either as *lyt* ("not," resulting in: "he said, 'I do not know what I see'") or *lyh* ("to him," resulting in: "he said to him, 'I know what I see'"). The majority of manuscripts agree on the reading that also makes the most sense conceptually— that Jacob would *not* know what he sees, would be confused, and hence the holy spirit would be enkindled in him so that he could gain some clarity. This is version which I follow in this chapter.

41. Why Jacob is suddenly confused by the presentation of the coat is not fully explicated in this midrash, but it may be explained further by another midrashic tradition, which is interpolated from *Tanḥuma* into editions of *Genesis Rabbah*:

> *Now Jacob saw that there was corn in Egypt.* Was Jacob in Egypt, that Scripture says, "Now Jacob saw that there was corn in Egypt"? Did he not say to his sons, "Behold, I have heard that there is corn in Egypt" (Gen. 42:2)? Since the day that Joseph was stolen, however, the holy spirit departed from him [Jacob], so that he saw yet did not see, heard yet did not hear. (*Gen. Rab.* 91:6)

Thus, Joseph's confusion, his inability to determine what he sees, may be explained by the idea that in that moment, the prophetic spirit departed from him. But this later midrash need not be invoked to explain Jacob's confusion—in fact, the very next line suggests that the holy spirit did guide Jacob towards the truth. Rather, his confusion may simply reflect his inability to jump to conclusions based on the evidence presented to him.

42. The section in brackets appears in several manuscripts, but others simply end with the preceding sentence. The clause does make sense, however, as a segue into the next passage and an expression of the dilemma this midrash describes.

BIBLIOGRAPHY

Adamiak, Richard. *Justice and History in the Old Testament: The Evolution of Divine Retribution in the Historiographies of the Wilderness Generation.* Cleveland, Ohio: Zubal, 1982.

Albeck, Shalom. *Harʾayoth Ba-Dine Ha-Talmud.* [*Evidence in Talmudic Law.*] Ramat Gan, Israel: Bar-Ilan University Press, 1987.

Alexander, Elizabeth Shanks. *Transmitting Mishnah: The Shaping Influence of Oral Tradition.* New York: Cambridge University Press, 2006.

Alter, Robert. *The David Story: A Translation with Commentary of 1 and 2 Samuel.* New York: Norton, 1999.

———. *Genesis: Translation and Commentary.* New York: Norton, 1996.

Altmann, Alexander. "The Gnostic Background of the Rabbinic Adam Legends." *Jewish Quarterly Review* 35 (1945): 380–384.

Armstrong, A. H. *An Introduction to Ancient Philosophy.* London: Methuen, 1949.

Avemarie, Friedrich. "Aporien Der Theodizee: Zu Einem Schlusselthema Fruher Rabbinischer Martyrererzahlungen." *Journal for the Study of Judaism in the Persian, Hellenistic and Roman Period* 34.2 (2003): 199–215.

Barmash, Pamela. "Blood Feud and State Control: Differing Legal Institutions for the Remedy of Homicide During the Second and First Millennia B.C.E." *Journal of Near Eastern Studies* 63.3 (2004): 183–199.

Barton, John. "Imitation of God in the Old Testament." In *The God of Israel: Studies of an Inimitable Deity,* ed. R. P. Gordon, 35–46. Cambridge; New York: Cambridge University Press, 2007.

Baumann, Gerlinde. *Love and Violence: Marriage as Metaphor for the Relationship between Yhwh and Israel in the Prophetic Books.* Collegeville, Minn.: Liturgical Press, 2003.

Bentham, Jeremy. *The Theory of Legislation,* ed. C. K. Ogden.1802; Littleton, Colo.; Rothman, 1987.

Berkowitz, Beth A. *Execution and Invention: Death Penalty Discourse in Early Rabbinic and Christian Cultures.* New York: Oxford University Press, 2006.

Berlin, Adele. *Poetics and Interpretation of Biblical Narrative.* Sheffield, England: Almond Press, 1983.

Bernstein, Alan E. *The Formation of Hell: Death and Retribution in the Ancient and Early Christian Worlds.* Ithaca, N.Y.: Cornell University Press, 1993.

Blackstone, William. *Commentaries on the Laws of England* 3, ed. Wayne J. Morrison. London: Cavendish Press, 2001.

Blidstein, Gerald. "Capital Punishment: The Classic Jewish Discussion." In *Contemporary Jewish Ethics,* ed. M. Kellner, 310–325. New York: Hebrew Publishing Co., 1978.

Block, Richard. "Death, Thou Shalt Die: Reform Judaism and Capital Punishment." *Journal of Reform Judaism* 30.2 (1983): 1–10.

Boecker, Hans Jochen. *Law and the Administration of Justice in the Old Testament and Ancient East,* trans. Jeremy Moiser. Minneapolis, Minn.: Augsburg, 1980.

Bourdieu, Pierre. "The Force of Law: Toward a Sociology of the Juridical Field," trans. Richard Terdiman. *Hastings Law Journal* 38.5 (1987): 805–850.

Boustan, Ra'anan. *From Martyr to Mystic: Rabbinic Martyrology and the Making of Merkavah Mysticism.* Texts and Studies in Ancient Judaism. Tubingen: Mohr Siebeck, 2005.

Boyarin, Daniel. *Border Lines: The Partition of Judaeo-Christianity.* Philadelphia: University of Pennsylvania Press, 2004.

———. *Carnal Israel: Reading Sex in Talmudic Culture.* Berkeley: University of California Press, 1993.

———. *Dying for God: Martyrdom and the Making of Christianity and Judaism.* Stanford, Calif.: Stanford University Press, 1999.

Braiterman, Zachary. *(God) after Auschwitz: Tradition and Change in Post-Holocaust Jewish Thought.* Princeton, N.J.: Princeton University Press, 1998.

Brooks, Peter. *Troubling Confessions: Speaking Guilt in Law and Literature.* Chicago: University of Chicago Press, 2000.

Broyde, Michael J., and Michael Hecht. "The Return of Lost Property according to Jewish and Common Law: A Comparison." *Journal of Law and Religion* 12.1 (1995–1996): 225–253.

Budd, Philip J. *Numbers.* Word Biblical Commentary 5. Waco, Tex.: Word Books, 1984.

Carmichael, Calum. *Biblical Laws of Talion.* Oxford: Oxford Centre for Postgraduate Hebrew Studies, 1986.

Childs, Brevard. *The Book of Exodus: A Critical, Theological Commentary.* Louisville, Ky.: Westminster Press, 1974.

Coats, George W. "Parable, Fable, and Anecdote: Storytelling in the Succession Narrative." *Interpretation* 35.4 (1981): 368–382.

Cohen, Aryeh. *Rereading Talmud: Gender, Law, and the Poetics of Sugyot.* Atlanta, Ga.: Scholars Press, 1998.

Cohen, Boaz. "Evidence in Jewish Law." In *La Preuve. Recueils de la société Jean Bodin pour l'histoire comparative des institutions* 16 (1964): 104–115.

Cohn, Haim. *Jewish Law in Ancient and Modern Israel.* New York: Ktav, 1971.

———. "The Secularization of Divine Law." In *Jewish Law in Ancient and Modern Israel,* 1–49. New York: Ktav, 1971.

Cover, Robert. *Narrative, Violence, and the Law: The Essays of Robert Cover,* ed. Martha Minow, Michael Ryan, and Austin Sarat. Ann Arbor: University of Michigan Press, 1993.

Crenshaw, James. *Defending God: Biblical Responses to the Problem of Evil.* New York: Oxford University Press, 2005.

Daube, David. "Law in the Narratives." In *Studies in Biblical Law.* Cambridge: The University Press, 1947, 1–73.

———. "Nathan's Parable." *Novum Testamentum* 24 (1982): 275–288.

Davies, Andrew. *Double Standards in Isaiah: Re-Evaluating Prophetic Ethics and Divine Justice.* Leiden: Brill, 2000.

Derrida, Jacques. "Force of Law: The 'Mystical Foundation of Authority,'" trans. Mary Quaintance. *Deconstruction and the Possibility of Justice,* ed. Drucilla Cornell, Michel Rosenfeld, and David Gray Carlson. New York: Routledge, 1992.

Destro, Adriana. "The Witness of Times: An Anthropological Reading of *Niddah.*" In *Reading Leviticus: A Conversation with Mary Douglas,* ed. John F. A. Sawyer. Journal for the Study of the Old Testament Supplement Series 227, 124–138. Sheffield, England: Sheffield Academic Press, 1996.

Dershowitz, Alan M. *The Genesis of Justice: Ten Stories of Biblical Injustice that Led to the Ten Commandments and Modern Law.* New York: Warner, 2000.

Dillon, John. *The Middle Platonists: 80 B.C. to A.D. 220.* Ithaca, N.Y.: Cornell University Press, 1977.

Dorhmann, Natalie. "The Boundaries of the Law and the Problem of Jurisdiction in Early Palestinian Midrash." In *Rabbinic Law in its Roman and Near Eastern Context,* ed. Catherine Hezser, 83–104. Tübingen: Mohr Siebeck, 2003.

Dorff, Elliot N., and Arthur Rosett. *A Living Tree: The Roots and Growth of Jewish Law.* Albany: State University of New York Press, 1988.

Douglas, Mary. *Purity and Danger: An Analysis of the Concepts of Pollution and Taboo.* 1966; New York: Routledge, 1992.

Ellickson, Robert C., Carol M. Rose, and Bruce A. Ackerman, eds. *Perspectives on Property Law.* New York: Little, Brown, 1995.

Elman, Yaakov. "The Suffering of the Righteous in Palestinian and Babylonian Sources." *The Jewish Quarterly Review* 80.3/4 (1990): 315–339.

Elon, Menachem. *Jewish Law: History, Sources, Principles.* Translated by Bernard Auerbach and Melvin Sykes. Philadelphia: Jewish Publication Society, 1994.

Falk, Ze'ev W. "Forensic Medicine in Jewish Law." *Dine Israel* 1 (1969): 20–30.

Fish, Stanley. "The Law Wishes to Have a Formal Existence." In *The Fate of Law,* ed. Austin Sarat and Thomas Kearns, 159–208. Ann Arbor: University of Michigan Press, 1991.

Fishbane, Michael A. *Biblical Interpretation in Ancient Israel.* New York: Oxford University Press, 1985.

Fonrobert, Charlotte Elisheva. *Menstrual Purity: Rabbinic and Christian Reconstructions of Biblical Gender.* Stanford, Calif.: Stanford University Press, 2000.

———. "On *Carnal Israel* and the Consequences: Talmudic Studies since Foucault." *Jewish Quarterly Review* 95.3 (2005): 462–469.

Foucault, Michel. *Discipline and Punish: The Birth of the Prison.* 1977; New York: Vintage, 1995.

Fraade, Steven D. *From Tradition to Commentary: Torah and Its Interpretation in the Midrash Sifre to Deuteronomy.* Albany: State University of New York Press, 1991.

———. "Navigating the Anomalous: Non-Jews at the Intersection of Early Rabbinic Law and Narrative." In *The Other in Jewish Thought and History: Constructions of Jewish Culture and Identity,* ed. Laurence J. Silberstein and Robert L. Cohn, 145–165. New York: New York University Press, 1994.

———. "Priests, Kings, and Patriarchs: Yerushalmi Sanhedrin in its Exegetical and Cultural Settings." In *The Talmud Yerushalmi in Graeco-Roman Culture,* ed. Peter Schäfer and Catherine Hezser, 315–334. Tubingen: Mohr Siebeck, 1998.

———. "Rabbinic Polysemy and Pluralism Revisited: Between Praxis and Thematization." *AJS Review* 31.1 (2007): 1–40.

———. "Rhetoric and Hermeneutics in Miqsat Ma'ase Ha-Torah (4QMMT): The Case of the Blessings and Curses." *Dead Sea Discoveries* 10 (2003): 150–161.

———. "'The Torah of the King' (Deut. 17:14–20) in the Temple Scroll and Early Rabbinic Law." In *The Dead Sea Scrolls as Background to Postbiblical Judaism and Early Christianity,* ed. James R. Davila. Studies on the Texts of the Desert of Judah, 25–62. Leiden: Brill, 2003.

Franklin, James. *The Science of Conjecture: Evidence and Probability before Pascal.* Baltimore, Md.: Johns Hopkins University Press, 2001.

Fretheim, Terence E. *The Suffering of God: An Old Testament Perspective.* Philadelphia: Fortress Press, 1984.

Friedman, Shamma. "Pereq ha'isha Rabbah babavli." In *Mehqarim umeqorot,* ed. H. Dimitrovski, 277–441. New York: Jewish Theological Seminary, 1977.

Frymer-Kensky, Tikva. "Tit for Tat: The Principle of Equal Retribution in Near Eastern and Biblical Law." *Biblical Archaeologist* 43.4 (1980): 230–234.

Furman, Nelly. "His Story Versus Her Story: Male Genealogy and Female Strategy in the Jacob Cycle." *Semeia* 46 (1989): 141–149.

Gold, Moshe. "Ethical Practice in Critical Discourse: Conversions and Disruptions in Legal, Religious Narratives." *Representations* 64 (Autumn 1998): 21–40.

Goldin, Judah. "On the Account of the Banning of R. Eliezer ben Hyrqanus: An Analysis and a Proposal." *The Journal of the Ancient Near Eastern Society* 16–17 (1984–1985): 84–96.

Greenberg, Blu. *On Women and Judaism: A View from Tradition.* New York: Jewish Publication Society, 1981.

Greenberg, Moshe. "Some Postulates of Biblical Criminal Law." In *The Jewish Expression,* ed. Judah Goldin, 18–37. 1970; New Haven: Yale University Press, 1976.

Grey, Thomas C. "The Disintegration of Property." In *Property,* ed. J. Roland Pennock and John W. Chapman, 69–85. NOMOS XII (NOMOS Series). New York: New York University Press, 1980.

Griffiths, John Gwyn. *The Divine Verdict: A Study of Divine Judgement in the Ancient Religions.* Leiden: E. J. Brill, 1991.

Gunkel, Hermann. *The Folktale in the Old Testament.* Translated by Michael D. Rutter. Sheffield, England: Almond Press, 1987.

Halberstam, Chaya T. "Encircling the Law: The Legal Boundaries of Rabbinic Judaism." *Jewish Studies Quarterly* (forthcoming).

———. "Negotiating Law and Religion in Ancient Jewish Texts." *Law, Culture and the Humanities* 3 (2007): 189–204.

Halbertal, Moshe. *People of the Book: Canon, Meaning, and Authority.* Cambridge, Mass.: Harvard University Press, 1997.

Halivni, David Weiss. *Peshat and Derash: Plain and Applied Meaning in Rabbinic Exegesis.* New York: Oxford University Press, 1991.

Handelman, Susan. *The Slayers of Moses: The Emergence of Rabbinic Interpretation in Modern Literary Theory.* Albany: State University of New York Press, 1983.

Hartley, John E. *Leviticus.* Word Biblical Commentary 4. Dallas: Word Books, 1992.

Hauptman, Judith. *Rereading the Rabbis: A Woman's Voice.* Boulder, Colo.: Westview, 1998.

Hayes, Christine E. "Authority and Anxiety in the Talmuds: From Legal Fiction to Fact." In *Jewish Religious Leadership: Image and Reality* v. 1, ed. Jack Wertheimer, 127–154. New York: Jewish Theological Seminary, 2004.

———. "Displaced Self-Perceptions: The Deployment of Minim and Romans in Bavli Sanhedrin 90b–91a." In *Religious and Ethnic Communities in Later Roman Palestine,* ed. Hayim Lapin, 249–289. Bethesda, Md.: University Press of Maryland, 1998.

———. "The Midrashic Career of the Confession of Judah (Genesis 38:26), Part I: The Extra-Canonical Texts, Targums, and Other Versions." *Vetus Testamentum* 45.1 (1995): 62–81.

———. "The Midrashic Career of the Confession of Judah (Genesis 38:26), Part II: The Rabbinic Midrashim." *Vetus Testamentum* 45.1 (1995): 174–187.

———. "Rabbinic Contestations of Authority." *Cardozo Law Review* 28.1 (2006): 123–141.

Herzog, Isaac. *The Main Institutions of Jewish Law: Volume 1: Property.* New York: Soncino Press, 1965.

Heschel, Abraham Joshua. *Heavenly Torah: As Refracted through the Generations.* Translated by Gordon Tucker. New York: Continuum International, 2005.

Holmes, Oliver Wendell. "The Path of the Law." *Harvard Law Review* 10 (1897): 457–478.

Hyde, Alan. *Bodies of Law.* Princeton, N.J.: Princeton University Press, 1997.

Jackson, Bernard. "Religious Law in Judaism." *Aufstieg und Niedergang der römischen Welt* 2.19.1 (1979): 33–52.

Jacobs, Louis. *The Talmudic Argument: A Study in Talmudic Reasoning and Methodology.* New York: Cambridge University Press, 1984.

Kaminsky, Joel S. *Corporate Responsibility in the Hebrew Bible,* Journal for the Study of the Old Testament Supplement 196. Sheffield, England: Sheffield Academic Press, 1995.

Kelsen, Hans. "The Principle of Sovereign Equality of States as a Basis for International Organization." *Yale Law Journal* 53.2 (1944): 207–220.

Klawans, Jonathan. "Idolatry, Incest, and Impurity: Moral Defilement in Ancient Judaism." *Journal for the Study of Judaism* 29.4 (1998): 391–415.

———. *Impurity and Sin in Ancient Judaism.* New York: Oxford University Press, 2000.

Kirschenbaum, Aaron. "The Role of Punishment in Jewish Criminal Law: A Chapter in Rabbinic Penological Thought." *Jewish Law Annual* 9 (1991): 123–144.

Koch, Klaus. "Is There a Doctrine of Retribution in the Old Testament?" 1955. Translated by Thomas H. Trapp. In *Theodicy in the Old Testament,* ed. James L. Crenshaw. Issues in Religion and Theology 4, 57–87. Philadelphia: Fortress Press, 1983.

Kraemer, David. *Responses to Suffering in Classical Rabbinic Literature.* New York: Oxford University Press, 1995.

———. *The Mind of the Talmud: An Intellectual History of the Bavli.* New York: Oxford University Press, 1990.

———. *Reading the Rabbis: The Talmud as Literature.* New York: Oxford University Press, 1996.

Lauterbach, J. Z., trans. *Mekilta de-Rabbi Ishmael.* Philadelphia: Jewish Publication Society of America, 1976.

Levine, Baruch A. *Numbers 21–36: A New Translation with Introduction and Commentary.* Anchor Bible Series 4A. New York: Doubleday, 2000.

Levenson, Jon D. *Creation and the Persistence of Evil: The Jewish Drama of Divine Omnipotence.* New York: Harper and Row, 1988.

Levinson, Bernard M. *Deuteronomy and the Hermeneutics of Legal Innovation.* New York: Oxford University Press, 1997.

Lorberbaum, Yair. *Image of God: Halakha and Aggadah.* Tel Aviv: Schocken Publishing House, 2004.

Maccoby, Hyam. *Early Rabbinic Writings.* Cambridge Commentaries on Writings of the Jewish and Christian World 200 BC to AD 200, 3. Cambridge: Cambridge University Press, 1988.

Matthews, Victor H. "The Anthropology of Clothing in the Joseph Narrative." *Journal for the Study of the Old Testament* 65 (1995): 25–36.

McCarter, P. Kyle, Jr. *II Samuel: A New Translation with Introduction, Notes, and Commentary.* Anchor Bible Series 9. Garden City, N.Y.: Doubleday, 1984.

Menn, Esther Marie. *Judah and Tamar (Genesis 38) in Ancient Jewish Exegesis: Studies in Literary Form and Hermeneutics.* Supplements to the Journal for the Study of Judaism. Leiden; New York: Brill, 1997.

Milgrom, Jacob. "Israel's Sanctuary: The Priestly 'Picture of Dorian Gray.'" *Revue Biblique* 83.3 (1976): 390–399.

———. *Leviticus 1–16: A New Translation with Introduction and Commentary.* Anchor Bible Series 3. New York: Doubleday, 1991.

———. *Leviticus 23–27,* Anchor Bible Series. New York: Doubleday, 2001.

———. *Numbers [Ba-midbar]: The Traditional Hebrew Text with the New JPS Translation [and Commentary].* The JPS Torah Commentary. New York: Jewish Publication Society, 1990.

Miller, Patrick D., Jr. *Deuteronomy.* Louisville, Ky.: Westminster John Knox Press, 1990.

———. *Sin and Judgment in the Prophets: A Stylistic and Theological Analysis.* Chico, Calif.: Scholars Press, 1982.

Nesson, Charles. "The Evidence or the Event? On Judicial Proof and the Acceptability of Verdicts." *Harvard Law Review* 98 (1985): 1357–1392.

———. "Theories of Inference and Adjudication: Agent Orange Meets the Blue Bus: Factfinding at the Frontier of Knowledge." *Boston University Law Review* 66 (1986).

Neusner, Jacob. *The Theology of the Oral Torah: Revealing the Justice of God.* Kingston and Montreal: McGill-Queens Press, 1999.

Nielsen, Kirsten. *Yahweh as Prosecutor and Judge: An Investigation of the Prophetic Lawsuit (Rîb-Pattern).* Sheffield, England: University of Sheffield Press, 1978.

Noth, Martin. *Exodus: A Commentary,* trans. J. S. Bowden. Philadelphia: Westminster Press, 1962.

Nussbaum, Martha. *Poetic Justice: The Literary Imagination and Public Life.* Boston: Beacon Press, 1995.

Phillips, Elaine. "The Tilted Balance: Early Rabbinic Perspectives of God's Justice." *Bulletin for Biblical Research* 14.2 (2004): 223–240.

Piattelli, Daniella. "*Zedaqa*: Pursuit of Justice and the Instrument of *'Ius Talionis*.'" *Israel Law Review* 29 (1995): 65–78.

Plato. *The Laws*. Translated by Trevor R. Saunders. Baltimore, Md.: Penguin Books, 1972.

Pool, David De Sola. "Capital Punishment Among the Jews." In *Jewish Eugenics, and Other Essays*, ed. Max Reichler, 53–103. New York: Bloch, 1916.

Posner, Richard A. "The Jurisprudence of Skepticism." *Michigan Law Review* 86 (1988): 827–842.

Pyper, Hugh S. *David as Reader: 2 Samuel 12:1–15 and the Poetics of Fatherhood*. Leiden: Brill, 1996.

Reichman, Ravit. *The Affective Life of Law: Legal Modernism and the Literary Imagination*. Stanford, Calif.: Stanford University Press, 2009.

Ricoeur, Paul. *The Just*. Trans. by David Pellauer. Chicago: University of Chicago Press, 2000.

Rose, Carol M. "Possession as the Origin of Property." In *Perspectives on Property Law*, ed. Robert C. Ellickson, Carol M. Rose, and Bruce A. Ackerman, 181–190. New York: Little, Brown, 1995.

Rosen-Zvi, Ishay. "Measure for Measure as a Hermeneutical Tool in Early Rabbinic Literature: The Case of Tosefta Sotah." *Journal of Jewish Studies* 57.2 (2006): 269–286.

———. "The Ritual of the Suspected Adulteress (Sotah) in the Tannaitic Literature: Textual and Theoretical Perspectives." Ph.D. diss., Tel-Aviv University, 2004.

Roth, Joel. *The Halakhic Process: A Systemic Analysis*. New York: Jewish Theological Seminary, 1986.

Rubenstein, Jeffrey. "Nominalism and Realism in Qumranic and Rabbinic Law: A Reassessment." *Dead Sea Discoveries* 6.2 (1999): 157–183.

———. *Talmudic Stories: Narrative Art, Composition, and Culture*. Baltimore, Md.: Johns Hopkins University Press, 1999.

Sarat, Austin, Lawrence Douglas, and Martha Merrill Umphrey. *How Law Knows*. The Amherst Series in Law, Jurisprudence, and Social Thought. Stanford, Calif.: Stanford University Press, 2007.

Satlow, Michael. "'Texts of Terror': Rabbinic Texts, Speech Acts, and the Control of Mores." *AJS Review* 21.2 (1996): 273–297.

Schofer, Jonathan Wyn. *The Making of a Sage: A Study in Rabbinic Ethics*. Madison: University of Wisconsin Press, 2005.

———. "Protest or Pedagogy? Trivial Sin and Divine Justice in Rabbinic Narrative." *Hebrew Union College Annual* 74 (2003): 243–278.

Scholem, Gershom. "On Sin and Punishment: Some Remarks Concerning Biblical and Rabbinic Ethics." In *Myths and Symbols: Studies in Honor of Mircia Eliade*, ed. J. M. Kitagawa and C. H. Long. Chicago: University of Chicago Press, 1969.

Schwartz, Daniel R. "Law and Truth: On Qumran-Sadducean and Rabbinic Views of the Law." In *The Dead Sea Scrolls: Forty Years of Research*, ed. Devorah Dimant and Uriel Rappaport, 229–240. Leiden: E. J. Brill, 1992.

Schwartz, Seth. *Imperialism and Jewish Society: 200 B.C.E. to 640 C.E.* Princeton, N.J.: Princeton University Press, 2001.

Segal, Peretz. "Post-Biblical Jewish Criminal Law and Theology." *Jewish Law Annual* 9 (1991): 107–121.

Shemesh, Yael. "Measure for Measure in the David Stories." *Scandinavian Journal of the Old Testament* 17.1 (2003): 89–109.

Silman, Yohanan. "Halakhic Determinations of a Nominalistic and Realistic Nature: Legal and Philosophical Considerations." *Dine Israel* 12 (1984–1985): 249–266.

Simon, Uriel. "The Poor Man's Ewe-Lamb: An Example of a Juridical Parable." *Biblica* 48 (1967): 207–242.

Simon-Shoshan, Moshe. "Halachah LeMa'aseh: Narrative and Legal Discourse in the Mishnah." Ph.D. diss., University of Pennsylvania, 2005.

Spitz, Elie. "The Jewish Tradition and Capital Punishment." In *Contemporary Jewish Ethics and Morality: A Reader,* ed. Elliot N. Dorff and Louis E. Newman, 344–349. New York: Oxford University Press, 1995.

Stern, David. *Midrash and Theory: Ancient Jewish Exegesis and Contemporary Literary Studies.* Evanston, Ill.: Northwestern University Press, 1996.

Stone, Suzanne Last. "In Pursuit of the Counter-Text: The Jewish Legal Model in Contemporary American Legal Theory." *Harvard Law Review* 106 (1993): 813–896.

Sugden, Robert. "The Economics of Rights, Cooperation and Welfare." In *Perspectives on Property Law,* ed. Robert C. Ellickson, Carol M. Rose, and Bruce A. Ackerman. New York: Little, Brown, 1995.

Summers, Robert. "Formal Legal Truth and Substantive Truth in Judicial Fact-Finding: Their Justified Divergence in Some Particular Cases." *Law and Philosophy* 18.5 (1999): 497–511.

Tribe, Laurence. "Trial by Mathematics: Precision and Ritual in the Legal Process." *Harvard Law Review* 84 (1971): 1327–1340.

Urbach, E. E. *The Sages: Their Concepts and Beliefs.* Jerusalem: Magnes Press, 1975.

VerSteeg, Russ. *Law in the Ancient World.* Durham, N.C.: Carolina Academic Press, 2002.

Von Rad, Gerhard. *Genesis: A Commentary.* Philadelphia: Westminster Press, 1972.

———. *Deuteronomy: A Commentary.* Philadelphia: Westminster Press, 1966.

Wilson, Robert R. "Israel's Judicial System in the Preexilic Period." *Jewish Quarterly Review* 74 (1983): 229–248.

Wolde, Ellen J. van. "Sentiments as Culturally Constructed Emotions: Anger and Love in the Hebrew Bible." *Biblical Interpretation* 16.1 (2008): 1–24.

INDEX OF SCRIPTURAL VERSES

Hebrew Bible/Old Testament

Genesis

2:7	136
3:11	148
4:10	97–98
18	110
25:8	126
31:34	174
37:32	151–53
37:33	171
38	148–51, 164–65
38:16	172
38:24	165
38:26	165, 167
39:19–20	172–73
42:2	171
44:2	151–53
44:13	174
44:16	175
45:5	153, 171–72
45:8	153, 171–72

Exodus

	46, 47–48
11:4–6	177–78
20:5	117
20:5–6	119
20–23	45
21:18	91–93
21:23–24	78
21:31	117

22:21–24	132–33
22:22	132–33
23:1	195n15
23:1–9	45–46
23:2	183–84n21

Leviticus

5:1	98, 98–99
11–15	18–22
12	29
13–14	18–19, 21, 22, 31
13:3–4	19
14:1–2	20
15	17–18, 19, 21, 29, 35
15:2	22, 23–24
15:2–3	19
15:17	27
15:19	19, 27, 34
15:25	19
15:31	21, 25, 31
15:32	21
19:17	130
24:13–14	78
24:17	78
26:18	118
26:21	118
26:24	118
26:28	118

Numbers

5:11–31	123–26
16–21	78–80

29–34	78–80	28:7	111
35	79–80, 82	28:15	111
35:23	92–93	28:21–22	111
Deuteronomy	45, 46, 56, 57, 129	28:25	111
4:37	198n18	30:11	1
6:15	198n18	30:19	119
8:1	128, 131	32:4	135–36, 140–41
8:2–5	131		
8:3	131	PROPHETS	112
8:5	131		
10:17	198n18	Judges	
13:6	82	2:10	126
13:11	82, 83	1 Samuel	
13:15	83	15	158–59
16:17	111	15:15	159
16:19	111, 114	15:23	158
17:4–5	83	15:24–25	159
17:7	82	15:26	159
17:8–9	1	15:28–29	159
17:8–11	81–83	31:3–6	155, 157
17:9–11	184n24	2 Samuel	154–58
17:11	7	1:3	154
17:12	82	1:9–10	155
19:11–21	80–81	1:11	157
19:13	82, 120, 197n42	1:14	155
19:13	82	1:16	155, 157
19:15	135	12:1–4	160
19:17	81, 99	12:5–6	160
19:19	23, 82, 83	12:13	161
19:20	82, 83	1 Kings	195n15
21:9	82	Isaiah	113
21:21	82	5:1–4	163
22:1–3	46–48, 50–51, 53, 54	11:2–3	1
22:3	66	11:4	1
22:21	82	40:2	118
22:22	82	58:6–8	126
22:24	82	58:11	126
24:7	82	64:5	188n25
24:12	130	Jeremiah	
25:5	148–49	32:19	141
28	118–19	Hosea	
28:1	111	4:6	117
28:4	111	7:11–12	116–18

Amos	112
2:6–8	130
8:1–2	203n18
Micah	
6:2–4	113–14
6:10	113–14
6:13	113–14
Nahum	
1:2	115

WRITINGS

Psalms	
7:12	115
11	138
11:7	138
31:20	139
32:34	139
51:6	139–41
67:4	115
76:12	165
82:1	2, 99
Proverbs	
11:10–11	98
Job	112
15:18	165
37:7	139–41
Ecclesiastes	112
7:29	136–38
Daniel	
3:28	165
2 Chronicles	
19:6	2, 3, 99

MISHNAH

Shabbat	
2:6	128–29
Rosh Ha-Shanah	
2:8–9	185n38
Yebamot	
16:3	69–70

Sotah	
1:7–9	124
Qiddushin	
1:10	128
Baba Metsiʿa	
1:2	49
2:1	56, 66–67
2:2	56
2:5	54, 58, 65
2:6	71
2:7	49–50, 55, 69–70
Sanhedrin	85–89, 97
3:3	85
3:6	85
4:1	85
4:5	85, 98
5:1–2	85
5:2	85, 104
5:5	85
6:2	90
6:6	90
Makkot	
1:10	88, 89, 102, 104, 196n36
Abot	
2:1	129
Niddah	26–27
2:6	31
8:2	33–34
8:3	34

TOSEFTA

Sanhedrin	
1:9	2–3, 99
9:5	100
12:3	91–92
Menahot	
13:22	129–30
Negaim	22
Niddah	22
4:1	187–88n19

BABYLONIAN TALMUD (BAVLI)
58, 65–75

Berachot
 3b 178
Baba Metsiᶜa
 21a–22b 67–68
 27b–28b 68–73
 59a–59b 184n24
Baba Batra
 154a 96
Makkot
 7a 103–104
 23b 168
Niddah 188n21, 194n35
 57a 189n32
 59a 35
Zabim 22, 29

PALESTINIAN TALMUD
(YERUSHALMI) 58–65, 74–75

Berachot
 9:5 145
Baba Metsiᶜa
 9a 59–60, 60–61, 61–62,
   63–64

Midrash

Genesis Rabbah 203n27
 12.1 136
 84.19 171
 85.11 169–70
 85.12 167
 87.9 173
 91.6 204n41
 92.8 174

 92.9 175
Sifra Leviticus 22–24
Metsoraᶜ, Zabim
 1.2 22–24
 4.3 27
Exodus Rabbah
 30.19 166
Numbers Rabbah
 13.4 165
Song Rabbah
 2.16 145
Ecclesiastes Rabbah
 2.12 136
Mekilta (of Rabbi Ishmael) 55, 92–96
 Beshalaḥ 203nn27,30
 Bahodesh
  10 131
 Neziqin
  6 92–93
  18 132–33
 Kaspa
  3 109
  38 134–35
  2 50–53
Mekilta of R. Simeon b. Yoḥai
 21.18 93
Sifre Deuteronomy 55, 133–34, 143
 48 6
 223 52–53
 224 54

New Testament (Christian Bible)

Matthew
 5:21–22 201n69
Romans
 3:20 181n6

INDEX OF SUBJECTS

Aaron (High Priest), 137–38
Abba Oshaiah, 60–62
Abbaye, 67
Abraham (Genesis), 110, 116
Absalom, 124, 125
Acquittal, 85, 95, 103–104, 196n33
Adam (Genesis), 148
Adultery: David and Bathsheba, 154–59,
    160–63; Judah and Tamar story,
    148–54, 157, 160–62, 164–71, 175, 177,
    202n7; laws related to, 69, 123–26
Afterlife, 139
Aggadah (narrative), 40, 58–65, 178
Albeck, Shalom, 186n44
Alexander, Elizabeth, 183n16
Alexander of Macedon, 62–64
Alter, Robert, 160, 161
The Amalekite, 154–59
American law, 43, 188n21
Anger (divine), 114–15, 118–20
Anglo-American law, 43
Animals, lost, 54–55, 59–60, 191n27,
    192n27
Anonymous redactor (*stam*) of the
    Bavli, 68, 70, 71, 73, 74
Apostasy, 81
Aqiba, R.: on capital punishment, 88,
    102–105, 145; martyrdom, 145–46; on
    post-mortem examination for signs
    of puberty, 96; rejection of physical

evidence from criminal trials by, 91–
    92, 93–96, 103; on restoration of Jew-
    ish independence, 87; on ritual pu-
    rity laws, 34–41, 74, 95; view of the
    unfathomable God, 202n85
Ashi, R., 103–104
Assyria, 116–17
Asylum, 79, 81–82
Atonement, 90, 100, 101, 119–20
Avemarie, Friedrich, 134
Azariah, 165

Babel, 137–38
Barbarians, 59–60
Barton, John, 119
Bathsheba, 160
Baumann, Gerlinde, 115
BDQ, 51
Bediqat'edim (the examination of wit-
    nesses), 51. *See also* Witness
    testimony
Ben Zakkai, 104
Benjamin (Genesis), 151, 152–53, 173–77
Bentham, Jeremy, 190n18
Berkowitz, Beth, 88, 97, 100, 183n16
Berlin, Adele, 156
Bernstein, Alan, 113
Biblical law: ambiguous cases of, 35–36;
    cannot be overridden by rabbinic
    enactments, 68; differentiation be-

tween public and private law, 30–31; observance of, 119, 128–29; "protective fences" built around, 35

Bilhah (Genesis), 175

Birth, 192n27

Blasphemy, 94, 118

Blidstein, Gerald, 86, 196n36

Block, Richard, 86

Blood (*dam*), 25, 27–28, 34–38. *See also* Menstrual impurity (*niddah*)

Bloodstains (*ketem*), 19, 20, 25, 28–29, 33–41, 189n9. *See also* Ritual purity laws

Bodies, identification of, 69–70, 192n27

Borrowing, 49, 69–70, 192–93n27

Bourdieu, Pierre, 4, 29–30, 31, 39–40

Boyarin, Daniel, 4, 145, 184n23, 185n27

Braiterman, Zachary, 141–43

Bush, George W., 194n4

Cain (Genesis), 97–98

Candle lighting, 128–29

Capital punishment, 76–105; absolute authority of the court, 90–91; acquittal, 85, 95, 103–104, 196n33; admission of doubt in a death penalty case, 77, 81–83; anxiety of judges, 99; as atonement, 90, 100, 101; biblical law on, 77–85; for blasphemy, 94; conflicting rabbinic opinions of, 102; corresponding to substantive reality, 81; death of an injured person, 103; divine arbitration, 79, 81, 86, 87, 98, 134–35; *ʾemet* (objective truth), 90, 103; evidentiary procedures, 80–86; execution methods and ritual, 97; exoneration of the accused, 80; for idol worship, 83, 94; infrequency of, 102–103, 104; justifications for, 82–83, 87, 98, 104; measure for measure, 128–29; murder weapons, 91–96; physical evidence and judicial responsibility, 83, 91–96, 103; talmudic restrictions on the death penalty, 86; trial process, 85, 88–90, 94–95; in the United States, 194n4; witness testimony, 76–80; witness testimony, accountability for outcome of the verdict, 96, 97–101; witness testimony, anxiety of witnesses, 98; witness testimony, false, 77, 80–81, 82–85, 95, 96, 197n43; witness testimony, mistaken, 77, 197n43; witness testimony, motivation for, 98–99; witness testimony, nullified through legal maneuvering, 103–104; witness testimony, qualifications and requirements of, 85, 94, 182n8; witness testimony, reliance on witnesses alone, 91–94; witness testimony, two-witness rule, 80–81, 84, 135; wrongful judgment, 76, 77, 84–85, 89–91, 95, 96–102

Carmichael, Calum, 195n15

Carnal Israel (Boyarin), 4

Childbirth, 128–29

Children, 96, 132–33

Childs, Brevard, 45–46

Christians and Christianity, 201n69

Cities of refuge, 79, 81–82

Civil suits, 97–98

Clothing. *See* Garments

Coats, George, 161–62

Cohen, Boaz, 186n44

Cohn, Haim, 119

Commandments, observance of, 119, 128–29

Conscience, 147

Consistency of human jurisprudence, 119

Cover, Robert, 4, 162–63

Creation, 136–38, 143–44

Crenshaw, James, 113, 200n42

Cultic atonement, 119–20

Dam (blood), 25, 27–28, 34–38. *See also* Menstrual impurity (*niddah*)

Daube, David, 149, 153

David (King of Israel), 137–38, 154–59, 160–63, 177

Davidic kings and Messiah, 166

Davies, Andrew, 113

Death: in childbirth, 128–29; identification of bodies, 68–71; of an injured person, 103; levirate marriage, 148–49; martyrdom, 133–34, 141–44, 145–46; post-mortem examination for signs of puberty, 96; reward for the righteous at, 126, 139–40; *Yebamot*, 69–70. *See also* Murder

Death penalty. *See* Capital punishment

Democratic decision-making process, 5–6

Despair or mental abandonment of property, 60–61, 65–68

Destro, Adrianna, 26–27, 29, 32–33

Deuteronomistic History, 112

Dietary laws, 18

Dinah (Genesis), 175

Disciplinary suffering, 131–33

Disproportion of divine retribution, 122, 128–32

Divine "gathering," 126

Divine justice. *See* Theologies of justice

Divine surveillance, 3

Divorce decrees (*get*), 68–69, 191n27

Dohrman, Natalie, 183n16

Douglas, Mary, 17

DRSh, 51

Egypt, 114, 151–54, 177–78

El (the supreme god), 181n5

Eleazar, R., 103–104, 168

Eleazar b. Azariah, R., 88, 102–103

Eleazar b. Mahabai, 70, 192n27

Elman, Yaakov, 123

ʾ*emet*, 90, 103. *See also* Objective truth

Enemies, 46

Eve (Genesis), 148

Execution methods and ritual, 97

Exile, 112, 129

The Exodus, 131, 154

Extra-legal conduct, 46, 60, 65

False convictions, 76, 77, 84–85, 89–91, 95, 96–102

Fishbane, Michael, 77, 187n12, 190n15

The flood, 137, 138

Fonrobert, Charlotte, 28, 29, 35–36, 38, 188n21

Formal legal truth, overview, 10

Foucault, Michel, 118

Fraade, Steven D., 2, 4, 135, 144, 181n3, 183n18, 184n23, 185n32

France, eighteenth-century, symbolic punishments in, 118

Fretheim, Terence E., 114

Frymer-Kensky, Tikva, 115–16, 117–18, 195n14

Fugitives, 79, 81–82

Furman, Nelly, 151–52

Gamaliel, R., 196n36

Garden of Eden, 148

Garments: lost property laws and, 54–55, 58, 71, 72–73, 191–93n27; significance of, 151–53, 159

Gathering of the righteous at their death, 126

Genital-flux impurity, 22–41; biblical sources, 17–20, 31–32.; consequences of disobeying, 21, 25. *See also* Ritual purity laws

Gentiles, 59–60, 61–62, 63–64

Gnostic literature, 201n79

God. *See* Yhwh

Gomorrah, 110

Gonorrheal discharges, 20

Greece (ancient), 63–64, 196n37

Greenberg, Blu, 197n38

Greenberg, Moshe, 47

Griffiths, J. G., 112

Halbertal, Moshe, 6, 7, 8, 9, 184n22
Halivni, David Weiss, 6–7
Ḥallah, 128–29
Hammurabi laws, 117
Hananiah, 165
Haninah ben Teradion, R., 141–44
Hartley, John, 21, 31
Hashib (return), 48
Hasmonean period, 145–46
Hatred, 129–30
Hayes, Christine, 142, 165, 166, 167–69,
    183n16, 184n24, 188–89n29, 193n30
Hebrew Bible, authority of, 3
Heinemann, Isaac, 125
Hellenistic Greece, 63–64, 196n37
Heretics (minim), 142
Heschel, Abraham Joshua, 143
Holmes, Oliver Wendell, 119
Human suffering, rationale for, 116
Hume, David, 42–43
Huna Bibi bar Goslon, R., 59–60, 171
Hyde, Alan, 188n21

Idol worship, 83, 94, 129–31
Indices (natural signs), described, 148.
    See also Objects in narratives
"Is There a Doctrine of Retribution in
    the Old Testament?" (Koch),
    199n29
Isaac (Patriarch), 166–167
Isaac, R. Samuel b. R., 167
Ishmael, R., 92–93, 132–33, 202n85

Jackson, Bernard, 110–111, 112–13, 115,
    120–21, 199n26, 201n77
Jacob (Genesis), 116, 152, 153, 165–67,
    171–72, 176
Jacobs, Louis, 67, 68
Jehoshaphat, 182n7
Jeremiah, R., 167
Jesus Christ, 201n69

Johanan, R., 103–104
Jonathan (2 Samuel), 154, 159
Joseph (Genesis), 116, 124, 151–54, 171–77
Josephus, 155
Judah (Genesis): Joseph story, 171–72,
    175–77; Tamar story, 148–54, 157,
    160–162, 164–71, 175, 177, 202n7
Judah b. Tabbai, R., 134–35
Judah, R., 66
Judan, R., 170
Juridical parables, 161–64, 177, 178–79

Kaminsky, Joel, 115, 118
Kelsen, Hans, 10
Ketem (bloodstains), 19, 20, 25, 28–29,
    32–41, 189n9. See also Ritual purity
    laws
Ketubim ("writings"), 201n81
Kirschenbaum, Aaron, 87
Koch, Klaus, 199n29
Koraḥ, 137, 138
Kraemer, David, 123, 128, 184n24, 185n32

The Laws (Plato), 6
Leadership, 1
Legal systems: Anglo-American law, 43;
    Roman law, 91, 120, 182n9; within
    paterfamilias, 149–50
Leprous disease. See Scale-disease
    impurity
Levenson, Jon, 120
Levine, Baruch A., 79–80
Levinson, Bernard, 81
Levirate marriage, 148–51
"a life for a life" (talionic) principle, 77–
    78, 82–83, 112–13, 115–19, 196n35
Lost property law, 42–75; in Anglo-
    American law, 43; benefits of re-
    turning lost property, 60–62, 64–
    65, 71–72, 74; Bentham on, 190n18;
    in biblical law, 43, 44, 45–48, 50–51;
    broad application of, 54–55, 64;
    case-by-case basis of, 56–57, 68;

credibility of witnesses, 57; divorce decrees, 68–69, 191n27; eclipsed by uncertainty, 52–53, 56–57; items that are scattered about, 66–67; mental abandonment (*ye'ush*) of property, 56, 60–61, 65–68; moral imperatives, 47, 53, 55, 57, 62, 64–65; in rabbinic law, 43–45, 48–57, 57–75; in rabbinic law, in the Babylonian Talmud, 58, 65–75; in rabbinic law, in the Palestinian Talmud, 58–65, 74–75; real-world fulfillment of the divine law, 74–75; returning lost items as gift-giving, 55–58; safeguarding lost property, 46–47; *shinuy* (something unusual about the object), 43–44; *simanim* (signs upon the object), 43–44, 52–57; *simanim,* deception via, 50; *simanim,* distinctive vs. general, 50, 70–71; *simanim,* for identifying bodies, 69–70; *simanim,* items that are scattered about, 66–67; *simanim,* on animals, 191n27, 192n27; *simanim,* on divorce decrees, 68–69, 191n27; *simanim,* on garments, 191–93n27; *simanim,* purpose of, 43–44, 58, 68; *simanim,* text of *Baba Metsi'a* on, 191–93n27; utopian standards, 65; verbal claims of ownership, 48–49

Majority rule, 5–9, 183–84n21
Marriage, 69–70, 115, 123–26, 148–51
Martyrdom, 133–34, 141–44, 145–46
Materialism, 63 65
Matthews, Victor, 152
Maturity, 96
"Measure for measure" reward and punishment, 123–31
Meir, R., 66, 131
Men: genital-flux impurity, 17–21; as witnesses, 85

Menn, Esther, 150
Menstrual impurity (*niddah*): bloodstains inspected by rabbis, 19, 20, 25–26, 28–29, 33, 38, 40; bloodstains to prove a woman's virginity, 189n9; consequences of disobeying, 128–29; impermeable legal boundaries, 56; lack of physical inspection of blood by rabbis, 33, 188n27; monitoring of compliance, 31–32; "protective fences" built around biblical commandments, 35; reasonable doubt about bloodstains, 33–36, 39–41, 74; sex forbidden with a ritually impure woman, 188n28. *See also* Ritual purity laws
Mental abandonment (*ye'ush*) of property, 60–61, 65–68
Mercy, 86
The Messiah, 166
Milgrom, Jacob, 20, 79
Miller, Patrick, 116–17, 118, 119
Minim (heretics or sectarians), 142
Minority opinions, 7
Minors, 96
Miriam (Hebrew Bible), 124
Miscarriage, 187–88n19
Mishael, 165
Moles on skin, 70, 192n27
Money, lost, 56, 71, 74
Months, 8–9
Mooney, Chris, 8–9
Moral imperatives vs. law, 47, 53, 55, 57, 62, 64–65
Moses (Prophet), 124, 126, 131, 135–36, 142–43, 144, 154, 178
Murder: attempted, 83; blood-feuds between clans, 198–99n23; cities of refuge, 79, 81–82; deterrence, 82–83, 87; God as guarantor of ultimate justice, 79, 134–35; hatred of man for his fellow equal to, 129–30;

of an injured person, 103; one who destroys a single soul destroys the complete world, 98. *See also* Capital punishment; Death

Naboth's vineyard, 195n15
Narrative (*aggadah*), 40, 58–65, 178. *See also* Objects in narratives
Nathan (prophet), 160–63
Nathan, R., 92–93
Natural signs (indices), described, 148. *See also* Objects in narratives
Nebuchadnezzar, 165
Nehemiah, R., 37
New moon, 8–9
New Testament, 201n69
Niddah. See Menstrual impurity (*niddah*)
Nominalism vs. realism, 8–9
"Nomos and Narrative" (Cover), 162–63
Non-Jews, 59–60, 61–62, 64–65
Non-juridical suffering, 116
Noth, Martin, 46
Nussbaum, Martha, 118

Objective truth, 90, 103
Objects, lost. *See* Lost property law
Objects in narratives, 147–79; biblical narratives, 148–64; biblical narratives, David and Bathsheba, 160–63; biblical narratives, Joseph and his brothers, 151–54; biblical narratives, Judah and Tamar story, 148–54, 157, 160–62, 202n7; biblical narratives, juridical parables, 161–64, 177, 178–79; biblical narratives, Saul's death, 154–59, 177; biblical narratives, the Exodus, 154; divine providence and inner conviction, 177–79; indices and symbols, described, 148; in rabbinic narratives, 164–77; in rabbinic narratives, Joseph and his brothers, 171, 173–77;

in rabbinic narratives, Joseph and Potiphar's wife, 172–73; in rabbinic narratives, Judah and Tamar, 164–71
Observation (*re'iyah*), 27
Onkelos, 168
Orphans, 132–33
"Oven of Akhani" story, 184n24
Ownership rights. *See* Lost property law

Paterfamilias, 149–50
Patriarchal attitudes of rabbinic culture, 182n8
Patriarchs, 115. *See also* Abraham (Genesis); Isaac (Patriarch); Jacob (Genesis)
Paul (apostle), 181n6
Peirce, Charles, 148
"Perfection of divine justice," 120–21
Phillips, Elaine, 125
Plagues, 177–78
Plato, 6
Polysemy of the biblical text, 6–7
Polytheism, 181n5
Pool, David De Sola, 86
Poor, oppression of, 130
Potiphar, 151, 172–73
Potiphar's wife, 151–54, 171, 172–73
Predictability of human justice, 129
Pre-Sinaitic era, 22–24
Priests: cultic atonement, 119–20; law of blood vengeance and asylum, 79, 81–82; motif of heavenly judgment in tannaitic literature, 201n76; rejected by Yhwh, 117; as religious authorities after the destruction of the Temple, 2; scale-disease lesions inspected by, 19, 20–22, 23, 24, 25, 28–29, 32
"Primal androgyne" myth, 201n79
Property law. *See* Lost property law
Prophets, 112, 115, 183n18. *See also specific prophets by name*

"Protective fences" around biblical commandments, 35
Puberty, 96
Pyper, Hugh, 156–58

Raba, R., 67, 70–75, 192–93n27
Rabbinic jurisprudence: admission of doubt in a death penalty case, 77; biblical commandments vs. rabbinic decrees, 35–36, 68; creation of legally-defined facts necessary for the rule of law, 29–30, 31, 33, 37–41; imperfect human juridical activity, 3; majority rule, 5–9, 183–84n21; menstrual blood examined by rabbis, 19, 20, 25–26, 28–29, 33, 38, 40; nominalism vs. realism, 8–9; overview, 5–9; rabbinic contestations of authority, 34, 39, 40, 74, 188–89n29; rhetoric of universality, 30; rivalry between priests and rabbis following destruction of the Temple, 2; sanctioned by God, 3. *See also* Lost property law; Ritual purity laws; Theologies of justice
Rachel (Genesis), 174
Rainfall, 140–41
Rashi, 193n30
Redemption from Egypt, 114
Re'iyah (observation), 27
Refuge, 79, 81–82
"Religious Law in Judaism" (Jackson), 110–111
Remarriage after divorce, 69
Return (hashib), 48
"Reward and punishment" doctrine, 123–31
Righteous, reward for, 126, 139–40
Ritual purity laws, 17–41; consequences of disobeying, 21, 25, 31, 32, 34; fear of, 26–27, 28, 39–40; genital-flux impurity, 22–41; genital-flux impu-

rity, biblical sources, 17–20, 31–32; genital-flux impurity, consequences of disobeying, 21, 25; impurity manifest in time, 26, 33, 38; menstrual impurity, bloodstains inspected by rabbis, 19, 20, 25–26, 28–29, 33, 38, 40; menstrual impurity, bloodstains to prove a woman's virginity, 189n9; menstrual impurity, consequences of disobeying, 128–29; menstrual impurity, impermeable legal boundaries, 56; menstrual impurity, lack of physical inspection of blood by rabbis, 33, 188n27; menstrual impurity, monitoring of compliance, 31–32; menstrual impurity, "protective fences" built around biblical commandments, 35; menstrual impurity, reasonable doubt about bloodstains, 33–36, 39–41, 74; menstrual impurity, sex forbidden with a ritually impure woman, 188n28; modern bias vs. "unreality" of ritual purity and impurity, 194n35; observation (re'iyah), 27; pre-Sinaitic era, 22–24; as requirement for approaching the Temple, 17; scale-disease impurity, 17–41; scale-disease impurity, biblical evidence of, 17, 18–21; scale-disease impurity, inspections by priests, 19, 20–22, 23, 24, 25, 28–29, 32; zabah (flowing), defined, 38
Riverbanks, 66
"The Rock, his work is perfect," 135, 141–43
Roman Empire, 91, 120, 141–42, 182n9
Rosen-Zvi, Ishay, 123, 124, 125, 183n16
Roth, Joel, 184n24
Rubenstein, Jeffrey, 4, 8–9

Sabbath candles, 128–29
Sacrifices, 119–20

Safeguarding lost property, 46–47

Safra, R., 71–73, 76, 192n27

Samson, 124, 125

Samuel (first generation Amora), 189n32

Samuel (prophet), 158–59, 167, 168

Samuel b. R. Isaac, R., 167

Samuel bar Suseretai, R., 61–62

Satlow, Michael, 124

Saul (King), 113, 154–59, 177

Scale-disease impurity, 17–41; biblical evidence of, 17, 18–21; inspections by priests, 19, 20–22, 23, 24, 25, 28–29, 32. *See also* Ritual purity laws

Schofer, Jonathan, 4–5, 127, 133–34

Scholarship on rabbinic literature, overview of, 4–5

Scholem, Gershom, 118–19

Schwartz, Daniel, 8, 9

Schwartz, Seth, 182n9

Scientific inquiry vs. traditional understanding of the law, 9

Sea, items lost at, 66

Sectarians (*minim*), 142

Segal, Peretz, 122, 201n76

Semikhut, 50–51

Sexual abominations, 128–30, 188n28

Shem (Genesis), 165–66, 167, 168, 170

Shemesh, Yael, 122–23

Shepherds, 202n7

Shinuy (something unusual about the object), 43–44

Signs (indices), described, 148. *See also* Objects in narratives

Simanim (signs upon the object), 52–57; on animals, 191n27, 192n27; deception via, 50; distinctive vs. general, 50, 70–71; on divorce decrees, 68–69, 191n27; on garments, 191–93n27; for identifying bodies, 69–70; items that are scattered about, 66–67; purpose of, 43–44, 58, 68; text of Baba Metsi'a, 191–93n27. *See also* Lost property law

Simeon (Genesis), 175

Simeon, R., 132–34, 141–42

Simeon b. Eleazar, R., 67

Simeon b. Gamaliel, R., 88, 102, 104, 192n27

Simeon b. Shetaḥ, 59–60

Simeon the Temanite, 91–96

Simon, Uriel, 161, 163

Simon-Shoshan, Moshe, 183n15

Skin lesions (*negaʿim*). *See* Scale-disease impurity

Snow, 140–41

Sodom, 110, 116, 137–38

Solomon, King, 167, 168

Song of the vineyard, 163

Sotah (adulteress), 123–26

Spitz, Elie, 77

Squatters, 49

Stam (anonymous redactor) of the Bavli, 68, 70, 71, 73, 74

Stern, David, 183–84n21, 184n32

Substantive truth, overview, 10

Suffering, rationale for, 116

Summers, Robert, 10

Symbols (conventional signs), described, 148. *See also* Objects in narratives

Talionic ("a life for a life") principle, 77–78, 82–83, 112–13, 115–19, 196n35

Tamar (Genesis), 148–54, 157, 160–62, 164–71, 175, 177, 202n7

Tarfon, R., 88, 102–103, 104–105

Temple era, 2, 17, 129–30, 201n67

Ten plagues, 177–78

Testimony. *See* Witness testimony

Theft, 59–60

Theologies of justice, 109–46; in the Hebrew Bible, 110–20; in the Hebrew Bible, disproportionality of divine justice, 122, 128–32; in the Hebrew Bible, interconnection between planes of human and divine legal authority, 110–20; in the Hebrew Bible, "reward and punishment" doctrine, 123–31; in the Hebrew Bible, talionic ("a life for a life") principle, 115–19; in the Hebrew Bible, "the perfection of divine justice," 120–21; in the Hebrew Bible, variability of divine justice, 119, 122, 128–32; in the Hebrew Bible, Yhwh's favorable judgment of himself, 113–15; in rabbinic literature, 120–46; in rabbinic literature, evicting God from the courtroom, 144–46; in rabbinic literature, on the scale of the individual vs. the community, 121; in rabbinic literature, the different faces of God's justice, 134–44; in rabbinic literature, varying measures, 122–34. See also Capital punishment; Lost property law; Ritual purity laws

Time, 26, 33, 38
Tithes, 129–30
Truth (ʾemet), 90, 103

United States, 49, 194n4
Unusual (shinuy), 43–44
Urbach, E. E., 123
Uriah, 160

Van Wolde, Ellen, 114–15
Variability of divine justice, 119, 122, 128–32
Vengeance, 115
Virginity, 189n9
Von Rad, Gerhard, 46, 153

Wicked, reward for, 139
Widows, 132–33
Witness testimony: accountability for outcome of the verdict, 96, 97–101; anxiety of witnesses, 98; credibility

of, 51, 52–53, 55, 57, 71–73, 72–73; for criminal procedures, 76–77; for demonstrating ownership, 49–51, 68, 72–73; false, 77, 80–81, 82–85, 95, 96, 197n43; mistaken, 77, 197n43; motivation for, 98–99; for new moons, 8–9; nullified through legal maneuvering, 103–104; qualifications and requirements of, 85, 94, 182n8; reliance on witnesses alone, 91–94; test cloths as, 188n25; two-witness rule, 80–81, 84, 135

Women: adulteresses (sotah), 123–26; death in childbirth, 128–29; divorce decrees, 68–69, 191n27; marriage metaphor between Yhwh and Israel, 115; objectified by legal language, 188n21; patriarchal attitudes of rabbinic culture, 182n8; rights and roles, 85, 94, 182n8; virginity, 189n9; widows, 132–33. See also Menstrual impurity (niddah)

World-to-come, 139
"Writings" (ketubim), 201n81
Wrongful judgments, 76, 77, 84–85, 89–91, 95, 96–102

Yebamot, 69–70
Yeʾush (mental abandonment) of property, 60–61, 65–68
Yhwh: anger of, 114–15, 118–20; as both a party to the covenant and its guarantor, 113–15; divine "gathering," 126; divine surveillance, 3; as God of justice, 79, 109, 134–35; marriage metaphor between Yhwh and Israel, 115; "perfection of divine justice," 120–21
Yoḥanan ben Torta, R., 129–30

Zabim. See Ritual purity laws
Zodiac signs, 192n27

Chaya T. Halberstam is Assistant Professor in the Department of Religious Studies at Indiana University Bloomington.

www.ingramcontent.com/pod-product-compliance
Lightning Source LLC
Chambersburg PA
CBHW030303100426
42812CB00002B/548